The Roots of
Ireland's Troubles

Robert Stedall

PEN & SWORD
HISTORY
AN IMPRINT OF PEN & SWORD BOOKS LTD.
YORKSHIRE – PHILADELPHIA

First published in Great Britain in 2019 by
Pen and Sword HISTORY
An imprint of
Pen & Sword Books Ltd
Yorkshire - Philadelphia

Hardback ISBN 9781526742186
Paperback ISBN 9781526751614

A CIP catalogue record for this book is
available from the British Library.

Typeset in INDIA By IMPEC e Solutions

Printed and bound in the UK by TJ International Ltd.

Pen & Sword Books Ltd incorporates the Imprints of
Pen & Sword Books Archaeology, Atlas, Aviation, Battleground, Discovery,
Family History, History, Maritime, Military, Naval, Politics, Railways,
Select, Transport, True Crime, Fiction, Frontline Books, Leo Cooper,
Praetorian Press, Seaforth Publishing, Wharncliffe and White Owl.

For a complete list of Pen & Sword titles please contact

PEN & SWORD BOOKS LIMITED
47 Church Street, Barnsley, South Yorkshire, S70 2AS, England
E-mail: enquiries@pen-and-sword.co.uk
Website: www.pen-and-sword.co.uk

or

PEN AND SWORD BOOKS
1950 Lawrence Rd, Havertown, PA 19083, USA
E-mail: Uspen-and-sword@casematepublishers.com
Website: www.penandswordbooks.com

Contents

Also by the same author:

Hunting from Hampstead: The Story of Henry and Lucy Stedall and their children, Book Guild Publishing, 2002

A two-volume history of Mary Queen of Scots:

The Challenge to the Crown, Volume I: The Struggle for Influence in the Reign of Mary Queen of Scots 1542 – 1567, Book Guild Publishing, 2012

The Survival of the Crown, Volume II: The Return to Authority of the Scottish Crown following Mary Queen of Scots' Deposition from the Throne, Book Guild Publishing, 2014

Men of Substance: The London Livery Company's Reluctant Part in the Plantation of Ulster, Austin Macauley Publishers, 2016

Mary Queen of Scots' Downfall: The Life and Murder of Henry, Lord Darnley, Pen & Sword Books Limited, 2017

Website: www.maryqueenofscots.net

List of Illustrations

John Toland (1670-1722)
Rev. Thomas Emlyn (1663-1741)
Francis Hutcheson (1694-1741)
Henry Grattan (1746-1820)
Rev. William Steel Dickson (1744-1824)
James Napper Tandy (1739-1803)
Theobald Wolfe Tone (1763-1798)
Archibald Hamilton Rowan (1751-1834)
Thomas Russell (1767-1803)
Henry Joy McCracken (1767-1798)
Lord Edward FitzGerald (1763-1798)
Arthur O'Connor (1763-1852)
Robert Emmet (1778-1803)
Daniel O'Connell (1775-1847)
William Smith O'Brien (1803-1864)
Charles Gavan Duffy (1816-1903)
Thomas Francis Meagher (1823-1867)
Charles Stewart Parnell (1846-1891)

Preface

In writing my history of the London Livery Companies in Ulster, *Men of Substance*, published by Austin Macauley in 2016, I was always conscious that I had glossed over the background to sectarian violence in Ireland, particularly in Ulster, which remained, and continues to remain, an uncomfortable legacy of British colonisation. While *Men of Substance* outlined the Livery Companies' efforts to establish and maintain settlements in co. Londonderry, a second line of research was needed to explain the impact of religion, politics and rebellion on the Irish people, which seemed to be behind the causes of centuries of conflict. Inevitably, there would be some overlap between the two subjects. To provide a cohesive text, I needed to revisit those parts of *Men of Substance* covering the periods of the Great Rebellion of 1642 – 1643, the War of the Three Kingdoms of 1643 – 1649, the Williamite Wars and the period of the Great Famine starting in 1845, but the focus now was on inept management by Church and State, which was often imposed with military force. It may seem unfathomable that tempers have continued to run so deep with friction remaining stubbornly close to the surface. Yet the protagonists have been slow to forgive and forget, jeopardising continuing efforts to secure a lasting peace.

Ireland is inhabited by differing groups, who have remained dogmatically wedded to conflicting ideologies, even though intermarriage has sometimes made it difficult to define where one begins and the other ends. For nearly five hundred years, it has been dogged by a dangerous cocktail of excuses for continuing unrest. Conflict has become endemic in the psyche of all those who now call Ireland their home; but what were the root causes for so much acrimony?

The objective of colonising both English and Scots into Ireland in the sixteenth and seventeenth centuries was to establish peace, but the settlers faced stubborn resistance from the indigenous Celtic inhabitants. Their arrival only exacerbated conflict and has been the root cause of almost continuous sectarian violence between Gaelic Catholics and arriving Protestants ever since. In its attempts to maintain control, the minority Anglican 'Ascendancy' in Dublin forcibly imposed rule on the Catholic majority. It was unfortunate that, in the aftermath of the English Civil War, the battleground for control of Britain between Jacobite Royalists and Williamite Parliamentarians was fought out on Irish soil. This left its residents, whether native Irish or British settlers, as the cannon fodder in between.

Another problem was the failure of absentee British landlords to ameliorate the abject poverty of their tenantry. Their insensitive and grasping estate management brought destitution and famine to an ever-increasing peasant population, until the only remedy was wholesale emigration to America and Canada, leaving those left behind determined on revenge. Even in the late nineteenth century, Irish calls for tenant rights and home rule fell on deaf ears in the British Houses of Parliament. These were dominated by members of the landed classes, who benefitted from maintaining the status quo. With their sole interest being to score points off their political opponents, they remained oblivious to the realities of the growing hardship. This forced the destitute Irish down a route that led inevitably to the formation of an Irish republic and partition.

Another influence for writing this book was to establish an understanding of Dissenter theology. My grandmother, a Miss Holmes, was a member of a well-established Dissenter family from Belfast. Research into her antecedents had provided an opportunity to understand the growth of Dissenter theology in Ireland and elsewhere. This led to an exploration of the unexpectedly republican nature of the United Irish rebellions of 1798 and 1803, when, in the wake of the French Revolution, idealist Presbyterians sought the help of dissident Catholics to end British rule. Their rebellion may have been doomed to failure, but the objectives of those involved were morally justifiable, even if history has treated them with contempt.

Ireland's beautiful coastline and fertile countryside make it a sought-after holiday destination, but its story is not a comfortable one. British settlement has fragmented its population, so that, particularly in the north, sectarian unrest never remains far below the surface and no one is faultless.

Introduction

Sectarian unrest in Ireland is generally blamed on Catholic violence provoked by insensitive English efforts to establish control of a belligerent Gaelic and adamantly Catholic people. The Catholic Irish faced great provocation, but this is only part of the story. Non-Conformist settlers, who arrived during the seventeenth century as Presbyterians from Scotland and Independents (generally Cromwellian soldiers) from England, also suffered from oppression and unrest. Throughout the eighteenth century, the Anglican Ascendancy in Dublin, with support from the Tory establishment at Westminster, propped up a corrupt Irish Government, from which both Catholics and Non-Conformists were debarred. In the 1790s, it was Non-Conformists who led initial calls for the creation of an Irish Republic in the hope of gaining French Jacobin (republican) support. They joined in an uneasy alliance with the impoverished and 'seethingly angry' Catholic peasantry, who were ready to support any project to remove absentee British landlords from their ancestral lands.

In contrast, the Catholic hierarchy in Dublin had no sympathy for an Irish republican rebellion supported by French Jacobins, who had not only toppled the French monarchy and its aristocracy, but had torn down the French Catholic Church. Their objective was to achieve emancipation, making them full members of the Irish community with the right to vote and to hold professional offices. The British Government managed to retain their loyalty by dangling this carrot before them, but neither the Tories in Britain nor the Irish Establishment in Dublin had any desire to grant it to them. If Irish Catholics should gain a majority in the Irish House of Commons, it was feared that they would seek to restore their ancestral estates, which had been sequestered from them and granted to British landlords over the previous two hundred years.

The solution reached by William Pitt's Tory Government in 1800 was to disband the Irish Parliament in Dublin and allow 103 Irish Members to sit at Westminster. This required the prior approval of the Irish Parliament, dominated as it was by the Irish Establishment. Pitt turned a blind eye to republican unrest as it developed in Belfast and Dublin until, in 1800, it became a sufficient threat to persuade the Dublin establishment to support the union of the two parliaments, albeit encouraged by a liberal scattering of bribes. The Catholics, who had no vote, supported the Union as the means of obtaining emancipation, which Pitt had promised to them.

Once parliamentary union was achieved, influential members of the Establishment in Dublin persuaded George III that granting Catholic emancipation contravened the terms of his Coronation oath, and he vetoed it. Pitt resigned in protest. It was not until 1829, thanks to the efforts of the Irish Catholic Daniel Collins, that full emancipation was eventually granted. By then the Irish Catholic interest had become focused on re-establishing home rule by restoring a parliament in Dublin. With most Irish estates continuing to be held by absentee British landlords, the British majority in the Westminster Parliament adamantly opposed home rule and were blind to the rural abuses that absenteeism caused. The British Government had only itself to blame for the future difficulties that arose.

Part 1

The Reformation and its impact on British efforts to dominate Ireland

Chapter 1

The arrival of British settlers in Ireland
c. 1540 – 1635

Following the English Reformation, it was of critical importance for England's security that the Catholic powers in Continental Europe should be prevented from using Ireland as a base to launch a Counter-Reformation into England. The obvious course of action for Henry VIII was to infiltrate Protestant preachers into Ireland to demonstrate to the Gaelic Irish the shortcomings of Roman Catholicism. He had been extremely successful with this policy in Scotland, where visiting preachers were able to show up the moral shortcomings inherent in the extremely wealthy Scottish Catholic Church. Protestantism offered a less financially demanding alternative by promoting the Reformation as it swept across northern Europe. Yet Ireland was different. Its Roman Catholic Church, which had developed through monastic foundations, was neither overly wealthy nor morally depraved, and it was serving its nation well, providing schooling and teaching Latin, the only common language for communication with its neighbours in England and elsewhere. Yet only the educated minority learned Latin. Protestant preachers arriving from abroad could rarely communicate in Gaelic to impart their message, and the Irish were stubbornly determined to retain their traditional forms of worship and Gaelic culture. The English had no moral justification for their approach. Just as in Scotland, their motives were entirely political. To maintain their uncertain control, the English moved in politicians and Protestant clergy, supported by a formidable array of military garrisons. They 'established' a Government in Dublin to maintain English law and they created an Anglican Church, the Church of Ireland, which imposed its doctrines throughout the country through a diocesan structure with a hierarchy of bishops. Former Catholic Church lands were granted to the newly established church administered by a local network of Anglican clergy. Thus, the principals in the Irish Government and the Irish 'Established Church' supported the English Crown out of mutual self-interest. This new Church was expensive to maintain. It was funded out of a tithe, often paid in kind, and imposed on the entire populace regardless of religious persuasion. Even though it was very quickly realised that Irish Catholics were unlikely to conform, and efforts by the English to enforce conversion lapsed, the tithe remained as a bone of contention, paid in the main by the poor to fund the religious persuasion of the rich.

Having failed to enforce Irish conformity with the newly established Church of Ireland, the English concluded that a more promising means of achieving order would be to expropriate land from any Irish opposing their rule and to grant it to English settlers moved in to 'civilise' the natives. It was also a convenient way of settling overdue back pay for soldiers and other officials involved in trying to maintain control. By this time, considerable areas had been confiscated from those Gaelic chieftains who had dared to resist English incursions, and it was hoped that arriving settlers would be able to establish order by force of numbers and by introducing English customs, religious doctrine and farming methods to the local inhabitants.

Even before the arrival of the English, there had been almost continuous conflict between rival Irish clans, resulting in complex networks of allegiance between them. Every chieftain could call on his clansmen to provide trained fighting men when needed. In the meantime, these fighting men (or 'wood-kerne') foraged in the surrounding woodlands. They found themselves out of work when a Gaelic chieftain was deposed, but they hid away waiting for an opportunity to make a concerted push to rid the land of settlers. They survived by terrorising farming communities of both settlers and the more amenable native Irish in their quest for sustenance.

The process of expropriating land from Irish rebels was extremely unfair. Under Gaelic law, land was vested in native farmers as co-partners with their chief in return for an obligation to provide military service when required. It was the farmers who lost out from the confiscation of a chieftain's lands, even though they might not have transgressed against English rule. Yet, if the chief was rebelling, the English believed that it was reasonable to assume that his community was a part of it. They also argued that Irish farmers would be relatively more secure as tenants of British settlers. Although they were now required to pay rent to their British landlord, they no longer faced the uncertainty of their former military obligation.

The native Irish were also embittered by unfamiliar farming methods being imposed upon them. Irish farmers had been nomadic, driving cattle, sheep and pigs across-country to time-honoured grazing grounds. British settlers, who wanted to till their land, needed enclosure to keep livestock away from growing crops. This interfered with historic Irish practices, notwithstanding that these were often extremely primitive. The Irish would plough 'by the tails of their garrons [horses] and not after the manner of the English Pale [the area under English control around Dublin]', where the plough was harnessed to a horse with a yoke.[1] Their methods were self-evidently inefficient and cruel, causing the deaths of large numbers of animals. Furthermore, the Gaelic Irish made no effort to improve soil fertility, to drain bog-land or to reclaim salt marshes.

Despite being granted lands in Ireland, many English landlords had no intention of settling there and farming themselves. The land was offered to 'undertakers' who took over larger areas for subletting in smaller parcels to new arrivals. It was always assumed that the native Irish would provide farm labour. This was particularly necessary, because many settlers, often former soldiers, had little or no farming experience. English arrivals were thus completely dependent on Irish labour for farming support and to construct their dwellings. With the native Irish having been deprived of their ancestral lands, there were outbreaks of belligerence, which only detracted from Ireland's appeal to newcomers. Undertakers often found themselves with insufficient settlers to occupy the available lands, and found the native Irish only too willing to pay good rents to remain *in situ*. The Irish showed such determination that they outbid settlers when land became available to rent, almost regardless of price, enabling absentee English landlords to raise prices, which the Irish in their desperation agreed to pay. With the letting income finding its way back to Britain, Ireland was sucked dry of the resources necessary to develop its rural economy. Furthermore, large numbers of natives remained on the settled land, when the objective was to reduce them. This did nothing to improve farming methods.

With fewer settlers arriving than had been hoped, security was always an issue. This was worsened by a confusion over land measurement. There were no accurate maps, and Irish lands were divided into 'balliboes'. (There were different names in different areas.) According to traditional Irish measurement, a balliboe, which the English renamed a 'townland', was 'sixty acres of profitable land'. It was not a finite area but a measure of economic worth. This resulted in areas on the ground being much larger than indicated by initial estimates, and settlers were dispersed much more widely than anticipated. Although efforts were made to group them into fortified villages for mutual security, this was impracticable for those trying to farm areas some distance from their village. For settlers wary of the wood-kerne, Ireland was a lonely and dangerous place. Although the unexpected land surplus meant that there was often enough to allow native Irish to stay put, they were generally allocated to the more remote or less fertile areas and this rankled with them.

When James VI of Scotland became King of England as James I in 1603, he was anxious to attract inland Scots to move to Ireland, and wanted them to intermingle with their English counterparts. This proved impracticable, as many settlers arrived in family groups or from the same districts, and were determined to stay together. Poor weather conditions had caused several periods of crop failure in Scotland, particularly during a mini-ice age in the late sixteenth century. Scots were attracted by the opportunities of fertile land only four hours' boat ride from the Galloway coast. They began arriving in Antrim and Down in the late sixteenth century and, by 1606, were settling in large numbers. T. M. Devine has stated:

The Scots who made the move to Ulster seem to have been a
relatively balanced cross-section of the national population.
At the upper end of the scale were small landowners and
substantial tenants who saw the venture as an unprecedented
opportunity for economic advancement ... Below this élite
class was a broad social spread which included artisans and
labourers as well as farm servants and cottars. Significantly
for every four men, three women moved to Ulster ... this
was an important influence which helped to maintain the
distinctive identity of the Ulster Scots.[2]

There were soon far more of them than English settlers. They were
experienced farmers, who started to plough and grow crops with great
success, and they soon dominated the area round Belfast. In James's
attempt to assure security for the settlers, he insisted on making any
Irish presence in 'plantation' areas illegal. Yet the need for labour by
the English made this objective totally unrealistic.

The Scots faced a problem. They were Presbyterians, as established
by John Knox in 1560 to the exclusion in Scotland of all other creeds of
Christian worship. They did not conform to the 'Established' Church
of Ireland any better than the Catholics. Initially, this did not create
great difficulty, and many Presbyterians shared Protestant churches
and even services with the more puritan English Non-Conformists. Yet
they were obliged, like the Catholics, to pay a tithe to the Established
Church with its hierarchy of bishops, of whom they did not approve.
With Scottish Presbyterians starting to promulgate freedom of religious
belief, they soon formed their own congregations and meeting houses in
eastern Ulster and later in Dublin, holding, as a principal tenet of their
Calvinist faith, an absolute belief in the word of the bible. The Scots
were horrified when the later Stuart monarchs started to impose 'high
church' doctrine onto both the Church of Ireland and the Presbyterian
Church in Scotland. This placed them at odds with the Dublin
Establishment. It was a requirement for Presbyterians to conform to the
very Anglican principles that had forced these more dogmatic Scottish
ministers to leave their Scottish livings in the first place. Many brought

their congregations across the North Channel to Ireland, sowing seeds of 'dissent' on arrival against the Church of Ireland.

The arrival of the British in Ireland in large numbers resulted in Gaelic culture and language becoming frowned upon. This was a tragedy for the native Irish. 'They were a conquered people, and their illegal presence on lands assigned to under takers ... depended on the whim of landlords.'[3] They found themselves facing eviction from their properties at the beginning of winter before the harvest had been gathered in. Those from Ulster were generally offered smaller areas of inferior land in remote areas such as co. Monaghan. Very often they preferred to take their chances as labourers for British tenants in familiar surroundings rather than face the tortuous task of uprooting completely and starting elsewhere. They saw the arrival of Scots in large numbers as a greater threat. Not only were Scots at opposite extremes of religious doctrine, but, as successful and self-sufficient farmers, they had no need for their labour. Although the English arrived in lesser numbers than expected, the natives were still left not knowing when and if they would be forced to move.

Although some 'deserving' Irish, who had supported the English against rebellious clans, were offered freeholds, only 20 per cent of Ulster's total land area was retained by them. They were not restored to their traditional lands, and new land grants were generally significantly less than they had enjoyed previously. As 'freeholders', they were required to fulfil jury duty, which involved them in substantial expense and time in travelling to assize courts. Very often, they proved inefficient farmers and were forced to sell areas to make ends meet until left with nothing at all.

The wood-kerne caused continuous outbreaks of violence, forcing settlers to organise themselves into armed posses for protection. Until his death in 1616, the Irish in Ulster lived in the hope that the Earl of Tyrone, who had escaped with other Irish chiefs to the continent, would return with a powerful force supported by European Catholic powers to recover what had been lost. Sir Thomas Phillips, one of the military servitors retained to protect the settlers, stamped on an uprising in 1615 by arresting the ring-leaders before it began.

In 1635, Charles I was facing a growing conflict with Parliament in his desperate effort to raise money to finance his extravagant foreign policy. Having failed in his attempt to raise taxes without calling Parliament, he expropriated the London Livery Companies' estates in co. Londonderry granted to them in 1610 by James I. Charles was acting on the advice of Thomas Wentworth, his Lord Deputy in Ireland appointed in 1632. The Companies had been reluctant participants in the Ulster plantation, believing that this was not an appropriate role for merchants to fulfil, but the Crown had forced them into it. They had been required to build and fortify both Londonderry and Coleraine and to bring in British settlers to establish peace in the locality. In fairness to Charles, the Companies had failed to meet their obligations to attract sufficient settlers to ensure peaceful coexistence with their Gaelic counterparts. Yet, the King's expropriation of the land granted left any remaining tenant settlers completely unprotected. Furthermore, Wentworth alienated both settler and native Irish tenants by attempting to raise rents.

Chapter 2

The development of Protestantism in Europe
c. 1517 – c. 1567

The two principal branches of Protestantism that developed in sixteenth century Europe were Lutheranism, as espoused by Martin Luther (1483 – 1546) in the German-speaking territories of the Holy Roman Empire, and Calvinism, as developed by John Calvin (1509 – 1564) and others in Geneva. The theological thinking of both movements was designed to counter growing abuses and profligacy in the Roman Catholic Church.

Lutheranism adopted many of the liturgical practices and sacramental teachings of the Roman Catholic Church but differed from it in holding that scripture is the final authority in all matters of faith, while Roman Catholics held that divine authority came from both scripture and tradition as promulgated by the Roman Curia. Roman Catholic laymen had no authority to question their church hierarchy. It was only the clergy who could read and interpret the scriptures, but Lutherans wanted bibles to be translated from Latin into languages that everyone could read and assimilate for themselves. They advocated a doctrine of justification 'by grace alone through faith alone on the basis of scripture alone'. In the Edict of Worms in 1521, the Holy Roman Emperor banned Lutherans from defending or propagating ideas which sought to 'reform' traditional practices. This led to an inevitable Lutheran schism with Roman Catholicism. Yet Lutheranism retained the Eucharist at the heart of its sacramental teaching and adopted a structure of bishops to administer its clergy and church practices. There was always an ultimate hope of achieving reconciliation.

John Calvin was one of a number of 'Reformed' theologians who sought to redefine Christian faith by placing scripture as the source of all authority, but Calvinism denied the bodily presence of Christ in the sacrament, believing that his presence was spiritual 'as a means of grace'. This was an important distinction, as from the safety of republican Geneva, Calvin was questioning whether earthly kings were anointed as the embodiment of Christ with divine authority. Calvinists held that each member of a congregation could come to faith as he saw fit, and bishops and clergy had no right to impose any particular doctrine. This resulted in many variations of Reformed thinking being developed in 'confessions of faith', but there was consensus that the inclusion of bishops in a church hierarchy was superfluous.

When Henry VIII, who had been appointed by the Pope as his *fidei defensor,* the defender of the Roman Catholic faith, failed to persuade his Roman Catholic bishops that he should divorce Catherine of Aragon, so that he could marry Anne Boleyn to provide a male heir to the English throne, he turned to Lutheranism. His clergy adapted its dogma to make him, as a spiritually anointed king, head of an Anglican church in place of the Pope. He retained bishops, so important to his control of Church administration, and many of them conveniently and pragmatically switched from Catholic to Anglican, rather than face the less appealing alternative of martyrdom by being burnt at the stake.

In the meantime, a young Scottish Catholic priest, John Knox (c. 1513 – 1572), had been influenced by a group of English Protestant preachers, including George Wishart. Wishart had been sent to Scotland to destabilise both the Scottish Catholic Church and the Scottish Government led by the Queen Dowager, Marie of Guise, mother of Mary Queen of Scots. With Marie of Guise benefitting from powerful French and Catholic support, Henry lacked the military strength to impose his will on Scotland. Marie sidestepped his attempt to arrange a marriage between his son, Prince Edward, and her daughter, the infant Mary Queen of Scots, by sending her to France for her education and subsequent marriage to the French Dauphin, later Francis II.

Wishart was well received in Scotland by a group of the Scottish nobility seeking to break the power of Cardinal David Beaton (or Bethune) who dominated Scottish politics with his control of the purse-strings of the extremely wealthy Scottish Catholic Church. When, in 1546, Wishart was arrested in Edinburgh for spreading heretical doctrine, he was taken to the castle of St Andrews, where Beaton arranged for him to be burned at the stake. As a result, a group of Fife lairds managed to enter the castle, where they gained control and murdered Beaton. They were immediately surrounded by mainly French troops loyal to Marie of Guise, but the 'Castilians' received support by sea from Henry VIII and were able to hold out for fourteen months. Over Easter 1547, Knox gained entry to the castle during a period of armistice. By this time, he was already espousing Calvinism in his determination to belittle Catholic monarchs and the mass, and he preached to the Castilians with an evangelical zeal, for which he was to become renowned.

Eventually, in July 1547, the French broke the siege by launching a massive naval bombardment. The Castilians, including Knox, were consigned to French galleys for two years. When Knox was released, he was brought to England by the English general, Edward Seymour, Earl of Hertford, who, as Duke of Somerset, had become Protector for his nephew Edward VI. While in London, Knox befriended the young William Cecil, Somerset's secretary and already a rising political star, who arranged for him to become a chaplain to the young King.

On the death of Edward VI in 1553, the adamantly Catholic 'Bloody' Mary Tudor ascended the English throne and pushed the supporters of the English Reformation underground. Knox escaped to the Continent, eventually arriving in Geneva to train under Calvin. He was able to visit Scotland in 1556, where he galvanised a group of dissident Scottish peers under the banner of the Lords of the Congregation, ultimately led by Lord James Stewart, later Earl of Moray, the illegitimate half-brother of Mary Queen of Scots. They were flirting with republicanism as a means of thwarting Marie of Guise, who still retained powerful French military support. While he was waiting at Dieppe in 1557, Knox wrote his *First Blast of the Trumpet against the Monstrous Regiment of Women*, published in early 1558. This was a diatribe written in vituperative style against the governments of Marie of Guise and Mary Tudor, but it showed him up as a political embarrassment. He saw it as 'a subversion of good order, of all equity and justice' for women to rule men. His timing was unfortunate as Mary Tudor died in the following year. When, in 1559, Knox returned to England, Elizabeth was affronted. To make amends, he wrote to her in July conveying his unfeigned love and reverence but told her that she ruled by the will of the people and not by dynastic right. She now saw him as an anathema and would never have his name mentioned.

Knox remained insensitive to criticism, but Elizabeth's opposition forced him to return to Scotland, rather than gain a more glittering Protestant post in England. On arrival, he quickly went onto the attack against the Catholic Church. With many members of the Scottish nobility benefitting from grants of Catholic Church lands for their younger sons (Lord James Stewart was Commendator – a lay holder of a benefice – of St Andrews), the Lords of the Congregation needed to steer Knox into addressing the political concern of ending Marie of Guise's 'tyranny of strangers (foreigners)'. With the powerful invective of his oratory, Knox was extremely successful. He inculcated Calvinist doctrine into Scotland and, with the support of the Lords of the Congregation, manoeuvred Presbyterianism, as it became known, to become the established faith of the Church of Scotland, to the exclusion of all other forms of religion. The 'Kirk' dispensed with bishops and arranged for elected presbyteries of the people to administer each congregation.

Following the deposition of Mary Queen of Scots from the Scottish throne in 1567, the infant James VI became King and was raised as a Presbyterian. He was extremely astute. His principal objective was to ensure that he would be recognised as heir to the English throne, as was his dynastic right. If he were to rule successfully over both nations, it was desirable that the Established Church in Scotland should adopt liturgy similar to that of the Anglicans in England. He was well-aware of the republican threat posed by Presbyterianism, and already favoured Anglican dogma with its hierarchy of bishops. He recognised that the popularity of his Government would be enhanced by ceremony, which would benefit from bishops in golden copes and mitres rather than dour Presbyterians in sombre puritan dress.

Furthermore, he wanted to use the bishops' diocesan structures to administer church policy to suit his objectives.

Although the church in England had adopted Lutheranism, it too became progressively more puritanical and 'low church', with sombre dress becoming the norm away from court, where Elizabeth continued to bedazzle like a peacock. For a time, Presbyterians and puritan Anglicans sat comfortably together, but efforts by the later Stuart Kings to impose 'high church' Anglican doctrines caused a schism with Presbyterians.

Chapter 3

The effect of Presbyterianism on British political thinking c. 1567 – c. 1649

The development of Protestantism in both England and Scotland was not just a religious crusade against Catholic Church excesses; it had a political motive. Even in Tudor times, an anointed monarch's divine authority to govern was being questioned, and Parliament in both countries was seeking to make the Crown more accountable to the people. Resistance to Royal claims of divine authority was initially more pronounced in Scotland, where Calvinism fitted with a growing republican sentiment to be rid of its Catholic Mary Queen of Scots. Yet, even in England, Protestants, though Lutheran in outlook, wanted their monarch to be beholden to the people, particularly in reaction to the reign of the Catholic Mary Tudor. Both Elizabeth and James I fought tenaciously to uphold the divine authority of their monarchy, but matters came to a head when Charles I defied all criticism and attempted to raise taxes without calling Parliament. Opposition by Parliament (with its support from the City of London) led to the English Civil War, when a growing republican faction rebelled against the iniquities of its anointed King.

Even before he succeeded to the English throne in 1603, James had famously said: 'No bishops, no king', and successive Stuart Kings always remained more comfortable with Anglican theology than the dour Presbyterianism of the Scottish Kirk, where bishops continued to be resisted. Despite strong criticism from the English Parliament, later Stuart Kings went further and began to flirt with the Catholic faith.

On the arrival of the Stuarts as Kings of England, Anglicans and Presbyterians vied for recognition as the Established Church, although both supported the Stuart monarchy. Yet Calvinists among both

Scottish and English theologians were already questioning Christian doctrines that were not mentioned in the bible. Those at the extremes of radical religious thinking were often known as 'Dissenters', but initially Dissenters were those who 'could not accept the king's or the bishop's authority over their religious consciences'. They wanted to reach their own conclusions, and, as 'non-conformists', 'believed that a man can find his way to God through scripture …',[1] sharing a common view that 'individual Christians may relate to God, free from the intervention of priests and, more particularly, bishops'.[2] They steadfastly opposed the hierarchy of bishops now being imposed by both Anglicans and Catholics and they abhorred Papacy.

> Popery allegedly promoted superstition and idolatry and was thrust on a peasantry kept in ignorance and denied access to the scriptures. Popery denied any political and religious authority to a man's conscience or reason.[3]

Yet they held back from trying to force religious change on Catholics, believing that 'someone who changes their religion because of political oppression is not a convert but a hypocrite'.[4]

In the 1640s in England, 'Freeborn John' Lilborne led a group, known as Levellers, seeking universal male suffrage (the right to vote) alongside a demand for complete religious toleration, even for Catholics. These objectives became known as 'The Good Old Cause', but they were more than two centuries before their time. Leveller views were adopted by more far-reaching Presbyterian ministers in Ireland, when they too called for freedom of expression in religious matters. As a result, they found themselves sharing common ground with Catholics against the Church of Ireland. Opposition to Established Church tithes and hearth taxes resulted in an uneasy alliance of these two religious extremes against the middle.

Freedom of expression meant that Dissenters did not share a single set of beliefs. Those, who baptised their converts as adults, were soon known as Baptists and those who 'trembled in the fear of the lord' were known as Quakers. Quakers believed so strongly that everyone was equal before God that members of their congregation were forbidden from raising their hats in deference to their fellows.[5] Another area of concern among Dissenters was in belief in the Trinity. Although the bible refers to Father, Son and Holy Spirit, it makes no mention of them being incorporated as one being. This group of Dissenters, referred to as Unitarians, believed in just one heavenly God, while Jesus was an earthly being, a great teacher or master, but a human being and not God. This formed part of a broader questioning of sections of the bible which did not stand up to scientific scrutiny. There had been a view more than two hundred years before Charles Darwin that the Creation, as recorded in the book of Genesis, lacked credibility. Similarly, there was scepticism about the miracles of Jesus, adding support to the Unitarian view that he was not a deity. Such philosophies caused Unitarians to be considered heretical by the Established Church, whether Anglican or Presbyterian, but republicans latched onto a dogma presenting Jesus as a human being in their search for a theology to justify claims that earthly kings were not divinely anointed. Unitarians needed to keep their heads down; their theology was not only heretical but treasonable, but it suited those seeking moral justification for bringing down the monarchy.

During the English Civil War, Dissenters, both Scottish and English, supported the Parliamentarian cause and used their beliefs to justify action against the King. Meanwhile, the Established Churches, both Anglican and Presbyterian, continued to back the Royalist cause. There was thus a religious division between the two sides. 'The Presbyterian majority in Parliament was made up of moderate puritans, who sought to replace the Anglican Established Church with a Presbyterian church establishment', where authority resided with the synod and presbyteries, not with bishops.[6] Had the Stuart monarchs supported these moderates, Parliament would never have turned against the Crown.

Part 2

Events leading up to the English Civil War

Chapter 4

Growing conflict between Charles I and the English Parliament 1625 – 1641

Matters came to a head against Charles I, when he attempted to raise taxes to finance his extravagant foreign policy without calling Parliament. As has been seen, on the advice of Wentworth, he accused the London Livery Companies of failing to meet their obligations under the Plantation agreement, and in 1635 he took the Companies to the Court of Star Chamber, where he expropriated their estates for failing to bring in the required numbers of settlers. This had a major impact on what was to follow. It placed the City of London at odds with the King, and they now financed Parliament in its opposition to him. Fortified with Unitarian philosophies and City of London money, Parliamentarians felt better able to stand up to an anointed King.

This was not the only cause for disagreement. Up to this time, a wide range of Protestant views had been tolerated by the Established Church. When Scottish Presbyterians (particularly those in Ireland) did not have kirks of their own, they had happily attended Established Church services, where they followed Puritan dogma with plain forms of worship and sombre dress. Yet the High Church liturgy now being promoted by the King was an anathema to them. Scotland was soon up in arms, forcing the King to travel north to restore his authority. On reaching Berwick, he realised that he had underestimated the level of opposition he faced, leaving his forces insufficient to impose his will. In June 1639, he was forced to come to terms, which left the Presbyterians in Scotland in control.

Meanwhile Wentworth had raised an Irish army of nine thousand men to support the King in Scotland. While they were awaiting trans-shipment across the North Channel, his men were billeted on tenanted lands at Carrickfergus, but with Ulster's crops having failed, there was insufficient food to go round. Edward, Viscount Chichester wrote:

> [The] poor people … are so much impoverished that they can no longer subsist, and the plantation which was here begun and brought to some perfection is now much ruined as there is little hope to recover it.[1]

When five hundred troops were moved to billets at Londonderry, where the population was about one thousand, food prices reached ruinous levels.

When Charles I reached terms with the Scottish Presbyterians, Wentworth's troops remained in Ireland to enforce religious conformity on Scottish settlers in Ulster. Presbyterian ministers were castigated by the Established Church for not being ordained. They, in turn, criticised some of the forms of worship in the Book of Common Prayer as popish. When ministers were called upon to adhere to Anglican liturgy, some resigned. By depriving them of office and financial support, Wentworth forced them back to Scotland. When he insisted on all Scots in Ulster over the age of sixteen taking 'The Black Oath' (an 'oath of abjuration of their abominable covenant'), Presbyterians saw his action as the final straw.[2]

In January 1640, Wentworth received the thanks of a grateful King for his loyalty and was created Earl of Strafford. Despite having employed heavy-handed money-raising efforts to support the Royal coffers, he had proved an efficient administrator. He had streamlined Irish Government processes by replacing inefficient officials. He had also benefitted the Irish economy by improving agricultural methods, most notably by encouraging the manufacture of linen to take advantage of the availability of cheap Irish labour. In April, Charles recognised Strafford's worth by withdrawing him from Ireland to assist him in facing mounting hostility at home. Ireland was left under the temporary control of three Lords Justices. In 1640, Strafford's friend, the Anglo-Irish Protestant, James Butler, 12th Earl of Ormonde, took over command of Establishment forces left in Ireland to deal with sporadic outbreaks of Catholic rebellion.

Chapter 5

The Great Rebellion in Ireland 1641 – 1649

T he native Irish saw the growing conflict between Charles I and the English Parliamentarians as their opportunity to recover lost ground. Pockets of Irish unrest had been bubbling up on several fronts. Strafford had repatriated émigré Irish colonels, Catholic veterans from the European wars, to train his Royalist troops. With the cost of maintaining a Royalist Irish force running at £1,000 per day, the men were put on half pay, and, following his departure, they were disbanded. With the colonels left out of work, they had nothing better to do than contemplate a Catholic rebellion to capitalise on the Crown's difficulties and to advance a Counter-Reformation.

Initially rebellion broke out in Dublin, but in 1641 it spread all over Ireland. This laid to waste almost all the British rural settlements and gained control of the whole of rural Ireland other than the Pale, the area round Dublin. In Ulster only the fortified settlements of Londonderry, Enniskillen, Coleraine, Belfast and Carrickfergus survived under British control. It took until the arrival of Cromwell's New Model Army in 1649 for order to be restored.

The man who came to the fore on behalf of the down-trodden Gaelic lords was Rory O'More, an Irish army officer from Longford. He convinced the Irish chieftains in Ulster that, if they rebelled, they would be supported by the Catholic Anglo-Irish in the Pale. He assured them that, after Charles had reneged on his offer of 'graces' to the Anglo-Irish (he had promised them religious toleration, the right to hold Government posts and hope of regaining legal title to their forfeited estates), the Anglo-Irish would take no more. O'More's plan was to recruit soldiers from Wentworth's army before it was disbanded. He entered into an alliance with Sir Phelim O'Neill, one of a group of

Gaelic members of Parliament from Ulster, looking to take advantage of the lull caused by the English Parliamentarians' growing success against the King in England. Sir Phelim had been one of the deserving Irish under Stuart rule, who had converted to Protestantism. After being educated in the English manner, he had spent three years at Lincoln's Inn. Although he had attracted British settlers to his 4,500 acre estates in Armagh and Tyrone, like many of his compatriates he had failed to manage his affairs efficiently and was £13,066 in debt. After the success of the extra-parliamentary action against the King in Scotland, Sir Phelim with other discontented members of the Irish Parliament hoped to emulate them, despite fears that the Scottish achievement would cause 'a ferocious Puritan crackdown on the Catholic majority in Ireland'.[1]

Sir Phelim's somewhat limited ambition was to take the walled city of Londonderry. To do this he needed to challenge the settlers on the former London Livery Company estates, and he turned to the Papacy for help. To achieve success, he and his Gaelic colleagues needed to encourage the Ulster peasantry to rise up in support. On 4 November 1641, he resorted to subterfuge. He produced a forged commission under the Great Seal of Scotland, which he had detached from a land patent. This confirmed the King's authority for 'all Catholics of the Romish party both English and Irish' to 'seize the goods, estates and persons of all the English Protestants'.[2] On seeing it, many hesitant Catholics took up arms against the settlers.

While Sir Phelim raised the north, O'More planned a second line of attack. The colonels scheduled a surprise raid on Dublin Castle on 23 October. To maintain the neutrality of the Scottish settlers, the rebels had no plan to molest them, unless they proved hostile. The objective was to focus only on their opposition to the English Government.[3] On 4 November, when Sir Phelim was acclaimed Commander-in-Chief of all Irish troops in Ulster, he 'set the rebellion in motion, plunging the whole island into a state of perpetual warfare for more than twelve years'.[4] His approach was ferocious. He began by attacking every fort garrisoned with English troops. With the English being caught completely unawares, many forts fell to the rebels and authority in Ulster collapsed. Within two days much of Ulster was in rebel hands, allowing Sir Phelim to head south. When Dundalk fell on 21 November, the insurgents besieged and captured Drogheda.

The Lords Justices in Dublin were seriously rattled. Although they called the Catholic Anglo-Irish of the Pale to arms, there were doubts over their loyalty. After facing years of religious persecution and threats to expropriate their lands, the Anglo-Irish were in two minds where their sympathies lay. On reaching Drogheda on 3 December, they joined the rebels. In Ulster, the rebellion devolved into the wholesale butchery of Protestant settlers.[5] With the London Livery Companies no longer involved, Ulster settlers were in mortal danger.[6] Refugees from the surrounding countryside frantically strengthened Coleraine's defences, enabling it to withstand a siege of one hundred days until relieved from Londonderry. Yet, Strabane fell to the rebels.

Although some settlers had fled to the fortified towns, others escaped into the hills, where very often they starved to death.[7] The rebels soon controlled almost all of Ireland. Only the Dublin Pale, areas round Cork City, Londonderry and Belfast, with a few outlying garrisons remained Protestant. When Sir Phelim arrived with 9,000 men at Lisburn from further west, he was unable to break the defences of the garrison under Sir Arthur Tyringham, even when the rebels tried to force open the gates by charging at them with one hundred head of cattle. Lisburn was the key to control of Belfast, and, given its strategic importance, the rebels made three attacks on 8, 22 and 28 November. With veteran Lowland Scots troops reinforcing the garrison, each attack was repulsed, on the last occasion causing the rebels great loss.[8]

There were appalling atrocities. At least 100 men, women and children were imprisoned in the church at Loughhall by Manus Roe O'Cahan. Many were tortured by strangling and half-hanging. They were then forced onto the bridge over the Bann at Porterdown, where they were stripped naked and pushed into the river, causing many deaths. Any who tried to swim were shot in the water. Several groups of Protestant settlers were herded into houses and burned to death. Fifteen men with sixty women and children held out for several days at Tully Castle on Lower Lough Erne. When they surrendered on Christmas Eve, it was on the expectation that the women and children would be spared. Nevertheless, they were all stripped and, having been imprisoned in the vaults, were taken into the bawn, where they were murdered.

The rebels fought on showing great savagery. Within a fortnight, their Gaelic chieftains no longer had control over them. Any distinction between English and Scots was forgotten as they 'threw themselves with merciless ferocity on the settlers'.[9] Not only did the legacy of failed harvests leave them starving, but they had heard wild rumours of a Puritan plot for their massacre. They made such rapid progress that they could not handle the number of prisoners surrendering to them. In Cavan, their captives were robbed and stripped before being 'turned naked, without respect of age or sex, upon the wild, barren mountains, in the cold air, exposed to all the severity of the winter'.[10] Any who were set free made for Dublin, only to die of exposure on the way.[11]

The rebels' cruelty resulted in a determination to seek revenge. Sir James Montgomery, in command of a Presbyterian force in South Down, wrote that he could not contain his men, for they:

> had seen ... their houses burned, their wives and children murdered. So they were like robbed bears and tygers, and could not be satisfied with all the revenge they took ... being full of revenge ... most partys killed many, and giving no quarter.[12]

With many Scottish settlers returning home, the Scottish Privy Council ordered a food collection for their relief and urgently called on the English Government to send reinforcement to Ulster.

The rebellion spread all over Ulster with the insurgents sweeping all before them. Most settlements in co. Londonderry were abandoned. The rebels razed houses to the ground, slaughtering any occupants showing resistance. Nevertheless, the settlers tried to retaliate. Sir William Cole fortified the island town of Enniskillen, making it impregnable.[13] Although the numbers of settlers killed has been wildly exaggerated, it is thought that between 527 and 1,259 died in Armagh out of a total of more than 3,000. This would equate to 12,000 deaths in Ulster as a whole. Only the fortified towns of Belfast, Carrickfergus, Enniskillen, Coleraine and Londonderry held out. Settlers crowded into Londonderry and Coleraine, so that the parish church and churchyard in Coleraine were filled 'with little Hutts, pestered and packed with poore people'.[14] With food in short supply, 3,000 women and children were in need of sustenance. Disease claimed many deaths, and refugees huddled inside the parish church were killed when it was struck by lightning. Although a sortie was sent out to challenge the rebels, it was routed.

Being the principal place of refuge, Sir Phelim targeted Londonderry, but a slow approach lost him his element of surprise. The settlers made a stand on a line south from Londonderry through Strabane and Newtown Stewart to Augher. Despite being heavily outnumbered, they managed to hold the insurgents back. Yet Sir Phelim stationed 1,000 men between Limavady and Coleraine to prevent British troops from further east making a rescue attempt. Reports sent to Dublin recorded that 1,000 men, women and children were sheltering within Limavady's walls. Although many settlers' families in the vicinity were butchered, the castle held out after the Dublin authorities sent weapons, ammunition, money and food. At Londonderry, many settlers now formed the 'Lagan Army', divided into four regiments. They made ferocious counter-attacks to secure the City's western approaches before relieving Ballykelly and Limavady. They also routed insurgents at Dungiven, where Manus O'Cahan was holding many British men, women and children prisoner. Further south, Sir Ralph Gore came to the rescue to prevent Donegal Castle, Ballyshannon and Castle Murray from falling into rebel hands. Despite their estates having been expropriated by the King, the London Livery Companies sent four ships to provision those being besieged in Londonderry. Each of the twelve Great Companies provided two pieces of ordnance for the walls to supplement twenty pieces already there.

Sir Phelim also sought reinforcements. He called on Tyrone's nephew, Eoghan Roe O'Neill, to return from the Continent. Eoghan

Roe was the acknowledged leader of the Irish in exile, having distinguished himself at the siege of Arras in 1640, as a veteran commander of one of Philip IV's regiments. Pressure was applied by Pope Urban VIII for the Spanish to release him with Papal money to 'stiffen the ranks of the Ulster Irish'.[15] Support was also promised from Cardinal Richelieu in France and from Roman Catholic families in exile from England.

By now Charles I was under threat both in Scotland and from his own Parliament. Having failed to send support to the Ulster settlers, both Parliament and the City of London turned on him. His inaction led inevitably to the English Civil War. He was unable to protect Strafford, who was impeached and executed on 12 May 1641. This provided Eoghan Roe with a good opportunity to bring an expeditionary force into Ulster. At the end of July 1642, he sailed from Dunkirk round the north of Scotland, landing at Doe Castle in Donegal. Ulster was 'like a desert'. Despite the promises made to him, reinforcements failed to arrive from either France or Flanders. With France and Spain now at war, neither dared risk upsetting the English. On 29 August, Eoghan Roe took command of the Ulster army, but he found the quality of its men and their shortage of equipment disconcerting. Despite his misgivings, he was persuaded to challenge the Lagan army. On 13 June 1643, his raw recruits, outnumbered two to one, were routed at Clones. Far from being humiliated, he retired to Connaught to establish a force of native Irish Ulstermen trained in modern fighting methods.[16]

It was the Scottish Presbyterian 'Covenanters' under Major-General Robert Monro, who had come to the Ulster settlers' aid. On 15 April 1642, he landed a Scots army of 2,500 men at Carrickfergus. Parliament discouraged him from setting out to relieve Londonderry, as the English settlers, who were largely Anglican, were unlikely to welcome Covenanters any more than the Irish insurgents. On arrival in Belfast, the Covenanters were pinned down, but in May 1644, after receiving fresh reinforcements from Scotland, Monro began to pursue rebels in co. Down. He did not take prisoners; as a hardened veteran of the Thirty Years' War in Europe, he slaughtered everyone he caught.

On 1 May, he relieved Newry. He shot and hanged sixty men but refrained from allowing his men to throw the women in the river for use as target practice, despite several being shot.[17] When he returned into Ulster, the rebels hid in the woods, but he slaughtered any native Irish he came across and seized their cattle. When he recovered Mountjoy and Dungannon, the natives capitulated; this cleared both co. Down and co. Antrim of insurgents. Nevertheless, until the end of 1642, much of co. Londonderry remained at risk, with both Londonderry and Coleraine being left in a ruinous state.

Elsewhere in Ireland, the rebels were more successful. Ormonde's cousin, Richard Butler, 3rd Viscount Mountgarret, led rebel troops in the south, who, by 1642, had established control almost everywhere other than Dublin. He was well organised and, in October, gained support from Anglo-Irish Catholics from the Pale. Regular troops were raised to replace the militia and he formed a government, known as the Catholic Confederation, at Kilkenny in the south-east. This was authorised to appoint generals, issue writs and mint its own coinage. It also had Catholic Church support. On 22 March, Catholic bishops and priests from Armagh meeting at Kells declared the Catholic war to be just. Any Catholics still supporting Protestant settlers were excommunicated. In May and June, a nationwide meeting of Catholics at Kilkenny approved their action, but also confirmed their allegiance to Charles I, seeing the Stuarts as more sympathetic than the Parliamentarians.

Despite a rebellion in Dublin, the authorities retained control, with leading conspirators being seized and imprisoned. Ormonde, who had remained there, received Royalist reinforcements from England and Scotland. He was now able to mount expeditions to clear rebel resistance from the Pale. Given his close kinship to many of the Confederation leaders, the Lords Justices were initially suspicious of his loyalty, but, on 5 March 1642, he successfully challenged the Confederation forces by lifting the siege of Drogheda and, in April, he relieved Royalist garrisons at Naas, Athy and Maryborough. Following his return to Dublin, he defeated Mountgarret at Kilrush despite the Confederation's numerically superior forces. This not only gained him plaudits from Charles I, but the receipt of a monetary reward from the English Parliament. Nevertheless, the Confederation still controlled two-thirds of Ireland, and Ormonde was unlikely to expect further assistance from the hard-pressed King. Despite achieving an indecisive victory during a sortie to New Ross, south-east of Kilkenny, Ormonde's position was far from secure.

Ormonde's problems were nothing compared to those of Charles I in England. With a desperate need for more troops, Charles took the unenviable decision to withdraw Royalist forces from Ireland. Ormonde was required to make a complete *volte face*. He was now instructed to treat secretly with the Catholic Confederation, with whom he was fighting, to gain their support for the Stuart cause in return for 'religious concessions'. In September 1643, the King agreed a one year 'Cessation of Arms' with Irish Catholics in return for limited offers of religious toleration. The Catholics had concluded that Charles now offered better prospects of religious freedom than the Parliamentarians. In November, Ormonde was appointed Lord Lieutenant with the title of Marquess, but neither he nor the Protestant Establishment trusted the Irish Catholics to support them. This meant that Irish Catholic hopes of improving their status by supporting the Crown were misplaced. Although Ormonde withdrew 4,000 Royalist troops to England, half came from Cork City, where its Protestant residents promptly sided with the Parliamentarians.

In May 1644, with Monro's Covenanter army demonstrating untold cruelty, Eoghan Roe O'Neill now believed that his Irish force was sufficiently trained to challenge them. When Monro left Antrim to face them with 6,000 men and six field guns drawn by oxen, Eoghan Roe, with an equal number of men but no guns, attacked Monro from the rear at Benburb on the River Blackwater. Despite taking a pounding from Monro's cannon, Eoghan Roe called to his men:

> Let your manhood be seen by your push of pike! Your word is Sancta Maria, and so in the name of the Father, Son, and Holy Ghost advance! – and give not fire until you are within pike-length![18]

With this, the Irish pushed the Covenanters back into the river, where they slaughtered them. 'Monro escaped only after he had cast away his coat, hat and wig. Between a third and a half of the Scots were killed, the Irish sustaining only trifling losses.[19] On hearing the news in Rome, the Pope attended a *Te Deum*, thanking God for this Irish triumph. Monro complained: 'For ought I can understand, the Lord of Hosts had a controversie with us to rub shame in our faces.'[20]

In October 1645, the newly elected Pope Innocent X sent his Nuncio, Archbishop Giovanni Battista Rinuccini, from Italy with arms, 20,000 pounds of gunpowder and 200,000 silver dollars. This heralded calls for Irish independence. Despite the north being at his mercy, Eoghan Roe came south to help the Nuncio in establishing control of the Confederation at Kilkenny.

Nevertheless, the Irish Royalists were fatally divided. With little common ground and much squabbling between the rival factions, they were not prepared to make common cause with Protestant Royalists behind the King. Ormonde found himself trying to co-ordinate a group whose affiliation was uncertain. Had the Royalists worked together, there is no doubt that they would have retained control in Ireland, but were thwarted by 'fatal hesitation, conflicting aims and wasting disputes'. Loyalties in Ireland became almost unfathomable, with generals and their men varying between Royalist and Parliamentarian with bewildering frequency.[21] Even Monro's Scottish troops in Ulster were initially Royalist, then Parliamentarian, and then Royalist again.[22]

Both British and Irish Protestants had strongly opposed Ormonde coming to a truce with Irish Catholic rebels. Having intercepted Charles's instructions, they were horrified at his deal with 'malignants' and 'idolatrous butchers' of the 'popish party'.[23] This left Ormonde in a difficult position with almost all Ireland in Catholic hands. Despite now having a modicum of Irish support, Charles wanted more. Without advising Ormonde, he sent Edward Somerset, 2nd Marquess of Worcester, to Ireland, where, on 25 August 1645, he signed a treaty with the Irish Catholic Confederation in Kilkenny. Neither Ormonde nor the Irish

Protestant community were made aware of the terms beforehand. When they vented their fury, Charles realised that he was pushing them into allegiance with the Parliamentarians, and he was forced to repudiate this new agreement.

Chapter 6

The War of the Three Kingdoms 1642 – 1649

In 1643, a group of moderate Calvinist divines in England produced the 'Westminster Confession of Faith', which included adherence to the doctrine of the Trinity. Although all Protestants were expected to subscribe to it, there was resistance from both episcopal Anglicans and from the soldiers of Cromwell's New Model Army, who were fighting and winning the Civil War on Parliament's behalf. This army was drawn largely from East Anglia, where religious 'Independency' was stronger. Like Presbyterians, they believed that authority resided with individual congregations, who had the right to choose their own ministers. 'Their most frequent and vehement disputes were for liberty of conscience as they called it ... that every man might not only hold but preach and do in matters of religion what he pleased.'[1] The New Model Army strongly rejected an establishment of bishops and, from the outset, believed that 'the King should face justice for his crimes against the people'.[2]

Support for the King came from the British aristocracy and the Established Churches in both England and Scotland, but nowhere was it greater than in Ireland. Irish Catholics, both native Irish and the descendants of Anglo-Norman knights, originally sent by the Plantagenets to establish control, joined together to support the Stuart kings. As a Protestant, Ormonde faced a dilemma with his newly-established Irish Catholic allies, who varied in the extent of their loyalty to the Crown. The Lords of the Pale, who were English by descent, zealously supported Charles, particularly as the Stuarts seemed to harbour Catholic sympathies; the Gaelic Irish in Ulster were still determined to recover their lands expropriated by the plantations and to expel any remaining settlers; those in Connaught and Leinster wanted to gain approval of Charles I's promised graces; and those in the south-west and other Gaelic Irish wanted to achieve a country independent of Britain under a Catholic sovereign appointed by the Pope.

The English Parliament realised that it urgently needed to establish its authority in both Scotland and Ireland. On 23 September 1643, it had achieved a Solemn League and Covenant with the Scots. This had freed up further Scottish Covenant troops to come to Ireland in support of Monro. Yet bringing Ireland to heel was a bigger problem. It was going to require a powerful fighting force. The English Parliament passed the Adventurers' Act, under which it raised loans of £10 million to fund Oliver Cromwell with his New Model Army to embark on an Irish military campaign as soon as the Royalists had been defeated in England. The loans were to be repayable out of land confiscated from Irish Catholic rebels. Under the 1642 Act, anyone advancing £200 was promised 1,000 acres in Ireland. Parliamentarian soldiers agreeing to fight there were promised allotments of land in lieu of wages. Some 37,000 of them agreed to the terms and were promised an initial 2.5 million acres as security for loans granted under the Act. This was not enough. Under the Doubling Ordinance of 1643, lenders were promised double the land previously allocated, if they invested a further 25 per cent. To honour its terms, Parliament would need to subdue Ireland, but the extent of its offer would cause it future problems. By 1653, it had expropriated 11 million acres of Ireland from Royalist rebels to allocate to its supporters. In Britain, the Royalists' military position had become parlous. Two months after Benburb, the King was crushingly defeated at Marston Moor and, in 1646, he was captured at Newark.

On 28 March 1646, Ormonde met with Irish Catholics to conclude new terms on the King's behalf, which again granted them concessions. Nevertheless, the Nuncio did not consider that they gave Roman Catholicism sufficient prominence. He persuaded their General Assembly to reject these terms and to arrest those Catholics who had confirmed their agreement to them. Ormonde's Royalist forces remained divided. Although Protestants loyal to the King openly declared their dislike for their Catholic allies, Ormonde feared that they lacked sufficient strength to hold Dublin against Catholics seeking Irish independence. He made the difficult decision to negotiate with the English Long Parliament, rather than turn Dublin over to the Irish Confederation. On 19 June 1647, he signed a treaty to cede Dublin to the Crown's erstwhile enemies on terms which protected both Protestant Royalists and those 'innocent' Catholics, who had not joined the Confederation. Two months later, the Parliamentary commander, Lieutenant-General Michael Jones, arrived from England with 5,000 men. Ormonde handed over Dublin to him with the command of his remaining 3,000 Royalist troops. Jones, who was of Welsh descent, had been brought up in Ireland and had previously served under Ormonde in Ulster before establishing his reputation with the Parliamentary forces in England.

Ormonde now left for England, where, during August and October, he attended Charles at Hampton Court Palace. In March 1648, to avoid arrest, he travelled to Paris to join Charles I's wife, Queen Henrietta Maria, and their son, Charles, Prince of Wales, to develop a plan for the consolidation of Royalist support in Ireland, which was on the brink of becoming the main front in the Civil War.

With Jones's Parliamentary forces equipped with up-to-date artillery, the Catholic Confederation was soon on the back foot. After persuading Ormonde's 3,000 Protestant Royalist troops in Dublin to support him, Jones led his combined force out to face the Irish Confederation. After relieving a siege at Trim, he crushed a powerful Catholic force from Leinster at Dungans Hill in co. Meath leaving 3,000 dead. Another 4,000 Catholic Confederation troops died at Knocknanuss Hill in co. Cork.[3] These were body blows for the Confederation, but Jones's men were suffering from disease, and they returned to Dublin, where they were pinned down over the winter of 1647/48.

The King's arrest had hugely shocked both Catholics and Scots. At the end of 1647, the Irish Confederation joined forces with the Presbyterian Scots in Ulster, until so recently their bitter enemies, and with Ormonde's former Royalist allies, to provide a Royalist axis in support of their captured King.[4] Charles was already calling on Scottish Royalists to assist him in England, but, in May 1648, their invading army was defeated by Cromwell at Preston.

With Cromwell's New Model Army now in unassailable control in England, it began to promote its Dissenter principles. It believed that 'the King should face justice for his crimes against the people'.[5] In 1648, Cromwell's supporters staged a military coup known as 'Colonel Pride's Purge', which surrounded the House of Commons, expelling all members refusing to accede to its Non-Conformist demands. 'The soldiers maintained that a Parliament that would impose Presbyterianism [the Westminster Confession of Faith] was little different from that which they had overthrown.'[6] 'In a bitter cry for justice for the common soldier, Edward Sexby said: "We ventured our lives and it was all for this: to recover our birth right and privileges as Englishmen ... I wonder we were so much deceived."'[7] 'It was the remaining "Independent" members, the so-called Rump Parliament, who gave in to the army's demands and brought the King to trial and execution.'[8] The King's invitation to Scottish 'foreigners' had been seen by Parliament as the grounds they needed to justify his execution for treason, allowing the legal process against him to be open and transparent. His execution in 1649 brought the Civil War in Britain to a close, despite continuing shockwaves among Catholics and Scottish Presbyterians.

Chapter 7

Ireland under Parliamentary control
1649 – 1660

With the monarchy being replaced by a Commonwealth, over which Cromwell became Protector, the English Parliament threatened to call a vote to exterminate Catholicism in Ireland. The Irish lords and gentry within the Catholic Confederation lost their nerve. They intervened with the Catholic wood-kerne in Ulster to stop any further slaughter in Londonderry. With peace there restored, the London Livery Companies were able to return to reclaim their estates. They granted new leases and collected rents, but legal title was not regained until 1656. This did not signal the end of hostilities. Ireland was now the battle ground, not for Catholics against Protestants, nor for British against native Irish, but for the continuing campaign between Royalist supporters of the Stuarts and their Parliamentarian opponents. The local inhabitants were the cannon fodder in between. Ireland remained in turmoil, exacerbated by regular outbreaks of small-pox and dysentery afflicting all sides.

Although the Irish Establishment had little in common with Irish Catholics, both groups clung to hopes that the Stuarts in exile would gain French assistance to support their restoration. Both sides realised that they needed to set aside their religious differences. After its reverses at the hands of Jones, the Catholic Confederation became much more amenable to compromise and it expelled the Nuncio. In September 1648, Ormonde returned and, in the following January, concluded a peace uniting all Catholics behind the Royalist cause. With Jones hemmed into Dublin, the rest of Ireland was under Royalist control. After Charles I's execution in January 1649, Ormonde brought in more English Royalist troops from France and retained the support of Scottish Presbyterians horrified at the King's execution. When Ormonde declared Charles II as King of Ireland, he was made a Knight of the Garter by the Royalist Government in exile.

To re-establish control of the English Parliament, moderate Puritans also recognised the need to break the power of Cromwell's New Model Army. With the war in England over, some units were disbanded, and, in 1649, Parliament moved 'the more radical regiments out of the way by sending them to Ireland' to counter the Royalist threat.[1] The army knew that it was being marginalised, and Cromwell's continued support for his men caused him to be mistrusted. In August 1649, he was appointed Lord Lieutenant of Ireland and took command of the campaign to restore control against the Irish Royalists.

Expecting that Cromwell would want to disembark his men at the port of Dublin, Ormonde attempted a pre-emptive strike in the hope of disrupting the landing. Having deployed his troops at Rathmines, Jones made a lightning sortie from the city and crushingly defeated him. On 15 August 1649, Cromwell brought thirty-five ships with an army of 12,000 men across the Irish Sea and was able to land unopposed. On the next day, his son-in-law, Henry Ireton arrived with a further seventy-seven ships.

From the outset, Cromwell promised civil liberty to those who did not oppose him, but the Irish were in no mood to capitulate. He made clear that his objective was to avenge the atrocities caused by the rebellion in 1641 and 1642. He told them:

> You, unprovoked, put the English to the most unheard of
> and most barbarous massacre without respect of sex or age,
> that ever the sun beheld, and at a time when Ireland was in
> perfect peace.[2]

His first objective was to gain control of the ports on Ireland's east coast to assure his lines of supply. With this achieved, he moved forward, systematically capturing the line of fortified towns across the country, which Ormonde was trying to defend, but, in July 1649, an outbreak of plague added to the ravages of 'starvation, war, burned harvests and a ruined economy'.[3] On 11 September, Jones took Drogheda after a short siege, during which he desolated all food crops in the surrounding countryside. Cromwell was determined to make an example of the defenders. He forbade his men 'to spare any that were in arms in the town'.[4] To seal Jones's victory, he massacred its garrison of 3,000 Royalist and Catholic Confederation troops, including any civilians who had turned down his offer of quarter. He reported to Parliament: 'This is a righteous judgement of God upon these barbarous wretches, who have imbrued their hand in so much innocent blood.'[5]

Cromwell's next step was to regain eastern Ulster. He sent five thousand men north under Colonel Robert Venables, a veteran of Naseby, to challenge the Covenanters who had retained their Royalist allegiance. After taking Newry and Belfast, Venables besieged Carrickfergus before turning west to relieve the Livery Company settlers, who were again under siege in Londonderry, routing Irish Catholic troops as he approached. With Ulster now secured, Cromwell turned his attention to the south, despite an outbreak of typhoid and dysentery among his men. Those who succumbed included Jones and later Ireton. When Ormonde's Cork garrison mutinied in May 1650, Cromwell's forces gained control of Munster, forcing Ormonde back behind the Shannon.

With Ormonde suffering a string of defeats, he was discredited, and his alliance with the Scottish Covenanters fell apart. From exile in France, Charles II had to choose between the Covenanters, who were supporting him in Scotland, and Ormonde's defeated Royalist troops. He chose the Covenanters. With Ormonde ousted from his command, he rejoined Charles as a key member of his Court-in-Exile in France, leaving his troops to come to terms with the Parliamentarians as best they could. By mid-1650, Cromwell was able to return to England with his job as good as done.

History has seen Cromwell as a hated figure in Ireland, although some of his army's reported brutality may have become exaggerated in the telling. Irish Catholics described Cromwellians as 'merciless butchers' and 'the scum of England, a generation of mechanic bagmen who had come to power by conquest'.[6] This may be unfair. Although he had always relied on local food and other supplies for his men, he had treated those who provided his provisions properly. On his first arrival in Dublin, he had pronounced:

> I do hereby warn ... all Officers, Soldiers and others under my command not to do any wrong or violence toward Country People or any persons whotsoever, unless they be actually in arms or office with the enemy ... as they shall answer to the contrary at their utmost peril.

It is known that Ireton court-martialled one of his Parliamentary Colonels for atrocities committed by his men. Yet there is also no doubt that Cromwell exercised 'the utmost severity' on those trying to resist him, particularly after the siege of Drogheda, when his motive was to avenge the atrocities committed in the rebellion of 1641/42.

In April 1652, Parliament brought the war in Ireland to an end. It granted terms, which allowed Irish troops to join foreign armies abroad not at war with England. With the Catholic Confederation surrendering in co. Cavan, a handful of fanatical English Puritan soldiers had become Ireland's masters. Their campaign had been financed by the City of London, whose natural loyalty to the Crown had been wilfully alienated by Charles I. Even so, Irish pride still gleamed bright. Catholicism was embedded in the nation's psyche and would remain its bulwark against the English, despite the forces thrown against it. It took some time for peace to be completely restored. Low level guerrilla attacks and lawlessness by bands of peasant brigands were to continue until the Restoration.

Under the Act of Settlement of 1652, the English Parliament sought reprisals. It approved the execution of 80,000 adult males, including any remaining leaders of the Catholic rebellion of 1641/42, but, in the final outcome, only 200 were rounded up and brought to death. Nevertheless, the English Parliament needed more land to meet its commitments under the Adventurers Act. A new wave of penal laws authorised the confiscation of further Catholic-owned lands, even from those who had not fought against Cromwell. Only those very few able to prove 'constant good affection' to the Parliamentary cause retained their estates intact, but Protestant Royalists and Catholics prepared to adopt the Anglican faith were able to pay fines to avoid confiscation.[7]

After the destruction of so many crops, war was followed by widespread famine. This was exacerbated by outbreaks of bubonic plague. Although the local population had been decimated, this eased the process of confiscating land. 'Dr William Petty, the Army's Physician-General, estimated that 504,000 native Irish and 112,000 colonists and English troops perished between 1641 and 1652.'[8] He also estimated that 100,000 Irish men, women and children, including prisoners of war, were forcibly transported to the West Indies and North America as 'indentured labourers' (slaves). A further 54,000 enlisted with the armies of France, Spain and the Holy Roman Empire.[9] The collective effect of all this reduced the Irish population by as much as 40 per cent (although estimates differ widely). According to Colonel Richard Lawrence, some areas of Ireland were without 'a living creature, either man, beast, or bird, they being either all dead or had quit those desolate places'.[10] 'Packs of wolves became numerous and audacious, even invading the streets of Dublin.' Military commanders had to organise hunts to kill them.[11]

The total cost of Cromwell's campaign was £3,500,000, with British soldiers, particularly the New Model Army, being owed about half of this in back pay, to be settled in land in accordance with the terms of Adventurers' Act. With many of them facing the prospect of religious persecution on returning to England, prospects seemed better in Ireland, and 33,419 men received what were called 'debentures – pieces of paper entitling them to Irish land.'[12] A Cromwellian plantation in Leinster and Munster was pioneered, on a 'magnificent scale'.[13] Land was allocated by lot. In co. Down, Colonel Arthur Hill of Hillsborough headed a Commission of the Revenue to seize control of lands forfeited from the Irish for transfer to beneficiaries under the Act. In Donegal, almost every Catholic was forfeited, including about twenty members of the Gaelic nobility. Before reallocation, instruction was given for everything to be mapped. Only about 12,000 former Cromwellian soldiers chose to farm. Being widely dispersed, some 'went native' very quickly, ignoring an ordinance forbidding their marriage to Irish women.[14] Some even became Catholic, allowing their children to be brought up speaking Gaelic rather than English. Others congregated in towns such as Cork, Youghal and Bandon, where they established ministers to their liking. The remainder sold their debentures, usually at great loss, often to Scottish land speculators, previously responsible for colonising Ulster. A fresh influx of Scottish tenants soon arrived eager to restore the lands to full production.

In Dublin, many Cromwellians 'joined two of the more free-thinking congregations originally established by English Presbyterian settlers in Elizabethan times'.[15] Despite facing continued Catholic hostility, they remained a powerful force. They were soon calling for freedom to express their more radical religious views, sharing much common ground with Scottish Presbyterians. Cromwell's Welsh chaplain the Rev. John Owen, who preached in Dublin, brought in further ministers as bastions against popery. Although he wrote a treatise against Unitarianism in 1654, his Dublin congregations refined their theological thinking after his departure. They shed Presbyterian concepts that individuals were predestined 'to be elected or damned' and, until well into the nineteenth century, accepted Dissenter views embracing freedom of conscience. There was a reluctant split with Cromwell on his appointment as Lord Protector by those unable to accept his 'rule by one man'. Yet the great majority of Cromwellians, being offered the prospect of Irish property, agreed, pragmatically, to support him in his new role, and might even have supported him to become King.

Over time, Dissenters started to show sympathy for the downtrodden Catholic Irish, despite abhorring their religious views, but they remained unwavering in their opposition to Ireland's Anglican Established Church. The cause of religious friction was no longer the difference between Catholic and Protestant, but between the Established Church and growing branches of non-conformity. More extreme Non-conformists saw the execution of Charles I as the beginning of 'the age of virtue', which, in accordance with the Book of Revelation, would 'lead to a thousand-year rule by the godly'.[16] These were 'Fifth Monarchist' principles (a Fifth Monarchist was one who believed that the second coming of Christ was near at hand and that his reign should be established by force).

Except in co. Antrim, there were very few Catholic freeholders left in Ulster after the confiscations of the previous fifty years, but those remaining now lost their entire estates. Although they were promised alternative lands wherever Parliament might decide, this was generally in cos. Mayo and Galway. Almost all the O'Donnells ended up in co. Mayo. Despite being promised two-thirds of the areas being relinquished, they were rarely offered more than one-third. Regardless of their origin, other native landowners were consigned 'to hell or Connaught' or, in the case of vagrants, to America. Even in Connaught, efforts were made to stop new arrivals from moving into walled towns or from practicing their religion. 'Priests found in the exercise of their religious duties were hanged without ceremony', although some were expelled to the West Indies.[17] Anyone involved in the rebellion of 1641/42 was sentenced to death, if caught. The Earl of Antrim was a staunch Catholic and Royalist. He did not join the Covenanter rebellion, but, having served Charles II overseas, his vast estates were confiscated by the Commonwealth without recompense.

Even for the many British settlers in Ulster, it was not immediately apparent that their future was secure. Many Presbyterians had joined the Scottish Covenanter army, only to see it routed by Venables. Venables called on their ministers to swear allegiance to the Commonwealth, but the majority refused and fled back to Scotland. By the end of 1651, only six Presbyterian ministers remained in Ulster. Eventually, Covenanters in Antrim and Down were required to relinquish one fifth of their estates. Other Protestant proprietors, who failed to swear allegiance, were treated similarly. Some recalcitrant ministers were advised to accompany their congregations to co. Tipperary. This was easier said than done. When leading officials met Venables to work out how to implement this move, it was quickly concluded that forcing such determined colonists to give up their land 'might be well-nigh impossible'.[18] A softer line was approved. The Government started fining offenders twice the annual value of their estates, but very few paid. It resorted to transporting 'popular men ... of whose dutiful and peaceful demeanours [it] had no assurance'.[19]

It was soon realised that opposition to Presbyterian settlers was counter-productive. To improve security the area being settled was extended over almost the whole of Ulster, but the authorities needed to attract new arrivals. An estimated 80,000 Presbyterian Scots arrived during the 1650s allowing the process of reconstruction to begin. This caused a profound change in Ulster's religious make-up, challenging the authority of the Established Church.[20] Efforts to suppress non-conformists were forgotten, and seventy Presbyterian ministers were permitted to return to give the 'poor church ... a new sunshine of Liberty'.[21]

In 1652, Charles II was crowned King of Scotland at Scone, causing the English Parliament to place an embargo on Scottish shipping to Ireland. This did not prevent the Scots already in co. Londonderry from farming, but many of the remaining English settlers had moved to the towns or left altogether. There was now a strong desire to redress the imbalance of Scots in rural areas. Londonderry was now well supplied with arms for its defence, with an array of cannon on the walls.[22] With a new survey having been completed with Cromwellian efficiency, the Privy Council gave authority for the London Livery Companies to be formally restored to their estates. Cromwell signed the letters patent on 24 March 1656, but it took a further two years to finalise the conveyancing.

By 1660, Ulster's population was between 217,000 and 260,000, with nearly half being made up of settlers. With settlers continuing to seek out more fertile and accessible areas, the Irish were pushed onto poorer land. Yet, English settlers still relied on them for farm labour.[23] The effect of these changes on land ownership was dramatic. In 1659, there were 4,428 English and Scots and 5,306 Irish in co. Londonderry. By the 1660s, this had become a majority of settlers, with 1,770 British households and only 1,000 Irish. This left the native Irish in Ulster infinitely weaker than before the rebellion. Up to then, Irish Catholics had owned 60 per cent of Irish land; Commonwealth confiscations now reduced this to 8 per cent. Even after the Restoration, when Catholic Royalists were partially restored, Catholics still controlled only 20 per cent.

Part 3

The Restoration and the Williamite Wars

Chapter 8

Backlash against Dissenters following the Restoration 1660 – 1685

Following Cromwell's death in 1658, his son Richard became Protector in England, but, given his lack of military experience, he lost the New Model Army's backing. Without the army's support, non-conformists forming the Rump Parliament needed to demonstrate their legitimacy. It was clear that the election of a new Parliament or a return to the position prior to Pride's Purge would 'produce a majority in favour of some kind of restoration of the monarchy'.[1] Royalists now had sufficient influence to persuade General Monck to march south from Scotland with his Parliamentarian army to back Charles II's restoration.

The New Model Army realised that they would lose Parliamentary support if Charles were to be restored as King. When this became inevitable, they approached him to highlight their role in settling Ireland on the Crown's behalf, and Charles undertook to support its 'Protestant interest'.[2] On 1 May 1660, Charles II was declared King by a newly elected Parliament in London. Dissenters were now criticised for having been the key religious supporters of the Commonwealth, and crowds started to attack their meeting houses. On 14 May 1660, Charles was also proclaimed King in Dublin. His return was greeted with great enthusiasm by Irish Catholics, hoping to see the Cromwellian land settlement overturned. In August 1660, Parliament passed an Act of Free and General Pardon, Indemnity, and Oblivion, but one section 'specifically excluded all persons involved in the Irish rebellion from any acts of clemency'.[3]

Cromwellians faced attack in Dublin, where 'the heretics and sectaries are deservedly laid aside'.[4] Leading Dissenters and regicides were brought back to London to be hung and drawn as traitors. The Restoration was also a cause for concern for the newly rehabilitated settlers in co. Londonderry. Although Cromwell had approved their return in a Charter of 1657, Charles did not recognise any Commonwealth enactments. Nevertheless, when a City deputation met him in October 1660, he pronounced:

> that his Majesty would perform what his father had promised, and more, and that his Majesty would deny the City nothing; that his Majesty found they dealt honestly with him, and his Majesty would deny them nothing.[5]

On 10 April 1662, he provided a new Charter, which left James I's original almost unchanged. The London Livery Companies now took their obligations seriously. In 1668, much of the City of Londonderry was destroyed by fire. Despite still suffering the after-effects of the Plague in 1665 and the Great Fire in 1666, the Companies again provided resources for rebuilding.

Charles was also determined to restore those prominent men, Catholic as well as Protestant, who had stood by him while he was in exile. Although soldiers and 'adventurers' were to keep the lands granted to them, 'innocent papists' and other named individuals, who had served the King with special fidelity, were to be properly compensated. Having accompanied Charles on his return to England from France, Ormonde was rewarded with lucrative appointments, including that of Lord High Steward of England. He also became Earl of Brecknock in the peerage of England and, on 30 March 1661, was raised to Duke of Ormonde in the peerage of Ireland. His huge Irish estates were restored, and he received grants that went some way towards reimbursing his earlier expenditure in support of the Royalist cause. In November, he was reinstated as Lord Lieutenant of Ireland and was now positioned to plead with Charles to overturn some of the injustices of Cromwell's Act of Settlement of 1652. In 1662, a new Act in the Irish Parliament required all new settlers to return a portion of the lands they had been allocated to the 'Old English' and those defined by Commissioners as 'innocent Catholics'. Settlers were to receive equal amounts of land elsewhere in compensation. 'Unfortunately, the Court of Claims, set up to resolve matters, identified far too many "innocent Catholics", leaving insufficient land available to provide compensation.'[6] This meant that very few Catholics recovered their estates, although efforts to resolve the issue continued for the rest of the decade.[7]

Another complexity was that expropriated lands had been occupied just as much by Church of Ireland and Protestant Establishment colleagues as by Cromwellians. Pragmatically, Charles preferred to leave 'the property of nearly the entire country in the hands of "the Protestant and English interest"'.[8] He recognised that England's security would best be served by continuing to bar Irish Catholics from public office or from Parliament.

To provide a workable solution to the compensation difficulty, Ormonde, in 1665, steered an Act of Explanation through Parliament. This required Cromwellian settlers (with some named exceptions) to give up one-third of the lands they had received under the 1652 Act. This was made more complicated because the original grantees had very often resold their allocation. Although a 'favoured minority' of Catholics (including James Duke of York, later James II), generally Anglo-Irish Royalists (which included Ormonde), recovered much of their pre-war estates, most regained nothing. Once more, Catholics concluded that the Stuart monarchy had let them down. The outcome was unsatisfactory for everyone, and grievances continued. Moreover, those, who retained lands expropriated from Catholics:

> believed, and they believed justly, that if ever the Catholics and native Irish recovered political ascendancy, they would immediately demand the restoration of the forfeited estates; they lived therefore in a state of continual alarm and excitement, and they were forced to place themselves completely under the control of England in order to have British aid in protecting the property which they had acquired. ... They felt like a garrison in a conquered country.[9]

It was not just Catholics who faced Irish Government discrimination. Dissenters had to keep their heads down to avoid charges of heresy and treason. To restore peaceful coexistence, Ormonde cracked down on religious dissent and political militancy. The Established Church demanded adherence to the Thirty-Nine Articles, the articles of faith of the Church of England.

> In January 1661 the Lords Justices forbade all meetings of 'Papists, Presbyterians, Independents, and Anabaptists and other fanatical persons' as unlawful assemblies. These included Presbyterian congregational church sessions, which not only enforced church discipline, excommunicating if necessary, but also had functions similar to those of a court of petty sessions.[10]

The influx of Presbyterian settlers, now the lifeblood of the rural economy, proved more confrontational in Ulster. Radical Presbyterian ministers, with little sympathy for monarchy after being disenfranchised for supporting the republican cause at home, arrived in large numbers as refugees from Scotland. Mossom, the Anglican Bishop of Derry reported that 'fractious preachers run out of Scotland like wild boars hunted out of the forest and throw their foam of seditious doctrine among the people'.[11] They were joined by more than 50,000 uncompromising Scottish Presbyterian extremists, who acted 'as a stimulus to an independence of mind that already existed'.[12]

Ormonde had to act quickly. He evicted sixty-one dissenting ministers from their livings. Their choice was 'to flee or only continue their ministry by preaching in barns, houses and even open fields'.[13] Only seven or eight of them agreed to conform, and many Presbyterian settlers felt compelled to return to Scotland. Having re-established its authority, the Established Church 'insisted that non-conformist views were heretical. Dissenters were banned from civil and military office.'[14] Not unreasonably, they claimed that they were being treated more harshly than Catholics, who were still pressing to be restored to their estates.

Charles II had no time for radical Presbyterians and Independents. He blamed them for starting the Civil War, seeing them as guilty of 'overthrowing a protestant church and murdering a protestant king'.[15] In England:

> Chancellor Hyde [later Earl of Clarendon] introduced the Clarendon Code, designed to suppress religious dissent. This required ministers to subscribe to the Book of Common Prayer, and banned Non-Conformist ministers from coming within five miles of a town where they had served.[16]

Although the Clarendon Code only applied in England and Scotland, Ormonde introduced a similarly oppressive policy in Ireland. Under the Act of Uniformity of 1662, it became a requirement for clergy to be consecrated by a bishop. As a result, 2,000 ministers throughout Britain and Ireland were ejected from their livings, although, in many cases, their congregations stood by them.

In June 1666, sensing that Charles was at heart a Catholic, Roman Catholic bishops and clergy meeting in Dublin pledged their allegiance to him. At the same time, Ormonde purged the Cromwellian army, reducing its numbers from 15,000 to 6,000, and Charles called on both Presbyterians and Cromwellians to adhere to religious conformity. The desperate Cromwellians instigated two rebellions attempting to take Dublin Castle and to kidnap Ormonde but failed in both. Although Ulster Presbyterians had played no part in this Dublin rebellion, Ormonde used the attack to justify his imprisonment of all Presbyterian ministers in Ulster.

Politicians, who supported the King now became Tories (a term which had originally applied to Irish outlaws).[17] Despite their initial support for Charles II's heir, his brother James, Duke of York, when his conversion to Catholicism became apparent, they focused their loyalties on support for the Crown and the Established Church. Those believing that the Crown should be answerable to the people became Whigs and included Dissenters to a man.[18] 'Those opposing episcopacy and the Established Church were by definition also the enemies of monarchy.'[19] There was deep division between opposing camps, but, as so often, those who wrote the history were on the winning side:

> Royal propagandists transformed Charles I from a 'Man of Blood' into an Anglican saint. 30 January, the anniversary of his death, was designated a church holiday and Tory churchmen used it to praise passive obedience, to condemn rebellion and to attack religious dissent.[20]

Nevertheless, until the end of the eighteenth century, Dissenters in Belfast treated 30 January as a day for celebration.

In the aftermath of the Civil War, much of Ireland was devastated. Parliamentary forces had destroyed many Royalist strongholds. The loss of buildings, crops and livestock caused great depression, so that for much of the 1660s, those settlers who remained struggled to restore their farmlands. By its persecution of Presbyterian ministers, the Establishment delayed the Scots' return and exacerbated friction. The resultant labour shortage left land destitute and farm production in decline.

As religious discord started to settle down, Ormonde became more sympathetic, but the farming economy also faced external problems. In 1667, he challenged the English Government when it passed the Importation Act to prohibit Ireland's principal export of cattle being landed in Britain.[21] This Act had been promoted by the maverick George Villiers, 2nd Duke of Buckingham, to protect British farmers. With its cattle left unsold, Irish farmers faced economic catastrophe. In Antrim, huge numbers of livestock died from a shortage of feed. Tenants had insufficient corn remaining for planting or to make bread. The contraction in trade caused by the Dutch Wars of 1672 – 74 made matters even worse. Over the next few years, there was widespread famine, only worsened by absenteeism among landlords. 'Rural poverty and hardship [became] endemic'.[22] It was only when 'Ormonde retaliated by barring the import of English and Scottish goods into Ireland [that] the Act was eventually reversed'.[23]

Ormonde's efforts on behalf of the Irish lost him favour in England. Although Irish Catholics had been removed from any remaining authority, he was criticised for the mildness of his approach. He was attacked by the 'irresponsible' element at Court led by Buckingham, and an attempt was made to assassinate him in London.[24] He remained aloof, saying: 'However ill I may stand at court I am resolved to lye well in the chronicle.' Buckingham threatened him with impeachment, and, in March 1669, he was dismissed as Lord Lieutenant and from the committee for Irish affairs. He retired to his estates at Carrick-on-Suir in South Tipperary, where, in 1670, he established a woollen industry. He did not complain, but his removal was a token gesture. His son, Thomas Butler, Earl of Ossery, became Lord Lieutenant in his place, while other friends and relations, over whom he had influence, retained their posts. As a mark of the respect in which he was more generally held, he was appointed Chancellor of Oxford University.[25]

In 1671, Richard Talbot (later Viscount and then Earl of Tyrconnell), from a family of minor Catholic gentry, presented a petition on the Irish land settlement to the King on behalf of the Irish Catholic hierarchy. The King showed his sympathy by appointing a commission under Prince Rupert of the Rhine to examine it. In the following year, he made a 'Declaration of Indulgence', to relax the Penal Laws operating against both Catholics and Non-Conformists. He also authorised the grant of a regular stipend, the *'Regium Donum'*, to Non-Conformist ministers, even though they were not restored to their livings.[26] Scots now returned to Ulster in great numbers, particularly after a Covenanter uprising at Bothwell Bridge in Scotland was suppressed in 1679. Yet, the economy still took time to recover.[27]

The English Parliament had little sympathy for the King's more conciliatory approach and it declared his Declaration of Indulgence illegal. In 1673, it passed a Test Act, which required all office-holders to take the sacrament in accordance with the rights of the Established Church. Roman Catholic bishops and priests were banished, and their religious houses and schools were closed. In 1675, the King retaliated by establishing a commission to hear grievances from Catholics who had been transplanted to Connaught.[28]

Nevertheless, there were signs of economic improvement. During the final ten years to Charles's reign, Ireland enjoyed a sustained recovery. This encouraged a large influx of settlers from north-west England. Quakers moved up the Lagan Valley and into Armagh and beyond, planting grain wherever they settled. With a requirement that settlers should plant apple trees, a thriving cider business developed, and linen production expanded. In 1681, the expiry of the Navigation Act relaxed trade restrictions to allow goods to be shipped directly between Ireland and the American colonies. Even the exceptionally cold winter of 1683/84, which ruined the crops of many Ulster farmers, did not halt the recovery:

> Lands were everywhere improved, and rents advanced to nearly double what they had been a few years before. The Kingdom abounded with money, trade flourished, even to the envy of neighbours ... Gentlemen's seats were built or building ...[29]

Yet prosperity:

> depended on the support from the Government in London, on the permanence of land settlements, on the rule and observance of Law, and on the narrow band of political and bureaucratic powers held by the Protestant ruling classes.[30]

By now, only 4 per cent of Ulster's farmland remained in native Irish ownership, and 'the few Irish we have amongst us are very much reclaimed from their barbarous customs, the most of them speaking English'.[31] The great majority of residents at Kilroot were 'presbiterians and Scotch, not one natural Irish in the parish, nor Papist'.[32] A steady flow of English and Scots continued to arrive, despite the competing attraction of the American colonies. Ireland was more appealing being closer to home, and the native Irish provided a valued source of labour.[33] Although Gaelic farmers were also enjoying economic recovery:

this fragile structure was endangered by the resentment of those who had lost lands, power and public office, and who, as devout Roman Catholics, could only deplore the anti-Papist trends.[34]

In 1672, the appointment of Arthur Capell, 1st Earl of Essex, as Lord Lieutenant to replace Ossery heralded attempts to restore the authority of the Established Church, by limiting the political power of both Dissenters and Catholics. This was entirely against the King's objective. Essex also took steps to deal with corruption in the Irish Exchequer, not realising that it was feeding Charles II's almost limitless thirst for revenue. Charles would not condone such meddling and, in 1677, Essex was recalled, allowing Ormonde to be reappointed one more time. He now placed both the Revenue and the army on a proper footing.

Faced with the prospect of the Catholic James, Duke of York, as heir to his brother Charles II, anti-Catholic feeling in England was running high. In 1678, Titus Oates created a politically motivated story of a 'popish plot' to launch a Catholic invasion of England from Ireland. Although this implicated Ormonde, Ossery defended his father 'with great spirit'. The Roman Catholic Primate of Ireland, Oliver Plunkett, the saintly Archbishop of Armagh, was accused of conspiring to raise a force against the King. Plunkett (who was beatified by Pope Benedict XV in 1920 and canonised by Pope Paul VI in 1975) was brought to London, where, on spurious evidence, he was found guilty of treason. In 1681, he was hung, drawn and quartered at Tyburn. This led to renewed calls for the removal of Roman Catholic bishops and priests from Ireland, with their religious houses and schools being closed down. The result was to force Catholic services and schools underground.[35]

Ormonde was forced to defend himself, and he wrote an open letter explaining his actions during the Civil War. Charles backed him, and, on 29 November 1682, he was granted the English title of Duke of Ormonde. Although he returned to Ireland in June 1684, the knives were out for him and he was again brought back to London. With Charles dying a few months later, Ormonde's final task as Lord

Lieutenant was to proclaim James, Duke of York, as King James II in Dublin. Although he retired in England, he remained nominally as Lord Lieutenant, attempting to block James's efforts to promote Catholicism. On his death in England in 1688, he was buried in Westminster Abbey.[36]

Chapter 9

James II and the Williamite Wars 1685 – 1691

After his second marriage in 1673 to Mary of Modena, James had become a confirmed Catholic. The prospect of returning to papal authority and the oppression of Mary Tudor's reign appalled both Irish Protestants and the English Parliament. In 1679, the Whig majority had attempted to prevent his succession by passing an Exclusion bill, but Charles, who avowed his own Catholicism on his deathbed, dissolved Parliament to prevent it from passing into law. An attempt was made to assassinate James by Whig extremists as he returned from Newmarket races, but the Rye House Plot, as it was known, failed because a fire at the King's house forced the Royal party to leave earlier than expected.[1] After it was exposed, some of the principal conspirators, including Richard Rumbold, the ringleader, and the Duke of Monmouth, an illegitimate son of Charles II, escaped abroad. Yet, two senior Whig leaders, Algernon Sidney and William, Lord Russell, were executed after being convicted by the foul-mouthed and often drunken Judge Jeffreys.[2]

'Sidney had been a key figure in developing Dissenting principles. He had supported Cromwell and, for a short period in 1646, had acted as Governor of Dublin, although he fell out with him over the execution of Charles I.'[3] In his *Discourses Concerning Government* published after his death, he 'was one of the first writers in early modern history to question hereditary kingship and suggest that a free people should choose its government'.[4] He expounded the dictum: 'Where liberty is, there is my country'. He died proclaiming his loyalty and lifelong commitment to 'The Good Old Cause' (complete religious toleration and the Catholic right to vote) and was later recognised as the Whig's foremost martyr and a secular saint. Thomas Jefferson, the architect of the American Revolution, acknowledged his *Discourses* as 'a rich treasure of republican principles'.[5]

Despite facing the prospect of a Catholic monarch for the first time since Mary Tudor, Whigs 'shed no tears' on Charles II's death.[6] He had 'reneged on promises of religious toleration' made at his restoration and was considered to have 'presided over the persecution of dissenters'.[7] James's accession renewed Irish Catholic hopes for an end to their repression and for the restoration of their ancestral lands, leaving Irish Protestants in 'a state of profound anxiety'.[8] The Revocation of the Edict of Nantes in October 1685 added to the shock waves, when 400,000 industrious French Huguenots were forced to seek asylum throughout Protestant Europe.[9] This resulted in a loss of economic confidence in Ireland, made worse by an Act of Parliament, which restored the prohibition on direct trade between Ireland and the American colonies.

Although Irish Catholics sought James's assistance, their flirtation with Spain made him realise that Protestant settlers were 'the guarantors of English power'.[10] This made him turn down initial Catholic demands for fairer treatment, and he even appointed his brother-in-law, the Protestant, Henry Hyde, 2nd Earl of Clarendon, as Lord Lieutenant. Nevertheless, with Protestants controlling 80 per cent of Irish land, James was determined to dilute their dominant position. He issued a warrant for stipends to be granted to Roman Catholic archbishops and bishops. He also turned to Richard Talbot to build Irish Catholic support for the 'Jacobite' cause. Talbot took over joint command of the Irish army with another Roman Catholic, Justin MacCarthy, later Lord Mountcashel. In 1687, to the horror of Irish Protestants, Talbot, now Earl of Tyrconnell, replaced Clarendon as Lord Deputy, becoming 'James's principal agent in promoting the revival of Catholic fortunes in Ireland'.[11] As a result, the 'process of appointing Roman Catholic Irishmen to positions of power throughout the Kingdom gained momentum'.[12] Tyrconnell purged the Irish Army of its remaining Cromwellians, replacing them with Catholics. He also ensured that the Irish House of Commons was overwhelmingly composed of Catholics;[13] Catholic sheriffs were appointed in each county; and the banned Jesuit order was permitted to return from the Continent. Tyrconnell also amended the land settlement by returning about half of what had been acquired by Protestants to its former Catholic proprietors.[14]

By returning Irish Catholics to positions of authority, James could claim to be supporting the majority population, but his promotion of Catholics in England was seen as the manoeuvring of a tyrant. His Jesuit mentors encouraged the appointment of his colleagues from exile in France. This aligned him with Louis XIV, par excellence an absolutist monarch. 'The rich and well-established Catholics of England, and even the Pope thought James's links to the Jesuits and Louis ill-advised.'[15] Even the court of Rome recommended that 'if he joined with the interest opposed to France, he would have the hearts of the people'.[16]

Dissenters in Britain were forced into action. They sought Monmouth's assistance to promote religious toleration for all and placed him in command of a small group of rebels based in Holland. 'He arrived in England with eighty-two supporters, fully expecting the populace to flock to him. Although many did so, he was comprehensively defeated at Sedgemoor, where he was captured.'[17] On 15 July 1685, his executioner took five attempts to sever his head and, even then, finished the job with a knife. On James's instruction, Judge Jeffreys chaired the 'bloody' assizes, imposing the death penalty on more than 1,000 of Monmouth's Dissenter supporters. Of these, 250, including two women, were beheaded and quartered, with the remainder being sent as slaves to the West Indies.[18]

With James making a series of tactical errors, even Tory bishops could not bring themselves to tolerate his Jesuit leanings. Nevertheless, the birth of a male heir (Charles Edward, the Old Pretender) in June 1688 seemed to assure a Roman Catholic succession.[19] A week after the birth, a Royal Warrant reserved teaching posts in all British schools for Jesuits. Faced with his insensitive approach, Protestants of all persuasions became convinced that James should be deposed. Tories combined with Whigs to seek an alternative. Their choice was his eldest daughter, the Protestant Mary, who had married William,

Prince of Orange, leader of the Dutch and a grandson of Charles I (being the son of his eldest daughter, Mary). William proved a wise choice: he had already established a strategic alliance on the Continent to thwart French aggression. He even had Catholic backing, including the Holy Roman Empire, many German States, Poland, Savoy, Spain and most importantly the Pope, horrified at the French revocation of the Edict of Nantes in 1685. When William was invited to invade England, James scrambled around for allies, but caused outrage when he called on Tyrconnell to bring his Irish Catholic army to England to assist him.

On 5 November 1688, William landed his imposing Dutch army at Torbay ready to face James's 'Jacobites' with their French and Irish support. 'After fatal vacillation', James fled to France before Christmas, abandoning his kingdom without a fight.[20] The 'Glorious Revolution' was won without a battle on English soil. In February 1689, William and his wife Mary were declared joint sovereigns of England, Scotland and Ireland. Although the French declared war on the Dutch, Tyrconnell's army in England was forced to disband, but he still retained significant forces in Ireland.[21]

Although Irish Protestants supported William, Tyrconnell, despite his acute shortage of money, still held Ireland for James. He had the support of an army of 40,000, mainly Irish Catholics continuing to press their land claims. On 12 March 1689, James landed a well-equipped Jacobite army led by French officers at Kinsale and received backing from Tory members of the Irish Established Church.[22] Nevertheless, he became nervous of their loyalty and disbanded several of their regiments despite the imminent arrival of William and his 'Orangemen'. Dissenters in Dublin had little hope of any compassion from James's Jacobite troops. The Williamite objective was not just to retain control of Ireland, but to prevent Ireland from becoming a second front for a French invasion of Britain. As a member of the English Parliament concluded: 'If Ireland be lost, England will follow.'[23]

Just as in 1641, Ulster faced the prospect of a native Irish rising, this time in support of the Jacobites. Although Ulster settlers inherently backed King William, they had little prospect of success. The key was to control Londonderry with its impregnable fortifications. Tyrconnell sent William Stewart, 1st Viscount Mountjoy, to establish control with a Royalist Regiment of Foot. Being Protestant, Mountjoy and his mainly Protestant force of 7,000 men were welcomed. This gave Tyrconnell concerns over their loyalty to the Jacobites, and he gave instructions for them to withdraw to Dublin. He intended to replace them with 1,200 Catholic Jacobite troops led by the aging Alexander MacDonnell, 3rd Earl of Antrim, but Coleraine refused to provision them. When they were billeted at Limavady, the Londonderry authorities received warning of their arrival. This provided time for thirteen apprentice boys to take matters into their own hands. While Antrim was ferrying his Scottish Jacobite troops across the Foyle River, the boys, on 7 December 1688, closed the gates of Londonderry in their faces. They forced Catholics in the City to leave, but the remaining citizens made ready to defend the walls.

Tyrconnell had to act quickly. He sent two companies of Mountjoy's men back to Londonderry under the command of Lieutenant-Colonel Robert Lundy, a Scottish Episcopalian. With Mountjoy being recalled to Dublin with his remaining men, he was immediately sent on a diplomatic mission to France, where Tyrconnell had secretly arranged his detention in the Bastille, and he remained there until 1692. Lundy was appointed Governor of Londonderry and made a show of improving the defences against an impending Jacobite attack. 'His small garrison was supplemented by six companies raised by the citizens, who had heard that William was sending troops and supplies.'[24]

The settlers' prospects were not good. James II had moved his army from Kinsale to link up with Tyrconnell at Cork, where Irish Catholics had raised troops at their own expense to support the Jacobite cause.[25] With the whole of southern Ireland under Jacobite control, James was greeted at Cork by a huge Irish army. He rewarded Tyrconnell with a dukedom. Yet their combined forces, living off the land, placed the rural economy under great strain. 'They moved on to a rapturous greeting in Dublin before continuing north.'[26] Although

Protestant Ulstermen tried to organise resistance, their assault on the Catholic garrison at Carrickfergus was unsuccessful. In early 1689, they were shattered by Jacobite troops at 'the break of Dromore' in co. Down. This left the Jacobites in control of the whole of Ulster except for the island town of Enniskillen and the walled city of Londonderry.[27]

About 30,000 Protestant settlers sought sanctuary in Londonderry with the protection of its garrison of 7,000 men. They knew that Ireland's fate depended on them holding out.[28] 'They arrived with their cattle and as much food as they could carry.'[29] They knew that if Londonderry fell, Ireland would become the bridgehead for James's assault on England to recover his throne. Arms, ammunition and cash arrived at Londonderry from Scotland under naval escort. 'The settlers showed great determination. The Rev. George Walker, Rector of Donoughmore, nearby, took personal command of his own regiment.'[30] When he learned of the imminent arrival of James's formidable force, he entered the City to encourage Lundy to face the enemy in battle before it gathered in strength. Lundy has often been considered as a turncoat acting secretly for the Royalist cause, but this is not borne out by his movements after the siege, when he returned to Scotland. Yet he showed every sign of cowardice. With Londonderry lacking provisions to withstand a siege, he was very uncertain that it could be held and had already advised that Coleraine was indefensible. He was proved wrong. On 27 March, Sir Tristram Beresford mounted a sortie against Jacobite forces from Coleraine, inflicting considerable loss. Although Lundy made a half-hearted stand at the Finn Water to protect Londonderry, his men were pushed back, and he shamefully escaped back into the City, even shutting the gates against his own troops when they sought refuge. When Walker forced his way back into the City, he prevented Lundy and its other governors from capitulating.

Lundy remained faint-hearted. When two English regiments arrived in Lough Foyle by sea to reinforce the garrison and to bring provisions, his only interest was to remove unnecessary personnel, including the other governors and himself, leaving the inhabitants to come to terms as best they could. Furious at their betrayal, the inhabitants killed one of the governors as he attempted to escape.[31] At this point, Colonel Adam Murray, a popular Scottish settler, arrived with local reinforcements and was fêted when he called on the residents to defend themselves. They went to the walls preparing to fire on the approaching Jacobite army of 20,000 men. When James demanded entry as their monarch on his arrival, the defenders shot at his entourage, killing several of his men. With Lundy being forced to resign, he remained hidden in his house, before being permitted to escape to the waiting ships.

With Murray turning down the offer to take command, the garrison appointed the 'gallant' Rev. Walker and Major Henry Baker to replace Lundy. The garrison was now supplemented with townspeople and fugitive arrivals, formed into eight well-organised regiments, each responsible for its own area. Military personnel now totalled 7,020 men and 341 officers. Any inhabitants wishing to leave joined the ships still anchored in the bay. This reduced the provisioning problem for those remaining.

The besieging army lacked the artillery to make a full-scale assault against Londonderry's massive walls. Although Tyrconnell began an eleven-day bombardment, it failed to achieve a breach, and James began to fear that 'the unpopularity of such an act would destroy his chances of restoration in England'.[32] He retired to Dublin, very critical of Tyrconnell's Irish troops. Nevertheless, Jacobite mortars lobbed bombs with high trajectories from across the Foyle River, which crashed through the roofs of houses with deadly effect, despite the defenders responding with their artillery pieces.

It was hunger which proved the inhabitants' real enemy, and pestilence broke out as a result of their poor diet. With food in short supply, disease took an increasing toll. Some crept away, providing a constant flow of intelligence to the besiegers. The besiegers were little better off; the devastated countryside could barely sustain them, and their shelter was inadequate in the very wet conditions. Walker arranged random sorties 'in a manner unauthorised by military rules', and his irregular tactics disrupted them with considerable success.[33] On 30 April 1689, Murray's horse attacked the Jacobites at Pennyburn.

When forced to retreat, he led their pursuing cavalry into an ambush manned by his infantry, where the French commander, the Marquis de Maumont, was killed. On 6 May, Murray made another successful attack which recovered Windmill Hill outside the walls, captured by the Jacobites on the previous day, but a month later, he was driven back in a second battle there.

With Enniskillen also holding out, the Enniskilleners could mount 'aggressive expeditions' against the Londonderry besiegers, 'seriously weakening the effectiveness of [their] operations'.[34] This was of crucial importance to Londonderry's defence. In May, they routed a Jacobite force at Belleek in co. Fermanagh.[35]

On 28 June, the besiegers brought two pieces of artillery to bear on the Butcher's Gate and managed to dig a mine into a cellar under one of the bastions.[36] When the Jacobites made their attack, the French officers were critical of their commanders and they were repulsed after a fierce struggle. Walker rose magnificently to the occasion, despite very few horses, no forage, no engineers to give advice, no fireworks or hand-grenades and his guns not properly mounted.

When thirty ships under Admiral George Rooke arrived in Lough Foyle with troops led by Major-General Percy Kirke with arms, ammunition and provisions, the besiegers were in such strength that neither Kirke nor Rooke was prepared risk a relief attempt.[37] The Jacobites had positioned batteries on each side of a floating boom crossing the narrows of the lough near Culmore. This was constructed of strong timber, strengthened with thick cables joined by iron chains. Although the warship *Greyhound* attempted to sever it, it ran aground and was badly damaged by fire from the batteries. Kirke made no further attempt to break the boom but sent intelligence to the citizens that he would take provisions to Enniskillen before returning with a stronger force.[38]

With supplies of meat from cattle, sheep and horses rapidly being consumed, 'dogs, cats, rats and mice began to appear in the butchers' shops'.[39] The inhabitants even resorted to hides and tallow. From the pulpit, Walker continued to assure his congregation that the Almighty would grant them deliverance. With 30,000 people still

within the walls, 10,000 were permitted to leave when James offered
protection to any who would acknowledge his authority. Those who
remained deteriorated into a progressively poor state from disease and
starvation. One fatality was Baker, who was succeeded as Governor by
John Mitchelburn, another officer.[40] Despite being almost too weak to
support arms, the defenders were threatened with death if they should
contemplate surrender. The French General, the Lithuanian Conrad
von Rosen, issued an ultimatum that, if they failed to submit by
1 July, Protestants in the surrounding areas would be rounded up and
brought to perish under the walls. On arrival the captives beseeched
the defenders to stand firm. 'The garrison retaliated by raising gallows
in the besiegers' view, threatening to execute their Jacobite prisoners,
unless the captives were freed.'[41] This persuaded James to free any
who had survived three days under the walls.

With conditions in Londonderry 'beggaring description', Walker
authorised tentative negotiations with the besiegers as a means of
buying time.[42] Yet William could not allow the City to fall, and he
ordered his naval force to make another relief attempt. On 26 July,
four ships could be seen sailing towards the town. Kirke had returned.
The frigate *Dartmouth*, commanded by Captain John Leake, escorted
three armed merchant ships (including the *Mountjoy* and the *Phoenix*)
and a long boat down Lough Foyle towards Londonderry. When the
Dartmouth opened fire, the remainder sailed past under cover of its
cannonade's smoke.[43] Despite facing heavy bombardment, they moved
forward. 'The *Mountjoy* being the larger ship, sailed into the boom
"and broke the iron part thereof" while the crew of the longboat "cut
the wooden part of the boom" with axes.' Yet, the *Mountjoy* rebounded
and her stern stuck in the mud on the west bank. The Irish yelled with
triumph as they prepared to board her.[44] Captain Michael Browning,
who was on deck encouraging his men, was shot through the head by
a musket ball and died immediately.[45]

> In an attempt to halt the Irish advance, the *Mountjoy* fired
> three guns loaded with partridge shot. Their attempt
> succeeded [in] killing several of the Irish and causing the rest

to flee. The recoil of those three shots had set the *Mountjoy* off the mud, into deeper water, where she re-floated. Led by the *Phoenix*, she passed through the broken remains of the boom and continued on her way to the City.[46]

By 22.00, they were tied up at the quayside, from where Browning's body was carried to the Cathedral. The siege, which had lasted one hundred and five days, was over.[47]

It is estimated that 15,000 settlers died. Of the:

> nearly 7,500 men forming the Londonderry regiments, only 4,300 lived to see the ships' arrival, and of these 1,000 were incapable of service. By the evening of 31 July, the Jacobites were burning their encampments and marching off. They had lost 8,000 men and retired in disorder to Strabane.[48]

Reinvigorated with sustenance, the Londonderry residents chased after them, and some lost their lives in challenging their rear-guard. Although Protestant troops from Enniskillen destroyed a Jacobite force under Mountcashel at Newtownbutler, the retreating Jacobites wreaked havoc, destroying Limavady and burning and looting any remaining settlements in their path. Roads were left in a terrible state with bridges impassable. Virtually no livestock survived, and any grain was reserved to victual Danish troops, who terrorised the area.[49]

The City of Londonderry was seriously damaged. The spire of the Cathedral had been demolished before the siege, with its lead being used to make bullets. The roof of the nave, which had provided a platform for cannon, required major repair. Very few houses remained standing. Yet its defiance had bought King William time and provided a 'much-needed tonic for Williamite and Protestant morale'.[50] With Walker being fêted as a hero, his published account provided admirable propaganda for the Established Church. 'Although he was promised the bishopric of Londonderry, he was killed at the battle of the Boyne before he could' take up his appointment.[51] Adulation for him annoyed Presbyterians, who felt that their contribution was overlooked. The garrison's survivors were never paid; when Mitchelburn went to London to seek compensation for the destitute citizen army, he was thrown in the Fleet prison for debt, despite William's promises of 'recompense' for services and sufferings.[52]

Irish Roman Catholics still believed they had a good opportunity to recover lost ground. The Jacobites were still a force to be reckoned with; they continued to control the Irish Government and retained French, English and Scottish Royalist troops to fight alongside them. William had been pinned down in Scotland against Royalists, who won a great victory at Killicrankie, cutting a Williamite force to pieces. It was only when the Highlanders' advance was brought under control at the Battle of Dunkeld, that William could turn his attention to Ireland.[53]

The Protestants in Ireland had:

> viewed the rapid increase of Roman Catholic influence and power with dismay, and knew their position under an Irish Roman Catholic Parliament and State would be very weak, if not untenable.[54]

Although they supported William and Mary as their rightful sovereigns, William knew that they needed his belated support.

> On 13 August 1689, despite having deployed the bulk of his English army to face the French in the Netherlands, he sent the seventy-three-year-old Protestant Frederick Herman, Duke of Schomberg, to Ballyholme Bay with an Irish expeditionary force.[55]

This was made up almost entirely of Protestants, mainly inexperienced Irish, who had taken refuge in England, supported by hardened Dutch and Huguenot troops. Each side boasted large armies under professional soldiers displaying 'courage and verve'.[56] Although Schomberg recovered Carrickfergus after a punishing bombardment, 'the next ten months were spent in inconclusive campaigning',[57] particularly because Schomberg's transport and provisions failed to arrive. With his Irish troops unversed in basic hygiene, disease killed many thousands of his men.[58]

James had 'subsided into an apathetic lethargy', but Tyrconnell reorganised his army and marched north.[59] Although Schomberg was forced back to Lisburn, Tyrconnell failed to press home his advantage and retired for the winter of 1689/90 to Dublin. In March 1690, Schomberg disembarked a further 7,000 Danish mercenaries at Belfast Lough. During April and May, English, German, and Dutch troops, well supplied with guns and ammunition, also arrived in numbers. Their arrival enabled Schomberg to capture Charlemont.[60] Yet William knew that he had to come himself, and the very threat of his arrival caused Jacobite mass desertions. His fleet crossed the Irish Sea with about 300 vessels escorted by a squadron of warships under Sir Cloudesley Shovell. On 14 June 1690, he landed a further 36,000 men at Carrickfergus, made up of English, Dutch, Danes, French Huguenots and Germans, all members of the Grand Alliance against France formed at the Treaty of Vienna. Even Pope Innocent XI provided financial and diplomatic support in his effort to contain the 'overweening ambition' of the French King.[61] The eyes of Europe were now focused on the war between Williamites and Jacobites in Ireland.

On arrival, William secured the loyalty of the Scottish non-conformists by raising the '*Regium Donum*', the stipend supporting Presbyterian ministers, to £1,200. This overcame their resentment at being treated as inferior citizens by the Established Church. With William advancing south to a position on the left bank of the River Boyne, Ulster settlers, particularly those from Enniskillen, joined him as skirmishers.[62]

James also curried favour with his Irish troops. With Irish Catholics continuing to press their land claims, he rushed a repeal of the Act of Settlement through the Irish Parliament. Yet this failed to offer compensation to the lands' former Protestant occupants for improvements they had undertaken. A new Act of Attainder made it treasonable to join William. The combined effect of this legislation persuaded Presbyterians to join William in droves. It had gone far further than James had intended, restoring Ireland to its original Gaelic ownership. Ireland was now:

> an independent self-governing Kingdom with a Roman Catholic dynasty as its head. He recognised, only too late, the disastrous effect on British public opinion of disinheriting the settlers and removing the influence of England's Parliament.[63]

Irish Tories and the Established Church faced a dilemma. If they accepted that kings were above the law and that subjects should be passively obedient, they had to accept legislation they considered outrageous. It resulted in William and Mary gaining both popular support and the City of London's powerful backing.[64]

In March 1690, Louis XIV recalled Mountcashel's Irish Regiments to France. Their French Officers considered them far more effective fighting on the Continent. They were replaced by 7,000 additional French troops, which landed at Cork under the Compte de Lauzun. Although Tyrconnell still retained a substantial Irish force, it lacked military experience. Although de Lauzun superseded von Rosen as the French Commander-in-Chief, he proved far less willing to engage in combat. He even considered coming to terms with William, but broke off negotiations after being advised that James 'had every chance of recovering England'.[65]

On 1 July, James lined out an army of 25,000 men to face William's force of 36,000 at the Boyne River. Both sides were well-organised and evenly matched. James's French military officers wanted him to approach the Williamites from the west, but James overruled their advice. When William sent his right wing westward in a feint to divert Jacobite forces from his proposed line of attack across the river, the Jacobite command fell for his ruse and moved their main force to cover his manoeuvre. Tyrconnell now faced the full might of William's advance with only one-third of the Jacobite army.

Despite being spearheaded by Schomberg's hardened troops as they crossed the river, the Williamites faced a ferocious counterattack from Jacobite cavalry led by the Anglo-Irish Patrick Sarsfield, during which both Schomberg and the Rev. Walker were killed. The outcome seemed in the balance until William with his Enniskillen skirmishers broke the Jacobite line in a flanking manoeuvre. Yet a rear-guard action by the French further upstream allowed most of the Jacobite force to retire in good order. Nevertheless, the result was decisive, with many inexperienced Irish troops abandoning their equipment as they retreated.

> James left almost immediately, fearing that any further involvement would prejudice his dwindling popularity in England. On 4 July, he re-embarked for France at Kinsale and was never to return.[66]

This 'was a severe blow to Louis XIV's pretensions to European hegemony'.[67] The victory at the Boyne was greeted with 'delirious joy' not only in England, but in the central European heartland of the Holy Roman Empire and by the Papacy.[68] William moved on to Dublin and, on 6 July, demanded unconditional surrender. Tyrconnell and the French commanders were only too ready to conclude terms, but Sarsfield persuaded them to fight on.[69]

'By deserting Ireland, James had devastated his cause and sacrificed his Irish Catholic and French forces.'[70] 'The Catholic Irish suffered for their loyalty to a dynasty that regarded [them] as, at most, expendable pawns in a game, the objective of which was to rule Britain.'[71] Once refreshed and re-equipped, the Williamites marched west. Sarsfield regrouped the Jacobite forces at Limerick, and it was here and at Athlone that they made their stand.[72]

Both William and his Dutch General, Baron von Ginkel, underestimated the Irish resolve. In July, the Williamites failed to take Athlone. In early August, they besieged Limerick, but:

> Sarsfield's cavalry dealt a crushing blow by destroying a Williamite convoy of heavy guns, ammunition carts and baggage, which left them short of equipment.[73]

Although the walls of Limerick were breached, its defenders 'fought bravely and effectively'.[74] All attempts to storm the breach were resisted, helped by lightning strikes from Sarsfield's cavalry.[75] 'By the end of August, William had had enough; he raised the siege and returned to England.'[76]

On 23 September, John Churchill, Earl (and later Duke) of Marlborough arrived with fresh Williamite troops to tidy up the campaign. Despite his former close association with James, Marlborough had joined William on his arrival in England. By taking Cork and Kinsale, the Williamites cut the Jacobites' main supply lines from France. Louis XIV had always viewed the war in Ireland as a means of diverting Williamite troops from the Continent. Realising that he could achieve no more, he recalled his French army, bringing Tyrconnell with it. The Irish Jacobites were left under the command of James's twenty-year-old illegitimate son, James Fitzjames, Duke of Berwick, (by Arabella Churchill, and hence, Marlborough's nephew). Berwick's men were left 'uncertain and confused'.[77] Yet they fought 'doggedly behind the Shannon River for another year'.[78]

Despite Marlborough's arrival, von Ginkel retained overall command of the Williamites, convinced that he could end the hostilities by buying off the Irish. In June 1691, after storming Athlone, he offered a pardon and security of property to any who would surrender or change sides. This had little effect. Meanwhile, Tyrconnell pressed Louis XIV to send more assistance. In May, the able French General Saint-Ruth arrived to take command, but the French objective was still only to divert Williamite resources from the Netherlands.[79]

Although he had failed to relieve Athlone, on 12 July 1691, Saint-Ruth made his stand in defence of Aughrim Hill, nearby. The opposing armies each numbered about 20,000 men. The initial Jacobite attack drove the Williamites back over marshy terrain, almost overrunning von Ginkel's artillery. With victory almost certain, Saint-Ruth was decapitated by a cannonball, and, without him, the Irish could not be rallied, even by Sarsfield's cavalry. 'Von Ginkel's Dragoons moved forward in a concerted charge, cutting down the demoralised Irish troops'.[80] With 7,000 left dead, many from members of leading Roman

Catholic Irish families, it was the bloodiest battle in Ireland's history.[81] It was Aughrim Hill not the Boyne that proved more decisive. 'Ulster Protestants celebrated the end of the war with bonfires and would continue to do so annually thereafter.'[82]

Although the French second-in-command, d'Usson, attempted to hold Galway, its burghers surrendered to Von Ginkel on 21 July. In August, when Tyrconnell died in Limerick, von Ginkel renewed his sieges of Limerick and Sligo. When Sligo surrendered, von Ginkel offered generous terms, hoping to free up his troops to return to Europe. On 3 October 1691, he signed the Treaty of Limerick, which allowed Irish Jacobite forces to retire to France. 'Those willing to swear the Oath of Allegiance to William and Mary were to be permitted to keep their estates.'[83] On 20 October, the French sent transport ships to the Shannon estuary. Three months later, Sarsfield and the remaining Jacobite force were transported to France as the core of the 'the Wild Geese', the crack Irish regiments of the French army.[84]

With the Glorious Revolution assured of control, the Protestant Ascendancy in Ireland regained authority. Presbyterians were granted religious concessions under the Act of Toleration. Settlers could now begin the slow process of rebuilding for a third time. Yet Protestant landowners still feared their prospects, if the Irish should ever recover power. Roman Catholicism and Irish nationalism had not been stifled.

Chapter 10

The Protestant Ascendancy's assertion of its authority 1691 – 1714

The Establishment in Ireland now joined with Presbyterians and Whigs in England to acknowledge William as King and to confirm James's deposition. Although Dissenters loyal to The Good Old Cause would have preferred to avoid another monarchy, they supported William in the hope that he would respect Parliament, restore liberties and show religious tolerance. When he introduced the Act of Toleration in 1689, they believed that, at last, they had found an English King in sympathy with them.[1]

William's other great achievement was to modernise the Irish linen industry. He brought in Huguenot immigrants, who congregated at Lisburn outside Belfast, to develop linen production processes and improve quality. Most importantly:

> flax spinning became a constant occupation for women among Ulster's farming families, providing a significant source of income for their hard-pressed agricultural households. With their cheaper labour cost and the skill to spin finer yarns by hand, this Irish cottage industry continued to compete successfully with flax spinners elsewhere.[2]

'For Tories, the Glorious Revolution was an act of God; for Whigs, it was an act of the people.'[3] 'Did civil and religious authority reside in the person of kings and bishops, or did civil authority reside in the people and religious authority in a man's conscience?'[4] This great debate between Tories and Whigs over the role of monarchy would continue for the next century.[5] Tories believed that:

the Established Church and its convocation of bishops were the only legitimate source of religious authority. Anyone who refused to accept this was a blasphemer, a heretic or worse.[6]

'Any attack on the privileges of the Established Church was seen as an attack on the State as well.'[7]

With the Protestant Ascendancy in Dublin wielding complete control:

the Irish Parliament considered Von Ginkel's terms [to the Jacobites] to have been too lenient. It withdrew the repeal of the Act of Settlement and forced the Irish to recognise English title to areas previously settled. Under a succession of Penal Laws, Catholics were excluded from holding public office or from being able to vote.[8]

It was feared that if Catholics gained a majority in Parliament, they would seek to reverse the land grants made to settlers over the previous 200 years.

From 1692 until its abolition by the Act of Union of 1800, the Irish Parliament consisted only of Protestant landowners. When it met for six months every two years, it focused only on protecting its Protestant interest by enacting a further progression of Penal Laws. In 1695, the English Parliament passed an Act (7 William III. Cap. 4) prohibiting Roman Catholics from sending their children abroad for their education or from teaching in Irish schools. Two other Acts (7 William III, Cap. 5 and 7 William III, Cap. 21) quickly followed; the first prohibited Catholics from keeping arms or horses valued at five pounds or more. The second attempted to suppress armed robbery by forcing both Roman Catholics and Protestants to pay collectively for crimes committed by their co-religionists.[9]

In 1697, the Irish Parliament passed the Banishment Act, requiring all Jesuits, monks, Catholic bishops and other clergy to leave Ireland by 1 May 1698. In 1699, Papists were banned from the legal profession, and a Commission of Inquiry appointed trustees to arrange the disposal of forfeited estates. In 1704, further legislation prohibited Catholics from buying land or from acting as guardians. With land-ownership being a prerequisite for holding a parliamentary seat, this kept Catholics out of Parliament.[10]

> It might be assumed that the Penal Laws were imposed out of high-minded religious conscience, but 'they were designed solely to maintain the wealth and influence' of those enacting them.[11] Religion was merely 'a convenient cry to secure the prejudices of the English people in support', and the restrictions were enforced far more rigorously than legislation prohibiting Catholic worship.[12] Apart from continuing to require Catholics to pay tithes to an alien church, no real efforts were made to prevent them from practicing their religion.[13]

With the great majority of the Irish remaining Catholic, the Establishment felt insecure, particularly as 'France remained strong and hostile'.[14] The papacy only added to concerns by delegating the appointment of Irish Catholic bishops to James with his Jesuit leanings and now in exile in France. This left the Roman Catholic Church in Ireland 'avowedly Jacobite'.[15] On William's death on 8 March 1702 (with James having died in the year before), Louis XIV recognised 'James III and VIII' ('the Old Pretender') as King. The English Government retaliated by insisting that all Irish office holders, lawyers and schoolmasters should be 'required by Act of Parliament to take an Oath of Abjuration recognising Queen Anne as their rightful Sovereign and disowning the Stuart Pretender'.[16]

Although Irish Catholics considered it a breach of the terms of the Treaty of Limerick, it was only Protestants, who gained restoration of their lands. 'Roman Catholics were to become second-class citizens in the country they regarded as their own'.[17]

'Nine-tenths of Ireland now belonged to the English Interest', and 500,000 acres of expropriated land was put up for sale. With few buyers, a half of it was granted at knockdown prices. William Conolly, the son of a family of Irish innkeepers, became the richest man in Ireland by land-jobbing, later becoming Speaker of the Irish House of Commons.[18]

Although Catholics could continue farming as tenants, they were gradually eased off more fertile lowland areas. It was their resentment at losing more productive land, as much as the Penal Laws, which fostered their conflict with Protestant neighbours. Cultivating upland areas involved 'unremitting labour' to burn off the whin and heather and to prise out rocks and stumps.[19] In west Donegal, 'thin acid soil had to be painstakingly enriched with seaweed and sweetened with shell sand'.[20] 'The soil's variable quality led to the planting of potatoes, which could tolerate poorer conditions and eliminate scurvy by adding vitamin C to the Irish diet.'[21]

In an effort to alleviate food shortages among Catholic communities, who continued to graze cattle to the exclusion of arable crops, farmers with more than one hundred acres were required to plough at least five per cent of their land. Yet the real problem was landlord absenteeism. The income from rents received by those living abroad no longer circulated through the local economy. To encourage them to live on their estates 'and to contribute to the economic and cultural life of Ireland', non-residents were levied with a tax of four shillings in the pound.[22]

Although William III had offered Dissenters freedom of worship under the Act of Toleration of 1689, this did not extend to Unitarians. Yet this embargo was relaxed. On 3 November 1692, Parliament passed an Act (4 William & Mary. Cap. 2) 'for the encouragement of Protestant strangers to settle in the Kingdom of Ireland'.[23] This allowed settlers to 'worship in the form to which they had been accustomed'.[24] Presbyterian Scots had arrived in Ulster in large numbers before the Williamite war ended. Many had followed the army, purchasing booty scavenged by the military. It was a natural disaster at home which triggered their mass exodus from Scotland. In 1693, the volcano of Hekla in Iceland erupted and, for seven years, spewed huge amounts of volcanic dust into the atmosphere, causing a mini-ice age. Scandinavia faced terrible famine and Scottish harvests failed in each year. Some 200,000 starving Scots were reported to be begging for sustenance from door to door, with an estimated one-in-five dying.[25] With Ireland escaping the worst effects of the dust cloud, many Scottish survivors, particularly from lowland areas in the south-west, headed for Ulster. Claims that 50,000 Scots arrived in Ireland between 1689 and 1715 may be exaggerated, but their departure from their traditional tenancies caused great difficulties at home.[26] They were motivated by the availability of cheap land, and their arrival forced out Gaelic Catholics. They arrived with large numbers of cattle and adopted more intensive farming methods. By the time that Scotland's climate had started to recover, causing a decline in the flow of immigrants to Ireland, Scottish Presbyterians were outnumbering Catholics in Ulster. With Dissenters enjoying a period of relative religious freedom, Ulster recovered rapidly from its recent severe loss of life, and even this had borne no comparison to the blood-letting of 1641/42.[27]

The Irish Establishment did not relish the increase in the Presbyterian population. It was not just Catholics who now faced discrimination. Successive British monarchs felt threatened by the growing republican sentiment among Presbyterians. William III's concessions started to be chipped away. By 1702, Queen Anne's Tory Government was campaigning against non-conformists. With lingering taunts at them being regicides, they felt that they were being treated as badly as, if not worse than, the Catholics. New penal laws challenged all brands of Calvinism, both Scottish and Cromwellian, eager 'to establish the Presbyterian form of Church Government' with its traditional hostility to the appointment of bishops. In London, the Tory Government re-imposed the Westminster Confession of Faith on all new ministers. This was followed in Ireland by The Test Act of 1704, which 'made it necessary for all persons holding public appointments to take Communion in the Established Church within three months of their assuming office.'[28] Some non-conformists overcame their religious scruples and adhered to the Test so that they could sit in Parliament 'ready to embrace every opportunity to weaken the episcopal establishment'.[29] When the Act was extended to require all Presbyterians to swear an oath of allegiance to the Crown, those with republican leanings saw this as a denial of their rights won during the Glorious Revolution. With most aldermen and burgesses in Londonderry and Belfast being Presbyterian, they faced dismissal, if they failed to comply with the Test.[30]

> No Presbyterians could legally conduct a school, in many instances land would not be let to Presbyterian tenants and, if magistrates so wished, church services could be declared illegal and the building of churches prohibited.[31]

Nevertheless, the Scottish influx had made Belfast 'the most dynamic centre of trade in Ulster and, possibly, the fastest growing town in Ireland'.[32] It brought with it a period of unbroken peace and prosperity, which lasted from 1691 until the outbreak of the United Irish rebellion in 1798. The Earl of Donegall, who supervised the City, did much to encourage new arrivals. Although freemen were required to conform to the Church of Ireland in accordance with the Oath of Supremacy, Donegall, who was himself strongly Puritan, did not enforce this on Presbyterians. They were permitted to become 'freemen' of Belfast, benefiting from lower property rates, reduced customs, tolls, fines and court fees. With Belfast growing in importance, it now eclipsed Carrickfergus as the principal port for exporting Ulster's agricultural produce.

> A new bridge across the Lagan linked it to Lisburn and was for many years the longest in the British Isles. By 1706, its population had reached 5,000, almost exclusively made up of settlers, compared to 62,000 in Dublin and 17,500 in Cork.[33]

Despite the Penal Laws, Presbyterian Meeting Houses remained well-attended and their elders called on congregations to study the bible each day for guidance. With ministers laying great emphasis on reading skills, Ulster was soon the most literate corner of Ireland. Congregations were formed into presbyteries to maintain discipline and to supervise every area with regular visitations, co-ordinated by annual meetings of the Ulster synod. The more radical were soon expressing their republican ideals and were 'seethingly angry'.[34] The Church of Ireland remained highly suspicious; William King, Archbishop of Dublin, was determined to curb their 'arrogant pretensions'. He reported:

> They are a people embodied under their lay leaders, presbyteries and synods ... and will be just so far the King's subjects as their lay elders and presbyteries will allow them.[35]

Faced with having to comply with the Test Act and Catholic Irish belligerence, many Presbyterians left for America. Their ability to read made them better able than Catholics to learn of the opportunities offered by emigration, and America attracted Protestants of every persuasion. In 1718, five ships left Londonderry filled with emigrants bound for New Hampshire, and there was a further wave of emigration in 1729. Their departure caused great concern within the Dublin Establishment, who blamed Presbyterian ministers for inciting their congregations to leave. The Catholic Irish did not leave in similar numbers; they were still tied to the land of their ancestors and had difficulty in raising the cost of the fare. Although Presbyterians still outnumbered both Catholics and Anglicans in Ulster, there were fears of an upsurge in the Catholic population, 'being a breeding people'.[36] This threatened the security of settlers staying behind.[37]

Close bonds were developed between Ireland and America. Their colonies had been begun at a similar time and had attracted similar numbers of initial settlers. Americans shared with the Irish a sense of frustration at their treatment by the British Government. It was not only freedom of religious thought, but controls on trade designed to protect English businesses and farm prices. Settlers from Ireland arrived in family groups, becoming known as the Scotch-Irish. Their skills in clearing the Ulster hinterland were now put to good use in the American 'back country', and they successfully pushed hostile native Americans ever westward. It was the development of republicanism among impoverished Irish Presbyterian immigrants that did much to sway Americans towards calls for American independence. These new arrivals, representing about one-sixth of the total colonial population, were already 'implacable enemies of British rule, and were one of the most significant factors in the success of the American Revolution'.[38] It took fighting in America to curtail the flood of departures from Ulster, but, by 1779, between 100,000 and 200,000 Scotch-Irish are thought to have arrived there. This outflow of former Ulster tenants again resumed in 1783, as soon as peace was declared.[39]

Part 4

The development of Dissenter theology in the cause of republicanism

Chapter 11

The development of Dissenter thinking in Ireland c. 1690 – c. 1760

The great fear among the Tory Government in London and the Establishment in Dublin was that the development of Presbyterian thinking would lead to a growth in republicanism. If this gained the support of the Catholic hierarchy in Ireland, it was difficult to see how British rule could be sustained. Despite the later folk-hero status earned by early Irish republican leaders, they never gained the crucial support of influential Presbyterians and Dissenters in Belfast or Dublin, nor of the Catholic hierarchy. Senior Catholics were not disloyal to Britain. They wanted to use persuasion not revolution to achieve emancipation and the vote in Parliament. Yet republicanism gained a considerable following among rank and file Presbyterians and Catholics. Their economic woes led them to be influenced by a group of pioneering and charismatic leaders.

The man who stepped forward to champion the Dissenters' cause in Ireland was John Toland, a young Irishman born in Donegal in 1670, probably the illegitimate son of a Catholic priest. 'By the age of sixteen he had embraced Dissenting Protestantism, and had become, in his own words, "zealous against Popery".'[1] After being sponsored through university by Dissenting benefactors, he befriended John Locke and seems to have espoused Deism with its belief in 'a single God, who does not act to influence events'.[2] Deism holds that God is a divine creator unconnected to individual religions. Toland denied that 'priests have any special insight into scripture'.[3] He held that 'no person should believe anything that is clearly contrary to reason'.[4] While his objective was to attack popery, his views could also be taken as an attack on the Established Church, exposing him to charges of blasphemy.

After arriving in Dublin in 1697, Toland spread his controversial ideas with great charm to a ready audience in local coffee houses. Despite receiving patronage from the Cromwellian Robert (later Viscount) Molesworth, his outspokenness gained him many enemies among the Dublin Establishment, resulting in a Parliamentary order for his books to be burned. When he made a 'coffee house jest of the Trinity', he was arrested.[5] Even his friends, including Locke, considered him incautious. To the delight of the Establishment, who did not want to turn him into a folk-hero, he fled Dublin to avoid trial, in which he would have been at risk of hanging. While away, he prepared a history of the druids written as a parody on Christian priests. He even claimed that the early Christian church in Ireland was Unitarian, but this conveniently suited his thesis, as St. Patrick is known to have adopted the shamrock as a symbol of the Trinity. He never returned to Ireland, but travelled to Hanover, where he courted the Electress by asserting 'the equal intellectual capacity of men and women'.[6] She had been chosen to succeed Queen Anne, and, after her death, he remained there to win support for the accession of her son, George, to the English throne. Despite Toland's republican ideals, he preferred the Hanoverians as monarchs 'to the High Anglican intolerance that had marked the reign of Queen Anne', during which attempts were made to enact anti-Dissenter legislation.[7] His legacy was to popularise the works of the early Dissenting philosophers, bringing them to the attention of Thomas Jefferson, Benjamin Franklin and the later Irish reformers and United Irishmen, who continued to espouse the Good Old Cause.

Although the Irish Parliament was dominated by Established Church members, Dissenters 'wielded some influence' in the Dublin Corporation.[8] With the Catholics side-lined, 'civic political conflict was usually between Anglicans and Dissenters'.[9] Dublin Dissenters were led by the Rev. Joseph Boyse and the Rev. Thomas Emlyn at the Wood Street Congregational Church, both of whom were vilified by the Establishment for their controversial writings. When the storm against Emlyn broke, he held to his stance. In 1702, a senior member of his New Street congregation challenged him for not referring to the doctrine of the Trinity in his sermons. This forced him to admit that he did not subscribe to it. He was brought before the Dublin Presbytery, where Boyse, despite advocating freedom of conscience, arranged his dismissal.

Emlyn travelled to London, where he secretly published an anonymous pamphlet setting out his Unitarian views. This left him open to charges of heresy and blasphemy. On returning to Dublin in 1702, he was charged with having published it. He now faced the Lord Chief Justice (supported by two archbishops and five bishops of the Church of Ireland) in the Blasphemy Court, where he was told he could not speak in his own defence. Although the Court had no proof that he was the author, Boyse, to the horror of Emlyn's supporters, gave evidence against his old friend. He told the Court that the pamphlet outlined views that Emlyn had expressed privately in Presbytery. In 'an outrageous perversion of the law', the Lord Chief Justice told the jury: 'Presumption is as good as evidence.' Emlyn was imprisoned and fined. With William III having recently died, Boyse probably feared being prosecuted himself, but was considered to have betrayed a confidence. He lived to regret his actions and, in 1705, lobbied James, 2nd Duke of Ormonde (previously Ossery), to gain Emlyn's release after two years of imprisonment. Emlyn immediately left Dublin for London, where he was established as a symbol of liberal thought and freedom of conscience, vigorously upholding Unitarianism until his death in 1743.

The Test Act of 1704 provoked a strong reaction, particularly from the Rev. John Abernethy, whose siblings had all died during the siege of Londonderry in 1689. To avoid the Williamite war, he had been sent to Scotland, where, at the age of thirteen, he began studying for the ministry in Glasgow. On his return to Antrim, he formed the Belfast Society, made up of like-minded liberal ministers and a few lay philosophers. Society members would brook no restriction on their consciences or accept a man-made confession of faith; nor would they accept any limitations on office as imposed by the Test Act. Although Abernethy had visited Wood Street in Dublin during the Emlyn controversy, he refused a ministerial appointment there. Yet he became the most prominent of the liberals, often known as 'New Light' Presbyterians or 'Non-Subscribers'. These were not all Unitarian, but all believed in freedom of conscience, despite their desire to remain within the Presbyterian mainstream. They 'argued that "it was only by being tolerant of different theological views within Presbyterianism, could a church plausibly petition for toleration from the Church of Ireland"'.[10] Theirs was a call not just for religious but for civil liberty. Abernethy preached on 'Religious Obedience Founded on Personal Persuasion'. He argued that early Christians had adopted episcopacy in a mistaken carry-over from their Jewish roots. 'In 1726, Abernethy and sixteen of his ministerial colleagues were ejected from the Synod of Ulster.'[11] This caused a Presbyterian schism. He now established the Presbytery of Antrim, which formed 'a warm coalition' with the Dissenters of Dublin and Munster.

The new coalition of Dissenters received funding from members of the Presbyterian congregation in Dublin led by the publisher, William Bruce. Bruce had published sermons and other works by ministers and philosophers, which were widely read, and became the driving force behind a circle of liberals connected to Wood Street, which often met at the home of Molesworth, Toland's old benefactor. It espoused republican ideals and 'handed to a second generation a patriotic spirit that included all Irishmen in its loyalties and diffused a liberal philosophy throughout more than one city or country.'[12] Bruce's group was widely respected by Non-Subscribers. William Drennan later acknowledged it as his greatest political influence. The coalition's first task was to rationalise differences in spiritual thought between the descendants of English, Cromwellian and Scottish Presbyterians.

By 1730, Abernethy was aged fifty and, with his skills as a great preacher, became recognised as the leading Non-Subscriber in Ireland. On Boyse's death in 1730, he was appointed minister at Wood Street. By then, Boyse had refined his views on Unitarianism and the congregation accepted Abernethy, although, in the light of Emlyn's problems, he was careful not to broadcast his Unitarian sympathies. It was only after his death in 1740 that some 'pretty amazing passages' were found in his diaries by his friend, the Rev. James Duchal, who decided to keep them secret.

Another strong influence on later Dissenters was William Bruce's cousin, Francis Hutcheson, born of Cromwelliam stock in 1694 at Saintfield, co. Down. He had studied theology at Glasgow University, and, after making his name as an academic, joined his friend the Rev. Thomas Drennan (father of William) to teach at a new academy attached to Wood Street. This of itself was not without risk, as neither of them had the licence required from a bishop of the Church of Ireland. While living in Dublin, Hutcheson wrote *An Inquiry Concerning the Origins of our Ideas of Beauty and Virtue* in which he asserted: 'That which is good is what brings the greatest happiness to the greatest number.' This became a slogan for liberal reformers and was to be quoted by William Drennan in his proposal for the formation of the United Irishmen. Hutcheson's writing established him as one of the greatest philosophers of his generation. He provided a bridge to link Presbyterians and Anglicans by developing friendships with the Irish ruling elite. Although its members tried 'to woo him into the Established Church with promises "of great preferment"', he refused to desert his Presbyterian heritage.[13] Yet the Archbishop of Dublin, William King, protected him from prosecution despite him teaching 'without subscribing to the ecclesiastical canons'.

In 1730, Hutcheson accepted the chair of moral philosophy at Glasgow University, where he became renowned as a brilliant and innovative teacher, one of the first to provide his lectures in English rather than Latin. He was 'the father of the Scottish Enlightenment', which held that reason was the primary source of authority and legitimacy. His followers promoted his ideals, which included liberty, progress, tolerance, fraternity, constitutional government, and separation of church and state. These included David Hume, the Enlightenment's greatest philosopher, and Adam Smith, the father of modern economics, both of whom considered 'the never to be forgotten Hutcheson' as a formative influence on their thinking. Hutcheson averred that Government should be representative of the people and be administered by popularly elected assemblies, sentiments which gained him Thomas Jefferson's respect. He proclaimed:

> When the lower orders are liberated from poverty, tyranny, ignorance and superstition, the common citizen's moral sense would promote civic virtue and general happiness.[14]

In an age when social position was conveyed by birth, Hutcheson saw that 'all human beings are born free and equal'.[15] As one of the first to condemn slavery, his views profoundly influenced the anti-slavery movement. He believed that standing armies were potential agents of tyranny and proposed raising a citizen's army for a community's protection. 'Never to be forgotten Hutcheson' died in 1746 in his beloved Dublin, where he lies in an unmarked grave.

With Dublin being the centre of Irish Government, members of Parliament and peers needed fashionable town houses while they attended sittings for six months every two years. 'The extravagant tastes of this metropolitan elite' spawned artisans, who formed into guilds to supervise building works and the manufacture of the artefacts being demanded.[16] Members of these guilds became freemen of Dublin, with a right to elect ninety-six representatives to its Corporation's Common Council. As they became more forthright, 'they were inclined to resent the Council's subservience to the unelected and self-selecting Board of Aldermen', who 'were drawn from the wealthiest Protestant merchants and held office for life.'[17]

Dublin artisans found a champion in Charles Lucas, who was of Cromwellian stock. He had become an apprentice apothecary in about 1730 and some ten years later joined the Common Council through the Apothecaries' Guild. He was supported by Dissenters to lead a campaign to increase the influence of elected representatives by 'an aggressive assertion of Irish constitutional rights and an insistence on the primacy of representative institutions over monarchy and aristocracy'.[18] The Established Church backed his opponents, who dubbed his supporters 'King-Killers'. He caused more controversy by publishing a pamphlet in which 'he questioned the right of the King to legislate for Ireland'.[19] When the Irish House of Commons saw this as treasonable, the Dublin Corporation pounced. Despite having public support, Lucas was forced to flee abroad to avoid prosecution.

While away, he qualified as a physician in Leyden. His replacement on the Council was another prominent Dissenter, Thomas Read. The Anglican bishops viewed Read's appointment as an attempt by New Light Presbyterians 'to take over the management of the City and to tear down the Church'.[20]

When George II died in 1760, he was succeeded by his grandson, George III. This allowed Lucas to return to Dublin with no case for his alleged treason to answer. The sitting Member of Parliament for Dublin, a Dissenter, stood aside to allow Lucas to contest the seat. With a platform that denounced political corruption and attacked the subordination of the Irish Parliament to Westminster, he scored a big victory as a champion of the Dublin working class. He retained his seat as a focus against corruption until his death in 1771. During this time, he established the anti-Government *Freeman's Journal*, 'in whose writings the first dawning of a national and Irish feeling are to be found'.[21] It achieved such international repute that Benjamin Franklin visited him on one of his trips to Europe.

Chapter 12

Growing seeds of Dissenter unrest
c. 1714 – c. 1783

Having welcomed the accession of George I, it might seem that Dissenters flourished under the Hanoverian Kings, but, when the papacy refused to recognise Hanoverian rule, the monarchy did not initially feel secure, particularly as the Jacobites retained French support. This meant that, during the first half of the eighteenth century, 'Dissenters could not afford to indulge in republican flights of fancy', but they remained genuine in their support for the Hanoverians.[1] 'Their loyalty did not mean that they would be content to allow a Hanoverian monarch to exceed his authority or deny them freedom of conscience.'[2] It was only when the Jacobite threat was finally extinguished at the Battle of Culloden in 1746 that Dissenters dared to assert their beliefs more openly. They were soon criticising George III, who let it be known 'that any form of religious toleration was an anathema to him'.[3] He defended the privileges of the Established Church and resisted 'demands for reform of corrupt, oligarchic and unrepresentative parliaments at Westminster and Dublin'.[4]

When the Tithe of Agistment (a rate on land used for pasturage) was repealed shortly before the start of the American Wars of Independence, it had the effect of making pasturage in Ireland far more profitable than tillage. This resulted in Irish landlords consolidating their farms and expelling tenants involved in arable farming. These were mainly Presbyterian, as Catholics were rarely more than agricultural labourers. It triggered a wholesale emigration of Irish Protestant farmers, mainly from Ulster, to America. The migration had many causes, including economic recession, rent and land disputes and climatic uncertainties, but a principal one was religious persecution by the Church of Ireland. Dissenters were not permitted to set up new congregations, to perform weddings or bury their dead in accordance with their principles. They 'arrived in the New World with a strong sense of grievance towards the Established Church, the king and Tories in general'.[5]

It was in America that George III's policies created most tension. He took the Stuart view that the King had the 'right to introduce new taxes without the consent of the people's representatives in Parliament'.[6] In 1765, the British House of Commons approved a Stamp Act, which imposed taxes on Americans to meet the military cost of their protection. Americans argued that, as they had no vote to elect House of Commons' members, this amounted to 'taxation without representation'. The King had to employ his considerable military presence in America to bring the colonies to heel, but 'Irish and British Dissenters instinctively sided with the colonists.'[7] 'They supplied the United States with a body of brave determined soldiers ... [with] ... a thorough detestation of the supremacy of England'.[8] They viewed George III and his ministers as aggressors and 'saw the war as an unjust attack on the liberty of the colonists'.[9] At the outset of hostilities in 1775, 'some of the most enthusiastic soldiers in the new American army were natives of Ulster'.[10] They fought with distinction. George Washington recorded: 'If defeated everywhere else, I will make my last stand for liberty among the Scotch-Irish of my native Virginia.'[11] It was former Ulster tenants, who, in 1777, made up the principal part of the 'body which brought about the surrender of the British army at Saratoga'.

Although the Scotch-Irish may have felt aggrieved, they acted in a manner similar to their initial arrival in Ireland:

> When they found the most fertile portion of Massachusetts in the possession of the Indians, ... they convened a meeting ... and the following resolutions are said to have been passed unanimously:-
> Resolved, - That the earth is the Lord's, and the fullness thereof

> Resolved, - That the Lord hath given the earth as an inheritance unto his Saints
>
> Resolved, - That we are his Saints[12]

Dissenters left in Ireland watched the American Wars of Independence with interest, greeting each American victory with joy. They now had an example to follow for their own republican ideals. The Rev. William Steel Dickson, a Non-Subscribing minister in Belfast and later a United Irishman, viewed English efforts to retain control in America as 'an unprincipled mad crusade'.[13] He believed that 'even if the king won the war, the cost of keeping the defeated Americans in subjection would be more than Britain and Ireland could bear'.[14]

A group of American sailors captured by the Royal Navy at sea were brought for imprisonment to Kinsale, where their guards, the 14th Regiment of Light Dragoons, treated them as rebels. The Rev. William Hazlitt (father of the essayist), an 'ultra-Dissenter' and minister at nearby Bandon, a longstanding Cromwellian and Dissenter stronghold, became so shocked at the appalling conditions in which they were being held that he wrote to the Cork newspapers. He reported that, out of 260 men, 60 had died from the hardships meted out on them and a further 57 were in hospital. He helped three to escape, sheltering them among his friends. When the Light Dragoons harassed the citizens of Bandon, Dissenters and Catholics alike (they made the Catholics eat pork on Good Friday off the streets at sword point), Hazlitt had them prosecuted. Although they were acquitted, he reported them to the War Office after they threatened to murder him. He now won his case and the Dragoons were removed from Kinsale. When the harassment against him continued, he left for America, but his unorthodox beliefs lacked favour, and he returned to a congregation in Shropshire from where he viewed the 1798 Belfast rebellion from afar. He later provided a home for Robert Emmet's daughter, Kitty, 'the last surviving member of Dublin's pre-eminent republican family left on the Irish side of the Atlantic', until her death in 1824.[15]

With Irish Dissenters continuing to support the formation of an American republic, *The Belfast Newsletter* was the first journal outside

America to publish the Declaration of Independence in full. The founding fathers drew on Commonwealth and Dissenting literature 'to justify their rebellion in terms comprehensible to all "freeborn men"'.[16] America produced its own apostle of republicanism, Tom Paine, born in Norfolk, England, in 1737. On arrival in America in 1774, 'he became the propagandist *par excellence* of the American revolution.'[17] In the cold winter of 1776, he rallied the spirit of Washington's army with: 'These are times that try men's souls.' In his pamphlet *Common Sense* written in 1775, he recorded:

> Government by kings was first introduced into the world by the heathens, from whom the children of Israel copied the custom. It was the most preposterous invention of the Devil ever set on foot for the promotion of idolatry.

He went on to ask:

> But where say some is the King of America? I'll tell you Friend, he reigns above, and doth not make havoc of mankind like a Royal Brute of Britain ... let it be brought forth placed on the divine law, the word of God; let a crown be placed thereon, by which the world may know, that so far as we approve of monarchy, that in America THE LAW IS KING.

With disturbances in the American Colonies making heavy demands on British military resources, the British Government deemed it prudent to provide some relaxation of the penal laws, so that 'legislation against both Dissenters and Catholics tended to fall into abeyance'.[18] In 1778, a Catholic Relief Act allowed Catholics to take long leases on land, to educate their children in Catholic schools, to intermarry with Protestants if solemnised by a Protestant clergyman, to officiate in church (but without any symbols of ecclesiastical authority), and, if they subscribed to the oath of allegiance, to be called to the bar and become attorneys. Two years later, the Test Act was repealed. This resulted in the Catholic Irish hierarchy maintaining faith with Britain throughout the American wars.

> While the plight of the Catholics was vastly improved, and
> they were acquiring positions of importance in trade, the
> professions and the Army remained closed to them and they
> were still denied all share in the government of the country.[19]

With its troops being diverted from Ireland to America, Britain's
involvement in the Seven Years' War against France left Ireland
exposed. There were fears that it was vulnerable to an opportunist
French attack. It had to learn 'that, in times of necessity, it should not
rely on British regular troops but should look to itself for defence'.[20] In
1760, a small party of French troops landed at Carrickfergus, hoping
to garner Dissenter support to attack Belfast. Yet, the Belfast citizens
'mustered an impromptu volunteer army and marched to confront
the enemy'.[21] Dissenters had no reason to support a Royalist French
invasion force, and the French retreated to their ships, only to be
engaged by Royal Navy frigates.

In 1777, with the American war still in progress, as many as 40,000
self-financed Volunteers in resplendent uniforms sprang up to provide
Ireland with defence. The splendid Frederick Augustus Hervey,
Bishop of Derry and 4th Earl of Bristol, relished his appointment as
Colonel of the Londonderry Volunteers. The 'Earl-Bishop' had 'a
mind refreshingly free from cant and hypocrisy':

> He attended the Grand Convention of the Volunteers ... in
> 1783, accompanied by a troop of dragoons, proceeding from
> his diocese to Dublin with all the pomp and ceremony of a
> royal progress. 'Dressed entirely in purple, with diamond
> knee- and shoe-buckles, with white gloves fringed with gold
> lace, and fastened with long gold tassels, he entered Dublin
> seated in an open landau, drawn by six horses, caparisoned
> with purple trappings, and passed through the principal
> streets to the Royal Exchange ...'[22]

When the Volunteers developed a political objective, he supported
them in opposing penal laws, backing Catholic emancipation and
remaining on good terms with Dissenters. Yet, he:

deemed Presbyterians 'much more dangerous than Papists' for their principles were 'truly republican'. He said that a reasonable indulgence to the Presbyterian and Papist may save the Kingdom ... that trouble in Ireland could be avoided if everyone were to be treated with enlightened benevolence ... [that] the Crown 'should be the patron of all dissenters, seceders, and schismatics whatever', and should 'either pay [their ministers] or be the cause of them being paid, because their rebellion would be torn up 'by the roots' and preachers preach 'loyalty instead of disaffection': 'where the treasure is ... there would be the heart likewise'[23]

Despite the authorities' approval of displays of citizen loyalty, they were soon concerned at the radical element involved. Without British troops in Ireland, 'gatherings of armed propertied citizens demanding reforms brought pressure on government'.[24]

It may be asserted, without fear of contradiction, it was something less than loyalty alone and something more than the fear of invasion at all, that animated Ireland, and arrayed its spirit in the volunteer associations, when the voice from America was shouting 'Liberty!' across the Atlantic.[25]

Volunteers saw their conventions as opportunities for rooting out Government corruption and courting influence in the legislature. Citizen soldiers in Ireland corresponded with Benjamin Franklin and with like-minded Unitarian theologians in Britain and began to assert Irish independence in the cause of liberty.

Chapter 13

The development of the Unitarians' political objectives c. 1755 – c. 1792

Although Presbyterianism started from a position that the bible was the only source of religious truth, Unitarians rejected passages that did not stand up to scientific reason. Thomas Jefferson used scissors to cut them out, and after his death the *Jefferson Bible* was published without them. Tom Paine began *The Age of Reason* by saying: 'I believe in one God and no more.' Over time, Unitarians softened their rhetoric, admitting that much in the bible was useful to mankind, while rejecting any church doctrine lacking scriptural validity. Dissenting scholars had to be careful; they generally wanted to be recognised as upholders of Christianity. As 'Anglicans stressed ceremony and outward practice rather than doctrine as proof of orthodoxy, most philosophers and clergymen could sail close to the wind but maintain their personal liberty'.[1] More pioneering Unitarian ministers were sometimes in danger of leaving their congregations behind. Some rejected Christianity, and others were even agnostic or atheist, although such radical philosophies tended to evolve over time. They needed to be circumspect, if they wanted to retain support and maintain their livelihoods.

Despite changing attitudes as philosophies developed, Unitarians were consistently hostile to the ecclesiastical Establishment. In 1787, the Bishop of Cloyne reported that, in Ireland, Dissenters:

> are Independents in a civil view; though they are Presbyterians as to ecclesiastical discipline. Their principles do not, like those of the Roman Catholics, tend to set up, but merely to pull down, an ecclesiastical establishment.[2]

Leading Dissenters promoted a new moral order to fight what they considered to be corruption within the Establishment. If they were to achieve the delivery of the Good Old Cause, offering emancipation and freedom of worship for all, it was critically important for them to gain Irish Catholic support. With revolutionaries grasping on their philosophies as justification for their actions, Dissenters were open to hostile propaganda.

After the surrender of British forces at Yorktown, Virginia, Benjamin Franklin, on 30 November 1782, signed the Treaty of Paris. 'America had no king, no aristocracy, no Established Church, and no hereditary power. Universal male suffrage was introduced, though only for whites.'[3] All this was Dissenter theology, but it would take a bit longer for emancipation to be extended to blacks and to women. Back in Britain, Dissenters were blamed for the loss of America and 'were very often branded as traitors', but the Whig opposition led by Charles James Fox had also opposed war with the American colonists.[4]

It was the French working classes, not the Irish, who took revolution in America as their cue to rebel against their King and aristocracy. In 1789, a group of French activists, the Jacobins (named after the Dominican Monastery of St Jacques where they met), were spurred on by the American successes to propound a philosophy of 'extreme democracy and absolute equality'. This led to the republican thrust of the French Revolution. Events were closely watched by Dissenters in England and Ireland, whose sympathy with Jacobin views spread terror through the ranks of Tories and the Irish Establishment.

One of the most influential of the Dissenters supporting the Jacobins was Dr Richard Price, born in Glamorgan in 1723, a man, who 'advocated liberty of conscience in religious matters, the right to resist tyranny and the right of people to choose their own government'.[5] In a sermon at the Old Jewry Meeting House in London in November 1789, he expressed his joy at the fall of the Bastille, and reflected:

> the delight of all liberal opinion in Britain and Ireland at the recent events in France which had transferred power from an absolutist monarch to an assembly of representatives of the people.[6]

After telling his congregation 'that their struggle for universal liberty had not been wasted', he concluded:

> Behold the light you have struck out, after setting America free, reflected to France, and there kindled into a blaze that lays despotism in ashes and warms and illuminates Europe.[7]

Such views were hardly likely to win him favour with the British authorities.

Price was a member of a circle of London Dissenters, headed by the publisher Joseph Johnson. Guests included Benjamin Franklin, Tom Paine (who returned to England in the early 1790s), Dr Joseph Priestley, William Godwin, William Blake and Mary Wollstonecraft. They formed 'the intellectual leadership of the radical reformers'; being prolific writers, Johnson published their papers 'with a will'.[8] In 1756, Price had written a *Review of the Principal Questions of Morals*, which advocated that 'individual conscience and reason should be used when making moral choices.'[9] This was pioneering stuff at a time when convention dictated that laws came from God for interpretation within the hierarchies of Church and State. In 1776, he published *Observations on the Nature of Civil Liberty*, a pamphlet supporting the American cause. It sold 60,000 copies, making him widely known in both England and America. He was so much admired by both Jefferson and Franklin that Congress offered him American citizenship. Yet, he remained in London, where his views gained him wide respect among radicals, and he was made a freeman of the City. Dissenters in Ireland and the Ulster Volunteers wrote to seek his 'advice on their reform programme', and he encouraged them to admit papists to their franchise.[10]

Priestley had been born in Leeds in 1733, a man of prodigious ability. He was an able linguist as well as being a dissenting minister. Almost as a hobby, he became one of the foremost scientists of his day, a founder of chemistry as a branch of science, in which he isolated oxygen and experimented with electricity. He was elected to The Royal Society, from whom he won their Gold Medal. He became a friend of Benjamin Franklin (with whom he conducted electrical experiments) and John Adams, the second President of the United States, who described him as 'like a comet in the system, this great learned, this indefatigable most excellent and extraordinary man'.[11]

Despite being one of England's foremost scholars, Priestley was banned, as a Dissenter, from attending the great universities, which Blake described as 'dark satanic mills'. This resulted in Dissenters establishing rival establishments, and Priestley tutored at the Warrington Dissenting Academy from 1757 to 1762. These offered a broad education for those not permitted to attend universities and became one of 'the most effective weapons in the assault on the old order'.[12] After Warrington, Priestley became minister of a congregation in Birmingham and formed a club of intellectuals, including James Watt, the inventor of the rotary steam engine, Josiah Wedgwood, the porcelain manufacturer, and Erasmus Darwin, the physician and philosopher. (Both Wedgwood and Darwin were grandfathers of Charles Darwin.) This became known as the Lunar Society, as it met monthly. In 1780, he published a pamphlet advocating Catholic emancipation. He followed the *Book of Revelation* in his 'Millenarian' view that prophesies of the second coming of Christ would be fulfilled in his lifetime. He held that the American and French revolutions were:

> unparalleled in all human history, [and] make a totally new, a most wonderful, an important era in the history of mankind ... a change from the darkness to light, from superstition to a sound knowledge and from a most debasing servitude to a state of most exaulted [*sic*] freedom. We may expect to see the establishment of universal peace and goodwill amongst all nations ... This sir will be the happy state of things distinctly and repeatedly foretold in many prophesies, delivered more than 2,000 years ago.[13]

Priestley:

> regarded George III and all reigning crowned heads of Europe as the ten horns of the great beast in the *Book of*

Revelation, whose days he believed were numbered once the ancien régime and the head of Louis had fallen.'[14]

Not surprisingly, Priestley's views drew hostile propaganda from the Tory press. In 1787, he wrote: 'We are ... laying gunpowder, grain by grain, under the old building of error and superstition' as an analogy to show that 'scientific enquiry would defeat ignorance'.[15] He was now branded a 'political subversive' and was dubbed 'Gunpowder Joe'.[16] He was accused of sharing views held by Charles I's regicides nearly 150 years earlier.

One piece of doggerel [presumably sung to the tune of *God Save the King*] warned people not to be fooled by the gentle demeanour of Priestley and other Dissenters. It suggested that they were hypocritical subversives:

> Sedition is their creed
> Feigned sheep, but wolves indeed
> How can we trust
> Gunpowder Joe would
> Deluge the throne in blood
> And lay the great and good
> Low in the dust.[17]

In 1791, Priestley held a dinner to celebrate the fall of the Bastille, but had to flee when a Birmingham mob burned down his home, his laboratory and two Unitarian meeting houses. The mob had acted with the complicity of Tory magistrates and clergymen and received George III's subsequent approval. The establishment had hoped that he would be murdered; effigies of Tom Paine and Priestley were burned in several cities. Priestley's real crime was his opposition to slavery in a town making much of its livelihood from manufacturing guns to be exchanged for slaves, and iron shackles required as the accoutrements of their trade. In an editorial in *The Northern Star* on 25 April 1792, the radical Samuel Neilson reported:

There is not perhaps an instance existing, of a more successful deception, than that practiced on the people of Birmingham in exciting their indignation against Doctor Priestley. There is no doubt that the very people who destroyed his house and its contents, and who would have gladly destroyed him in it, would be among the first to idolize him, if they knew what his sentiments really are and what is the tendency of his meritorious labours. The great endeavour of his life is to soften and ease the condition of mankind: and as the condition of the lower orders of the people stands in most need of amendment ... they would consider his protection a debt of justice.[18]

The fall of the Bastille in July 1789 breathed new heart into Belfast Presbyterians. The French 'Revolution was toasted because it had delivered the country from "popery, slavery, brass money and wooden shoes"'.[19] While Irish religious and trading connections with France can easily be understood, France's close relationship with Protestant Ulster needs further explanation than the notion of a revolution which freed France from Catholicism. By now, the 6,000 Huguenot arrivals at Lisburn had gained positions of importance and great respect. Their trading links with family members still resident in France remained well-established. The up and coming Belfast middle classes all encouraged their children to learn French.

Part 5

Britain's determination to retain control over Irish Government

Chapter 14

The rise to influence of Henry Grattan and the Irish Whigs c. 1770 – c. 1791

Irish Government was supervised by a Lord Deputy (sometimes a Lord Lieutenant or Viceroy) on behalf of the British Crown. He was appointed, with the King's approval, by the Government in power in London. He supervised an Executive based in Dublin Castle, which was also appointed by the British Government. Parliament consisted of an Irish House of Lords, made up of Irish peers, and a House of Commons, whose membership was dominated by local Protestant landowners. Landowners delegated their interests to Irish Borough Owners (known as Underwriters), who controlled seats 'under the influence of corruption' for their parliamentary nominees, dictating to their Protestant tenants how they should vote. The British Government bribed these 'place seekers' to assure its majority in the Irish Lords and Commons. 'Infamous pensions were bestowed on infamous men.'[1] 'Trafficking in seats for parliament became so profitable, that every landowner became anxious to increase his interest in the counties by the manufacture of votes.'[2] Without Catholic emancipation, landowners depended on Protestant tenants, who were in short supply, for their candidate's support. The resultant legislature was 'viewed with contempt wherever it was not viewed with hatred'.[3] Parliament had no control over the Executive, managed by the Lord Lieutenant, Chief Secretary, and other members. Furthermore, the British Government retained steadfast control over the armed forces and the judiciary. Catholics were not permitted to sit in either House, nor could they vote. House of Commons members were generally Establishment figures with a strong affiliation to the Anglican Church of Ireland and to the Tory party in England.

Even in Britain, voting was limited to landowners. Many parliamentary seats were 'rotten boroughs' in the giving of wealthy individuals, who controlled the voters. These shortcomings brought calls for British parliamentary reform to expand the voting franchise. Reform was resisted by the Tory party led by William Pitt the Younger, and by those on the right of the Whigs led by William Henry Cavendish-Bentinck, 3rd Duke of Portland, who believed that Parliament should remain within the control of the landed classes. The Protestant Ascendancy in Ireland shared these views and was single-minded in its desire to keep Catholics out of Irish politics. Their concern was that Catholic emancipation would give them a majority, allowing them to redress land confiscations by Protestant settlers in earlier centuries and to disenfranchise the Church of Ireland. It was feared that if the gates holding back emancipation were opened, the flood of change could not be resisted.

There was no real disagreement, even among radical members of the Irish Parliament, that it was only landed and merchant classes who had sufficient understanding of politics to vote or sit in Parliament. Nevertheless, the British Government retained a second line of protection. It enforced Poynings' Law, imposed by Henry VII in 1494, under which all Irish Government bills required the approval of the British Privy Council before enactment. This rankled with the modest number of more radical members of the Irish House of Commons and with members of the Volunteer Regiments seeking greater autonomy for the Irish.

The man who came forward to promote the political objectives of the Volunteers and parliamentary radicals was Henry Grattan, a member of a well-to-do political dynasty of Irish Protestants from co. Wicklow. After graduating from Trinity College, where he had developed an interest in poetry, Grattan had, somewhat unenthusiastically, read for the bar, spending eight terms at the Middle Temple in London. It was politics, not the law, which captivated him, and he spent hours listening to debates in the houses of Westminster, where he became an admirer of Edmund Burke, the prominent right-wing Whig, and William Pitt the Elder, Earl of Chatham, who had led the Whig party as Prime Minister. Both were brilliant orators. In 1772, after his return to Ireland, Grattan became a Member of Parliament at the age of twenty-nine. He had been offered a seat in the giving of the influential James Caulfeild, 1st Earl of Charlemont. Charlemont had met him in London and found 'his conversation was lively without being pert and ... able to discuss intelligently French and Italian literature'.[4] He became a keen and eloquent debater, always happier in opposition, where he used his oratory to attack Government motions, preferring the 'chase' to the 'kill'. He was by inclination a Whig, as much because the Irish Whig party in opposition, led by the brothers, George and William Ponsonby, provided a platform for him to criticise Government, rather than making him a supporter of their policies. He resisted taking office on their behalf when the opportunity arose; he was a British patriot at heart, supportive of war against France, whose peasantry had brought down both its Crown and its aristocracy. He favoured the use of the Volunteer movement to defend Ireland from foreign invasion, after the redeployment of British garrisons from Ireland to America and Europe. He was no revolutionary and, although he called for emancipation for Catholic landowners and burghers, their involvement would still have left a Protestant voting majority in Parliament. He had no time for the Catholic peasantry and strongly disapproved of its sporadic rioting, as initiated in Munster.

Grattan always courted popularity. A desire for approbation was sometimes thought to colour his objectives. In the company of senior British politicians, he generally appeared to side with the Establishment. Yet he fought vigorously to achieve Irish political autonomy and a fair deal for Irish merchants in commerce, with calls for even-handed customs duties and Navigation Laws. (The initial Navigation Ordinance of 1651, passed by Cromwell's Protectorate, had restricted the shipment of goods from Britain's colonies, including Ireland, to British ships. It was replaced in 1660 by the English Navigation Act, under which Ireland, along with other colonies, received some trading rights, but, in the first instance, all goods were to be shipped on an English vessel to England, where they were unloaded, inspected and charged with duty. They were then reloaded onto a second English vessel for delivery to their intended destination. This cumbersome arrangement added substantially to the cost and speed of delivery. It not only depressed colonial trade, but Irish and other colonial ports were deprived of duties. Irish goods, already beset with restrictions, saw prices pushed up.[5] (This arrangement, which also applied to goods from America, was a principal cause of the American Revolution.) Grattan also opposed trade restrictions being imposed because of the American wars. These caused great hardship in Ireland. Above all he believed that the Irish Parliament should be autonomous. He was determined to end Poynings' Law and to allow the Parliament to operate independently of Westminster.

By 1780, Grattan was already 'the most popular Irish MP, admired and supported by the Volunteers'.[6] The Volunteers used their new-found influence to gain concessions that would allow Ireland to 'become a nation and to acquire a national character'.[7] When the Dublin Volunteers broke away to form the Dublin Independents, they elected Grattan, 'one of the real ornaments of society', as their colonel, and he attended a great review in Belfast as ADC to Charlemont, the reviewing General.[8]

Britain's capitulation in the American Wars of Independence in October 1781 resulted in the fall of Frederick Lord North's Tory Government. He was replaced as Prime Minister by the Whig Charles Watson-Wentworth, 2nd Marquess of Rockingham. Rockingham was determined to demonstrate 'a more liberal and understanding approach to imperial problems', particularly in regard to Irish rights.[9] The Whigs called for:

> an Anglo–Irish settlement to recognise Ireland's constitutional rights and to provide for co-operation between the two countries on matters of common interest.[10]

At their convention at Dungannon in 1782, the Volunteers demanded electoral reform to redistribute seats in the Irish Parliament. They strongly asserted Ireland's right to parliamentary independence. Their objective was to abolish Poynings' Law, ending the need for the endorsement of Irish enactments at Westminster. On 2 February 1782, Grattan promoted the Volunteers' proposals in the Irish House of Commons. He declared:

> that the Kingdom of Ireland was a distinct kingdom with its parliament the sole legislature thereof, and that Great Britain would be greatly strengthened by renouncing the claim to legislate for Ireland.[11]

He concluded that Ireland:

> 'a community of different religions but one political faith', was expressing itself through the Volunteer movement: 'it is the property – it is the soul of the country armed'.[12]

The Irish Government deferred any decision on the repeal of Poynings' Law, when it became clear that the Whigs in London, including Rockingham and Fox, remained worried about conceding parliamentary authority to Dublin while Catholic emancipation was also being discussed. Grattan had encouraged Catholics seeking to join the Volunteers to back him by calling for a Catholic Relief bill to place Catholic landowners on an equal political footing with Protestants. Yet it became clear that his plan would need to be shelved if a bill for Irish parliamentary independence were to be taken forward. When Whigs in London asked Grattan and Charlemont to extend their earlier adjournment of the vote on Poynings' Law, they reported back that this was not feasible. To resolve the crisis, the Whigs appointed Portland, already a senior member of the British Government, as Lord Lieutenant of Ireland. On his arrival in Dublin on 14 April 1782, Grattan still refused to delay bringing his bill forward. Two days later, with ranks of Volunteers drawn up outside the Parliament House in Dublin, Grattan asserted that:

> Ireland was a distinct kingdom and that it was the birth right of Irishmen that no body of men could legislate for their nation except the King, Lords and Commons of Ireland.[13]

Despite a recent operation for a small fistula, he was exhilarated to find himself championing his country's rights. His eloquence was electrifying. He went on:

> I remember Ireland when she was a child, I have seen her progress from injuries to arms, and from arms to liberty. Spirit of Swift, spirit of Molyneux, your genius has prevailed! Ireland is now a nation! ... [If England] wishes well to Ireland she has nothing to fear from her strength. I do believe the people of Ireland would die for England...

Jonathan Swift (1667 – 1745), the author of *Gulliver's Travels*, had been born in Ireland and spent part of his career as an Anglican clergyman, latterly as Dean of St Patrick's Cathedral in Dublin. While there, he used his satire to criticise English dominance over Irish Government, particularly in *A Modest Proposal*, written in 1729. This recommended that children of the Irish poor should provide sustenance for the English rich. In 1698, William Molyneux (1656 – 1698), founder of the Dublin Philosophical Society, published *The Case of Ireland's being bound by Acts of Parliament in England*. This criticised English attempts to suppress the Irish woollen trade. The English House of Commons was sufficiently rattled to consider the publication as 'of dangerous consequence to the crown and people of England by denying the authority of the king and parliament of England to bind the people of Ireland'. Grattan concluded by expressing his confidence in Rockingham's Government and the new Irish administration. He intended to give it not 'a milk and water support' but a decided and responsible one. Yet, he refused to take office. 'I will', he said, 'go into the cabinet the friend of the people. I will come out of it unpaid and unpensioned.'[14]

Grattan's speech received a tremendous reception and his motion was carried unanimously. Although he was exhausted after a month of negotiation, his request to amend Poynings' Law was agreed. Portland detailed the English Government's concessions in a speech from the throne on 27 May. Grattan responded that 'all constitutional questions are at an end and we are now as much pledged to moderation as we were before pledged to a proper exertion ... [and a determination] to stand and fall with Great Britain'.[15] He immediately arranged that £100,000 should be pledged towards raising recruits for the Royal Navy.

Grattan was the hero of the hour. Statues were raised in his honour and his grateful countrymen made him a parliamentary grant of £100,000, which had to be reduced by half before he would accept it. Out of this, he purchased Tinnehinch, a country estate about twenty miles south of Dublin in co. Wicklow. Yet his success caused jealousy. He was criticised, particularly by Henry Flood, another influential Irish MP, who challenged him to a duel. Flood called for the Westminster House of Commons to reconfirm the Whig Government's decision. This delayed final approval until 22 January 1783. Grattan now agreed to join the Irish Privy Council and was invited to dine on a regular basis with Robert Henley, 2nd Earl of Northington, the new Lord Lieutenant, to discuss Irish Government policy. Although his subsequent proposals were frequently defeated in the House of Commons, he:

> held a special place in public life as the eloquent exponent
> of Ireland's right as a nation to a high degree of political
> autonomy within the British Empire.[16]

Grattan was less successful with his efforts on behalf of the Catholics. They were not granted emancipation, even on the limited basis that he was advocating. He was no rebel and remained close in his political thinking to Burke. He proposed a motion to provide £200,000 for the Royal Navy in the war against France. Although he backed Pitt's efforts to restore free trade between England and Ireland, Pitt was forced to withdraw his proposals. He faced concerted opposition from the protectionist lobby among English merchants, fearful that Irish goods would undercut English prices. Protectionist opposition gained support from English Whigs seeking to make political capital out of defeating Pitt. Grattan was also furious with the British Government when it tried to dictate comparable import duties in both Britain and Ireland for goods from the Commonwealth, but he was more concerned that this infringed Ireland's constitutional liberties, than the level of the duties.

Grattan also supported Volunteer efforts to achieve parliamentary reform. Despite believing that 'only a relatively small proportion of the population [was] fit for enfranchisement', he recognised the need for a broader electorate.[17] He focused on lessening the taxpayers' burden for the funding of patronage paid by candidates to gain parliamentary seats. He coupled this with a proposal to cut the pension list, recommending a 'resolution of restraint' to compel the Government to live within its income. Another proposal attempted to cut revenue collection costs. Although he gained support for his objectives after agreeing not to bring forward a bill for administrative reform, he was thwarted by the disreputable John Beresford, First Commissioner of the Revenue, who claimed that Grattan did not understand the collection process or the requirement to pay pensions. He also whispered that Grattan, having 'made insinuations of extravagance' in the management of the Revenue, had 'made no progress in the discovery of it'.[18]

Another project was Grattan's attempt to end agrarian rioting and robberies. These had begun as petty outbreaks of violence against tithes and hearth taxes, but, by 1770, fanatical groups of Irish subsistence farmers of all denominations were taking part in *vigilante* sectarian affrays. They broke into houses with guns and bayonets, treating occupants with great cruelty. Sometimes rioting was focused against unreasonable landlords or bigoted schoolmasters and clergy, but it was generally caused by sectarian differences and rivalries. It had become commonplace in southern Ulster, where the Protestant authorities blamed the Catholics. Yet, rival groups of both Protestants and Catholics unleashed hatred and bigotry against each other, pressaging the causes of violence of more recent times.

There was a growing recognition that it was 'want and wretchedness' among the agrarian peasantry that was the principal cause of social disorder. Legislation designed to suppress unrest included The Mendicity Act of 1772, which established work houses (or 'houses of industry') to take in itinerants and offer them occupations. The

Volunteers blamed the Irish tithe system, under which all religious faiths funded the Church of Ireland, as a principal cause of hardship. This 'flagrant injustice' involved 'heavily taxing the poorest sect for the support of the clergy of the richest sect from which they (the poorest) derive no advantage'.[19] It had been one of the first taxes removed in France during the French Revolution. When Grattan visited Munster to examine the situation for himself, he concluded that it was the root cause of all the rioting. He now became a devastating critic of tithes, proposing alternative means for the Church of Ireland to supplement its income based on the price of wheat. He insisted on exempting potato crops, which formed the staple diet of the poor. His scathing criticisms of the Munster clergy turned the Church of Ireland against him and the Irish House of Commons voted his proposals down. Although he had failed, his more moderate attempts to achieve reform on a basis acceptable to the English Government met with success. He gained an exemption from the hearth tax for houses with a single hearth occupied by the poor.

Although calls for voting reform in Parliament had fallen short of seeking emancipation for Catholics, the Irish Government offered an olive branch. In 1792, it extended Catholic relief beyond the limited concessions granted by the Catholic Relief Act of 1782, which Grattan had initiated. Grattan met with Theobald Wolfe Tone at Tinnehinch to discuss sectarian difficulties and to seek a way to end rioting by the Catholic peasantry (known as defenders). Although a petition for greater Catholic relief failed in the Irish House of Commons, Whig members, including Grattan and George Ponsonby, encouraged senior Catholics to summon a Catholic assembly to demand the vote for property owning Catholics. Grattan made several brilliant speeches to support emancipation as a means of breaking down sectarian barriers. He believed that 'enfranchised Catholics would reinforce the Protestant people against an encroaching executive and a monopolising borough oligarchy'.[20]

In February 1793, France's declaration of war on Britain triggered the Irish Government into heeding calls for Catholic relief. A new far-reaching Catholic Relief bill was drafted, and Grattan, as an independent MP, was able 'to play a congenial role … to give the government every necessary support and to give the people every constitutional redress'.[21] Yet he never sought the vote for all. He still believed that:

> a man who had no property could not complain that he had no vote – a passenger through your field or a labourer on your farm, has no right to make rules for the management of the same.[22]

Although Grattan supported a bill which would still leave more than half the Irish population without the vote, the Establishment mustered sufficient support to block it. Catholics were, however, granted the right to hold civil and military office and to obtain university degrees.

Catholics did not initially have support from the Volunteers, and those 'who tried to join the Volunteers were almost universally rejected and often "not without insult"'.[23] Yet Unitarian calls for freedom of conscience were never far below the surface. After the repeal of the Test Act in 1780, there was a growing sentiment among Volunteers for all Catholics to be offered emancipation, despite Grattan's opposition. Nowhere were calls for freedom of conscience more evident than in Belfast, where views were based entirely on political morality and social justice. In 1756, more than 93 per cent of the Belfast population was either Anglican or Presbyterian, and Catholics in the north were not perceived as a political threat. Even in 1791, 'Tone himself wrote that the people of Belfast know "wonderfully little" about the Catholics'.[24]

It was the Volunteers' support for the French Revolution that caused Grattan and the Whigs to lose faith with them. Republican sentiments among their largely Presbyterian membership made common cause with the French revolutionaries. These filled Irish Whigs with alarm. Many left the Volunteers and pulled back from supporting Volunteer attempts at Parliamentary reform. Without the Whigs behind them, the Volunteers became a 'feeble inefficient body'.[25] For Presbyterian republicans of the north to achieve a powerful reforming voice in Ireland, they recognised a need to 'form a frank conciliation with the Catholics of the south, on equal terms'.[26] These sentiments led to the formation of the Society of United Irishmen.

Chapter 15

British Government efforts to end the Dissenter threat c.1780 – 1797

Despite all Grattan's efforts, the Irish Establishment continued to dominate Irish politics, without having to garner support from the Irish Catholic hierarchy for British rule. With Presbyterian calls for Catholic emancipation falling on deaf ears, there was a real risk that Catholics would join the republican banner. It was Burke, so greatly admired by Grattan, who offered the Catholic hierarchy a lifeline, which they believed would lead to emancipation. For this he received the grateful thanks of both George III and the Tory Government.

Burke had been born in Dublin in 1729 from a Church of Ireland background (although his mother was a Catholic). After attending Trinity College, Dublin, he entered the Middle Temple in London in 1755, intending to sit for the Bar. Yet he abandoned the law to write philosophical treatises and entered politics. By 1765, he was Private Secretary to Rockingham, the Prime Minister, and, as a Member of Parliament, his eloquence gained him a respected position on the right-wing of the Whig party. He steered a fine line in politics, which often led to his motives being misunderstood. He criticised the imposition of taxes on Americans that led to the American War of Independence. He also attempted to gain relief for the Irish from the trade limitations being imposed on them by the British Government and wanted to alleviate restrictions on Irish Catholics. Although his views lost him Rockingham's support in Parliament, he opposed Charles James Fox in his backing of French Jacobins and deplored their revolutionary action to tear down France's crown and church. He was one of the first Whigs to desert Fox when he joined a coalition with the Tories in an attempt to avert the Jacobin threat. Yet he also opposed British imperialism, particularly in Ireland and India, where he attacked corruption, believing that colonial Government should be a trust. In 1788 he was instrumental in arranging the impeachment of Warren Hastings, Governor-General of Bengal. Hastings had returned from India after amassing a great fortune as Governor-General and was impeached by the House of Commons on twenty counts of crimes and misdemeanours during his governorship, especially for the alleged judicial killing of Maharaja Nadakumar. After a prosecution lasting 148 days over a period of seven years, Hastings was acquitted in the House of Lords on all charges. His prosecution had been conducted largely by Whig Members of Parliament including Burke.

Like most of his political colleagues, Burke did not advocate democracy, holding that:

1. Government required intelligence, which could only be provided by landed gentry,
2. the common people possessed dangerous and angry passions, and
3. it would tyrannize unpopular minorities, worthy of protection.

Most importantly he believed that Catholics should seek emancipation by linking with the Establishment rather than revolutionary Dissenters. He could see that the Catholic hierarchy lacked the appetite for rebellion and was unlikely to join a Dissenter-led revolt to achieve a republic supported by French Jacobins, who had torn down the French Catholic Church and its aristocracy. He argued that this would confuse their Catholic principles. The approach he took shaped British policy in Ireland during the 1790s. While the Society of United Irishmen attracted the Catholic rank and file to their revolutionary cause, the Catholic hierarchy remained aloof.

Catholic emancipation presented great risks for the British Government. There can be little doubt that Catholics would have sought to restore their ancestral lands if they regained control of the Irish Parliament. It was British Government policy to let them believe that offers of emancipation were on the table, but to find reasons to defer bringing them forward. In the meantime, it granted concessions so that Catholics believed that the British were in the mood to act reasonably. In 1785, the Government funded a Catholic seminary at Maynooth, providing it with £8,000 per annum. Thanks to Burke, the Irish Catholic hierarchy saw its future, once emancipated, as 'loyal defenders of George III'.[1] This neutralised the United Irish threat.

In Burke's efforts to weaken Dissenter influence, Price and his circle faced the full onslaught of his 'perverted eloquence'.[2] Price was denounced as dangerous and extremist, and, when Priestley moved to teach at New College, Hackney, which Price had founded, Burke described it as 'an arsenal for manufacturing revolutionary weapons, and a breathing ground for revolutionary ideas'. He also considered it a 'nursery of riot' and 'a slaughterhouse of Christianity'.[3] He:

> helped to ensure that Irish Roman Catholicism would be dominated by a group of churchmen who would see to it that never again would their flocks flirt with radical Protestant democrats. Religious division and sectarian hatred, rather than unity, would define relationships in Ireland thereafter.[4]

Nevertheless, Priestley's pioneering views were much revered both in America and by United Irishmen, and he rejoiced when, at one level at least, they linked 'the Papists and the Presbyterians'.[5] Although he was offered a post as minister of a Dublin Unitarian congregation, he turned it down. In 1792, when Priestley and Paine became honorary members of the Society of United Irishmen, they were forced into exile (Priestley went to Pennsylvania and Paine accepted a seat in the French National Assembly). Among their circle, Godwin was jailed for sedition and only Blake was acquitted. Mary Wollstonecraft was never charged but she died in 1797 with her reputation in tatters after Godwin, her husband, published an account of her life and loves.

In March 1791, Paine published *The Rights of Man*, written as a rebuttal of Burke's views. It gave rise to 'the most crucial ideological debate ever carried on in English'.[6] Paine directed his republican views in 'a blistering attack on Burke's notions of kingship, aristocracy and hereditary power'.[7] It was hailed 'with rapture' in Ulster, with its official edition selling 50,000 copies.[8] With the working classes starting to take an interest in constitutional reform and democracy, they purchased cheap pirated versions and 'embraced Paine's work as a Bible'.[9] Tone later described it as 'the Koran of Belfast'.[10] It 'confirmed rather than inspired the educated middleclass founders of the Irish republican movement in their adherence to their radical agenda'.[11] Dissenters believed that its popularity electrified 'the nation, and terrified the imbecile government into the most unjustifiable measures'.[12] With working class societies being suppressed, they were driven underground to become revolutionary cells.

Although Burke and the English Government had won the day, Burke died in 1797 before the relatively inconsequential United Irish rebellions began.

Chapter 16

Divergent political views in England on how to manage Catholic emancipation c. 1792 – c. 1795

During the American Wars of Independence, Charles James Fox, the leader of the Whig party in London, had sympathised with the justice of the American cause, and his attention now turned to events in France. While Pitt's Tory Government and those opposed to parliamentary reform in England followed George III in strongly condemning the French revolutionaries, Fox, with backing from the Irish playwright and politician, Richard Brinsley Sheridan, supported their desire for liberty. Fox's attitude alienated those on the right of the Whig party including Portland, Burke and William, 4th Earl Fitzwilliam, who had hitherto been closely associated with him. This caused an irretrievable split. Fitzwilliam was the archetypal English aristocrat, a man of unimpeachable integrity, commanding respect from all parties. In addition to his Fitzwilliam estates, he had inherited those of Rockingham, his uncle. These included 55,000 acres in Ireland, making him one of the wealthiest British landowners. Despite mistrusting Sheridan, Fitzwilliam did not initially publicise his differences with Fox over his support for the French revolutionaries, as he did not want to split the Whigs. Nevertheless, he strongly opposed Jacobin objectives. On 5 June 1792, he wrote to his friend the Reverend Henry Zouch:

> Now there is nothing but revolutions, and in that of France
> is an example of the turbulent and the factious instigating
> the numbers ... to the subversion of the first principle of

> civil society ... the protection of the individual against the multitude. ... The French revolutionists are just as anxious to bring into England their spirit of proselytism [conversion to their cause] as they have been to carry it into every other part of Europe.[1]

For the time being, he continued to back Fox as his old friend. Despite disagreeing with Dissenting principles, he followed Fox's lead by backing the repeal of the Test Act. This allowed Dissenters to vote and to hold public office without the need to confirm their adherence to the Anglican Church (although they had generally managed to circumvent this despite the Act). As he said in a letter to Burke on 18 September 1791, 'nothing can make me a disciple of Paine or Priestley';[2] yet he wanted to avoid having to say so in public. Despite Dissenters providing vocal support for the French revolutionaries, Fitzwilliam saw that they could use the Test Act as a justifiable grievance, which might gain them a greater following. Although he agreed with Burke's concerns about the formation of a French republic, he still hoped to broker a reconciliation with Fox. Yet Burke would not be moved; after publishing a pamphlet against the French revolutionaries, he wrote:

> I gave him [Fitzwilliam] such reasons why it could not be, yet at least, as made him not condemn me, though he left me, after our last conversation, in a mood sufficiently melancholy. He is, in truth, a man of wonderful honour, good nature and integrity.[3]

Fitzwilliam's anti-republican attitude towards France made him a target for Dissenter unrest in Birmingham. There was even a plan to burn down his home, Wentworth House, inherited from Rockingham and seen as a symbol of privilege. Luckily, he was warned beforehand. He tackled Fox privately over their differing attitudes. On 15 March 1792, they held a long meeting to discuss the state of the Whig party. Fitzwilliam took the opportunity to voice his fear that Jacobinism would spread into England. The next day Fox wrote to him:

Our apprehensions are raised by very different objects. *You* seem to dread the prevalence of Paine's opinions (which in most parts I detest as much as you do) while *I* am much more afraid of the total annihilation of all principles of liberty and resistance, an event which I am sure you would be as sorry to see as I. We both hate the two extremes equally, but we differ in opinions with respect to the quarter from which the danger is most pressing.[4]

Despite Tory opposition, the clamour for parliamentary reform continued to grow. In May 1792, Pitt approached Portland with a view to forming a coalition government to resist both parliamentary reform and Jacobinism. Although Burke was prepared to back Pitt, neither Portland nor Fitzwilliam was at that stage willing to break with Fox, who would not work with Pitt. Nevertheless:

they agreed Fox's conduct had been very ill-judged, and very distressing: that to separate from him would be highly disagreeable, yet that to remain with him after what he professed, was giving their tacit approbation to the sentiments he had avowed in the House of Commons, on the Parliamentary Reform, which sentiments were in direct contradiction to theirs.[5]

Perhaps more significantly, they did not consider the Cabinet positions on offer to Whigs in the coalition Government were of sufficient standing. Fitzwilliam wanted Pitt to take a lesser role in the coalition than that of Prime Minister and Pitt, in turn, objected to Fox joining them.

Following the mob violence (the September Massacres) in Paris in the late summer of 1792, it was again hoped by Fitzwilliam that Fox could be persuaded to condemn the French Revolution and to step back from his call for parliamentary reform in England. Yet, in December, Fox called on the Government to recognise the French republic. Although some conservative Whigs now sought a split from him, both Portland and Fitzwilliam hoped to hold the party together, but Burke defected to join Pitt. When Britain declared war on France in February 1793, Fox was quick to condemn the way it was being conducted. Fitzwilliam could no longer bring himself to back him, saying:

> France must start again from her ancient monarchy, and improving upon that is her only chance of establishing a system that will give happiness to herself, and ensure peace and security to her neighbours.

He now saw Fox's attitude to France rather than parliamentary reform as the cause of division in the Whig party. He strongly disapproved of Burke defecting to the Tories, and remained beside Fox, even contributing to a public subscription to settle his debts. Fox wrote to William Adam on 15 December 1793 that Fitzwilliam's:

> unremitting kindness to me in all situations quite oppresses me when I think of it. God knows, there is nothing on earth consistent with principle and honour that I would not do to continue his political friend, as I shall always be his warmest and most attached private friend.[6]

At last, on 25 September 1793, Portland agreed, in principle, to join a coalition with Pitt, who was determined to present a united front against growing Jacobinism as it had developed in France. He also wanted to stand up to Dissenter calls for parliamentary reform and to stamp out republican thinking, which was unsettling the working classes in both England and Ireland. Fitzwilliam persuaded Portland to ensure that the Whigs became equal members of the coalition. He continued to oppose the retention of Pitt as Prime Minister, unless the restoration of the Bourbon monarchy was made an objective of the war with France. On 25 December, Portland agreed to 'support the war with all the effect and energy in my power' and, on 20 January 1794, at a meeting of leading Whigs at Burlington House, he told them that he would support Pitt's Government and urged them to do the same. Fitzwilliam moved halfway, agreeing 'to take a more decided line than they had hitherto done, in support of the administration'. He shared Portland's determination to bring down France's republican Government, contending:

> that the safety of the country [England], the preservation of the constitution, of everything dear to Englishmen and to their posterity depended upon preventing the introduction of French principles, and the new-fangled doctrine of the *rights of man*; and that this could only be effected by the establishment of some regular form of government in that country upon which some reliance might be placed. [8]

It was Fitzwilliam's support for Portland's attitude towards France that sounded the death knell for Fox's leadership of the Whig party.

Portland knew that he needed Fitzwilliam's support in negotiations with Pitt over the form of the coalition. Yet Fitzwilliam continued to drag his feet. Portland met him at Burlington House on 25 May, to explain that he had seen Pitt on the previous day. Pitt had expressed his wish for a coalition to achieve:

> the expulsion of that evil spirit [of Jacobinism] ... and [said] that his wish and object was that it might make us act together as one great Family ... [he] lamented the scantiness of Cabinet employments he had it in his power at this moment to offer us. [9]

Pitt assured him that positions would be offered as they became available; Portland himself was to become Home Secretary with overall responsibility for Ireland. Fitzwilliam, who never wholly trusted Pitt, was determined to obtain clarification of what was on offer and confirmation that the aim of the war with France was to restore the Bourbon monarchy.

On 18 June, Pitt gave in and assured Portland:

> that the re-establishment of the Crown of France in such person of the family of Bourbon as shall be naturally

entitled to it was the first and determined aim of the present Ministry.[10]

The moderates' last hopes of breaking the Tory stranglehold over Irish Government lay in the appointment of a Lord Lieutenant sympathetic to their views. Portland, who remained a close ally of leading members of the Irish Whig opposition, including Grattan and George and William Ponsonby, favoured Fitzwilliam, whose wife Charlotte Ponsonby, daughter of the Earl of Bessborough, happened to be George's and William's cousin.

Pitt was willing to meet Fitzwilliam to discuss his future position personally, and Fitzwilliam now believed that the Government had moved to the Whig position. He told Portland that he would support the coalition, provided that new Whig peers were appointed 'after thirty years' exclusion from patronage'. Despite the pressure on him to accept office in the new Government, he would only agree if appointed Lord Lieutenant of Ireland, a role currently held by John Fane, 10th Earl of Westmoreland. When Pitt met Portland on 1 July, he agreed to offer the Lord Lieutenancy to Fitzwilliam as soon as Westmoreland could be compensated with another position. The real reason for delay was that Westmoreland condoned the granting of pensions to place seekers to assure support for Pitt's Government. On 3 July, Fitzwilliam agreed to join the coalition Government as Lord President of the Council for the time being. He wrote that day to Lady Rockingham: 'It is a time when private affection must give way to public exigency'.[11]

On 11 July, Fitzwilliam wrote to Fox to make his peace with him:

> I do not receive this honour (if it is one) with much exultation; on the contrary with a heavy heart. I did not feel great comfort in finding myself at St James's surrounded by persons with whom I had been so many years in political hostility, and without those I can never think of being separated from, publicly or privately, without a pang. (E. A. Smith, *Whig Principles and Party Politics. Earl Fitzwilliam and the Whig Party. 1748 – 1833.* p.169)

Some days earlier Fox had written to him:

> Nothing ever can make me forget a friendship as old as my
> life and the man in the world to whom I feel myself in every
> view the most obliged. ... Whatever happens I never can
> forget, my dearest Fitz, that you are the friend in the world
> whom I most esteem, for whom I would sacrifice every
> thing that one man ought to sacrifice to another. I know that
> the properest conduct in such a situation would be to say
> nothing, nor to inquire any thing from any of my old friends,
> and so I shall do in regard to all others, but I feel you to be an
> exception with respect to me to all general rules, I am sure
> your friendship has been so. God bless you, my dear Fitz.[12]

On 18 August he wrote to his nephew, Lord Holland:

> I cannot forget that ever since I was a child Fitzwilliam has
> been, in all situations, my warmest and most affectionate
> friend, and the person in the world of whom decidedly I
> have the best opinion, and so in most respects I have still,
> but as a politician I cannot reconcile his conduct with what
> I (who have known him for more than five-and-thirty years)
> have always thought to be his character. I think they have all
> behaved very ill to me, and for most of them, who certainly
> owe much more to me than I do to them, I feel nothing
> but contempt, and do not trouble myself about them; but
> Fitzwilliam is an exception indeed.[13]

With the coalition in place, Portland invited several Irish Whigs to
London, where they met Fitzwilliam, whose, appointment as Lord
Lieutenant had not at that stage been made public, and occasionally
with Burke. They agreed to join the Government in Ireland on
terms which included support for war with France, the dismissal
of John Beresford and his faction, and action to stop embezzlement
and improve the process of tax collection, over which Beresford had
been responsible since 1770. Burke called for immediate Catholic

emancipation and the promotion of a few Catholics to 'places of trust in the state'.[14] Yet, this was opposed by Grattan and his colleagues, but William Ponsonby believed, probably mistakenly, that Portland favoured it. Portland had always been diffident in his speech, failing to articulate his opinions clearly.

In addition to support for emancipation, Fitzwilliam saw, as his first task, the need to resolve the shortcomings of Irish Government. On 23 August 1794, he had told Grattan:

> The chief object of my attempts will be, to purify, as far as circumstances and prudence will permit, the principles of government, in the hopes of thereby restoring to it that tone and spirit which so happily prevailed formerly, and so much to the dignity as well as the benefit of the country.[15]

To achieve this, he needed support from Grattan and the Ponsonbys. In late August, George Ponsonby met with Grattan and other senior Irish Whigs:

> to prepare a programme for Fitzwilliam. They agreed that the country should be put into a proper state of defence by the formation of local corps on the lines of English Volunteers; that the Catholics should be conciliated; and that a system of government with the character of purity which would take away all pretence of censure should be pursued. It was also agreed to recommend FitzGibbon's [Lord Chancellor Clare's] removal from office.[16]

Clare was a supporter of Pitt, who was becoming extremely concerned that Portland and Fitzwilliam were attempting to turn Ireland into a 'private Whig desmene', at the expense of the spirit of the coalition.[17] He even feared that the coalition could be split over this comparatively trivial Irish issue, at a time when Britain was embarking on war in Europe. Loughborough, the English Lord Chancellor, attempted to reconcile opposing views with assistance from Burke and Grattan.

Grattan proposed Clare's retention as Irish Lord Chancellor if he played no further part in politics.

The terms being proposed by the Whigs were communicated to Pitt's Government. Up to this point Grattan had preferred a role outside Government but admitted: 'I think that places are now honourable, and, in taking one, I should be the friend of the people and His Majesty's government.'[18] According to Thomas Addis Emmet, Pitt sought a year's delay in the implementation of some of the proposals, but Grattan and his colleagues insisted on them being brought forward immediately. When Portland supported them, Pitt, who attended some of the later discussions, seemed to acquiesce and was certainly well acquainted with them. The Irish Whigs came away from their meetings with Pitt clearly believing that their requests had been agreed, although they were not formally confirmed in writing.

On 10 August 1794, Pitt confirmed Fitzwilliam as Lord Lieutenant of Ireland, but this was still not made public. Four days later, Portland wrote to Fitzwilliam saying that he had advised Ponsonby.[19] Yet Pitt was still dragging his feet over the public announcement. On 8 October, Fitzwilliam warned Portland of rumours in Ireland that Westmorland was to remain in office. He complained that, if no speedy announcement of his appointment were published, he would resign from the Government. Portland replied that Pitt 'harped' on needing to find Westmorland another office. He did not want Clare, who was unpopular for having defeated Grattan's efforts to reform the tithe system, to be removed. Yet Clare was using the Irish Privy Council, made up entirely of Crown appointees, to stultify parliamentary freedom. Fitzwilliam responded that he would not accept office without a free hand in both men and measures; he again threatened to resign if he were expected to 'step into Lord Westmorland's old shoes'.[20] At the beginning of November, Fitzwilliam and Grattan met Loughborough to clear the air. It was agreed that Ireland was not to be treated as 'separate from the general mass of the king's government' and Fitzwilliam was assured that Pitt would wholeheartedly support his administration'.[21]

On 15 November, leading Whigs met Pitt and William Wyndham, Lord Grenville, at 10 Downing Street to confirm Irish Government policy. At this time, Pitt was particularly distracted by events in Europe and may have had his mind on other matters. Neither Grattan nor the Ponsonbys attended but had prepared a memorandum for Fitzwilliam setting out the terms on which 'they and their friends will agree to support Lord Fitzwilliam's administration'.[22] These were raised by Fitzwilliam at the meeting, although he does not seem to have fully grasped all the issues, and only Fitzwilliam and Grenville made records of what was agreed. According to Fitzwilliam they decided: 'Roman Catholick [question] not to be brought forward by Government, that the discussion of the propriety may be left open'. He claimed this meant that, whilst the administration would not propose Catholic emancipation, they would not obstruct it, if approved in the Irish Parliament. Grenville's interpretation was that Fitzwilliam:

> should, as much as possible, endeavour to prevent the agitation of the question during the present session; and that, in all events, he should do nothing in it which might commit the king's government here or in Ireland without fresh instructions from hence.[23]

On hearing Fitzwilliam's summary of his discussions with Pitt and Grenville, the Irish Whigs seemed 'very disappointed (and possibly irritated by Fitzwilliam's ineptitude in committee)'.[24] Considerable doubts remained on exactly what had been agreed, but Fitzwilliam seems to have implied that the British Government would not stand in the way of granting Catholic emancipation, although he was asked to defer bringing the matter forward, and to take no action without further instructions.

Despite their concerns at Clare's retention as Lord Chancellor, the Irish Whigs told Fitzwilliam that they wanted him to accept the post. On 18 November, he wrote to Burke, explaining:

> the business is settled: that I go to Ireland—though not exactly upon the terms I had originally thought of, and I mean particularly in the removal of the Chancellor [Clare],

who is now to remain, Grattan and the Ponsonbys desire me
to accept: I left the decision to them.[25]

Burke was delighted that Fitzwilliam had joined the coalition. He
wrote to him on 21 June to give notice that he intended to resign
his seat in the Commons (and he died three years later). Fitzwilliam
offered Burke's seat at Malton to Burke's son Richard, who accepted.

It is clear, in retrospect, that Fitzwilliam did not understand or
accept that it was Tory policy, as promulgated by Burke, to woo the
Catholic hierarchy in Ireland with the hope of emancipation without
actually granting it. Fitzwilliam's objective as Lord Lieutenant was to
stamp out corruption in the Irish Establishment and he saw Catholic
emancipation as the means of achieving it. He failed to grasp the
strength of Tory opposition to his views. He did not understand or
was not aware of Pitt's later moves to seek Parliamentary Union with
Westminster, which would overcome the difficulty that emancipation
handed majority control of Irish Government to the Catholics.

Chapter 17

Fitzwilliam's Lord Lieutenancy in Ireland and its aftermath 1795

Fitzwilliam's ambitions to achieve emancipation for Ireland were not made any easier by them being leaked by the Irish Whigs, who saw his arrival as 'our redemption'.[1] Grattan, who had arrived back in Ireland in December 1794, immediately told Catholic leaders that Fitzwilliam would back full emancipation and they should bombard him with petitions from all over Ireland. This seems surprising, as Grattan was personally only in favour of granting emancipation to Catholic landowners. On 4 January 1795, Fitzwilliam landed at Balbriggan in the north of co. Dublin. His logic for supporting Catholic emancipation was diametrically opposite to that of more radical Dissenters. While they believed that emancipation would achieve support for republicanism as espoused by Priestley and Paine (with their links to the French revolutionaries), Fitzwilliam saw it as the means of reconciling Irish Catholics to British rule, thereby thwarting the threat of an invasion of Ireland by French Jacobins.

It was generally recognised that, if Irish Catholics sided with the French, not only would the Protestant Ascendancy be lost, but Britain's consequent loss of Ireland would weaken its sea power and make possible a French invasion of England. Yet, Irish Dissenters never gained the support of the Irish Catholic hierarchy for their republican ideals. When United Irish republicans tried to engineer a French invasion, the Catholic hierarchy felt no affinity with those who had overturned not only the French monarchy but the French Catholic church.

On arrival in Dublin, Fitzwilliam took immediate steps to reorganise the Irish Government's administration. Without consulting the Irish

Whigs, he made plans to replace the Attorney-General (Arthur Wolfe – who was appointed Chief Justice), the Solicitor General (John Toler), the First Revenue Commissioner (John Beresford) and the two Under-Secretaries. This seems to have been in accordance with his conversations with Pitt in London, although Pitt later denied it. He gained Portland's approval to make George Ponsonby Attorney-General and was on the brink of appointing him as Irish Secretary of State. Although Grattan was invited to join the Government, possibly as Chancellor of the Exchequer, he preferred to become leader of the house without portfolio, although Loughborough considered this absurd. He enunciated Government policy at the opening of Parliament, stressing solidarity with Britain in its war with republican France and promoting a grant of £200,000 for the Royal Navy.

George Ponsonby had persuaded Fitzwilliam to follow through with his plan to dismiss Beresford as Revenue Commissioner for alleged corruption, although his request was at least in part politically motivated. With both Clare and Beresford opposing Catholic emancipation, they had strongly disapproved of Fitzwilliam's appointment as Lord Lieutenant. With Beresford being seen to have milked his position as First Commissioner of the Revenue for his own pocket, Fitzwilliam was determined to be rid of him. He offered him retirement on full salary for life and confirmed the retention of the rest of his family in office, but he had a battle on his hands. Both Beresford and Clare were influential protagonists. Beresford was spoken of as the 'King of Ireland'. In 1768, he had joined the Irish Privy Council, and, as a close ally of Pitt, became an English Privy Councillor in 1786. In the light of Pitt's instruction, Fitzwilliam retained Clare in office. He had become Lord Chancellor in 1789, after having been Attorney General for six years before that, and 'was a powerful supporter of repressive policy towards Irish Catholics'.[2]

Following his dismissal, Beresford exerted all his influence with friends in England, describing himself as an injured and persecuted man. He arrived in London to lay his complaint before Pitt and other English ministers. He argued that a parliamentary enquiry was already investigating a tax collection fraud with a collector accused of defrauding the public of £60,000 (although there were grounds for believing that this involved collusion from one of the 'grasping' Beresford faction). The British Cabinet was suddenly perturbed at Fitzwilliam's dismissal of pro-Tory members of the Irish administration, and Portland had a change of heart. He objected to Ponsonby's appointment as Attorney-General. On 5 February, realising that Pitt was behind Portland's objection, Fitzwilliam wrote directly to him:

> I have every reason to expect a great degree of unanimity in support of my administration: nothing can defeat those expectations unless an idea should go forth that I do not possess the fullest confidence, and cannot command the most cordial support of the British Cabinet.[3]

Fitzwilliam's most immediate concern was to end continuing outbreaks of Catholic agrarian rioting. Six days after his arrival, he wrote to Portland that

> not one day has passed since my arrival without intelligence being received of violences committed in Westmeath, Meath, Longford and Cavan: Defenderism is there in its greatest force ... I find the texture of government very weak.

He also found both central and local government machinery to be chaotic. On 15 January, he reported that peasant violence was not political and could be solved if Catholics of rank were authorised to preserve law and order. This required emancipation. 'No time is to be lost, the business will presently be at hand, and the first step I take is of infinite importance.' Although he 'endeavoured to keep clear of any engagement whatever' on emancipation 'they are *all* looking forward to the repeal of the remaining restrictive and penal laws'. He continued:

> I shall not do my duty if I do not distinctly state it as my opinion that *not to grant cheerfully* on the part of government all the Catholics wish will not only be exceedingly impolitick, but perhaps *dangerous*. ... If I receive no very peremptory

directions to the contrary, I shall acquiesce with a good grace, in order to avoid the manifest ill effect of a doubt or the appearance of hesitation; for in my opinion even *the appearance of hesitation* may be mischievous to a degree beyond all calculation.[4]

He claimed that his calls for Catholic emancipation were made to support national security. Catholic disaffection required a new approach if Ireland were to be retained under British rule. On reading this, the King claimed that Fitzwilliam was:

venturing to condemn the labours of ages ... [which] every friend to the Protestant religion must feel diametrically contrary to those he has imbibed from his earliest youth.[5]

Even Portland was shocked at Fitzwilliam's forthright determination to agree emancipation so promptly, particularly after being told to delay matters, and the British Cabinet felt that it was being hustled. It postponed a discussion on the Catholic question and asked for more information on its likely impact. Beresford and his faction were expressing alarm at Fitzwilliam's policies, and, on 7 February, the British Cabinet decided that proposals for an Emancipation bill should be postponed.[6] Nevertheless, Fitzwilliam emphasised the need for urgency.

On 9 February, Pitt wrote to Fitzwilliam that Beresford's removal was never 'to my recollection ... hinted at even in the most distant manner ... much less ... without his consent' and that Fitzwilliam should have discussed it at the meeting held on 15 November. Furthermore, his policies were 'in contradiction to the ideas which I thought were fully understood among us.'[7] Fitzwilliam, 'whose reputation for veracity was unimpeachable', was perfectly clear that previous to his coming to Ireland he had informed Pitt of his intention to dismiss Beresford, and Pitt had 'made *no* objection, nor, indeed, any reply', which he took to mean that the decision was at his discretion. There had clearly been a misunderstanding, and it is probable that Pitt was focused on concerns about the war with France when they met. According to Fitzwilliam, Pitt now described Beresford's dismissal as an open breach of a most solemn promise.

On 12 February, Fitzwilliam gave Grattan leave to introduce a Catholic Relief bill, which had been approved in principle by Pitt. This fell short of seeking Catholic emancipation, but it followed a similar British Act of 1791 to allow Catholics to practice as barristers and attend university. Grattan continued to disagree with Fitzwilliam over full emancipation, being fearful of opening the vote to the masses, but had hoped it would be granted to Catholics of property, although even this proposal was opposed in London. His step by step approach to emancipation also lost him the respect of the United Irish. In other respects, the proposed concessions of the Catholic Relief bill had both Tory and Whig support, despite opposition from George III and Clare. (When Clare realised that it had Pitt's support, he recommended acceptance, despite his personal opposition for it.)

Fitzwilliam was still determined to achieve Catholic emancipation. He replied to Portland that:

> emancipation would have a good effect on the spirit and loyalty of the Catholics of Ireland, and Catholics of rank would be reconciled to British rule and put down disturbances. He also proposed a native yeomanry officered by Catholic gentry which would enable the British Army garrison to leave [for use] against the French.[8]

He linked Pitt's determination to defer Catholic emancipation with his insistence on retaining Beresford. Yet Pitt was arguing that deferment provided 'the means of doing a greater service to the British Empire, than it has been capable of receiving since the Revolution, or at least since the Union [with Scotland]'.[9] This seems to imply that he wanted to explore the possibility of uniting the Irish Parliament with Westminster. If he could achieve this, he could offer Catholic emancipation, without handing Catholics a majority in Parliament. Fitzwilliam believed that he had been thwarted by Beresford. He concluded that the objective was 'the certainty of driving this kingdom [Ireland] into a rebellion'.[10] This would make Irish self-Government impracticable. On 14 February, he wrote that he had had enough. His concerns about Beresford's 'power and influence' had been:

> too well founded: I found them incompatible with mine ... and after the receipt of this, you will be prepared to decide between Mr Beresford and me and that the matter is come to this issue is well known here.

If Pitt refused to accept his advice on emancipation, he asked to be recalled:

> These are not times for the fate of the empire to be trifled with. ... I will deliver over the country in the best state I can to any person, who possesses more of your confidence.[11]

Fitzwilliam was left in an invidious position. He had to remain in Ireland until the end of March, when his successor, John Jeffreys Pratt, 1st Marquess Camden, would arrive to replace him. He wrote two letters to his friend the Earl of Carlisle, which he circulated widely:

> I made proposals to [Pitt], for the removal of the attorney [Wolfe] and solicitor-general [Toler]; Mr. Pitt and the Duke of Portland knew perfectly well, that the men whom I found possessed of these ministerial offices, were not the men in whom I meant to confide in the arduous measures I had to undertake. Was I then to have two sets of men – one possessing confidence, without office; the other, office without confidence?[12]

In the second letter, he explained:

> And now for the grand question about Beresford:
> In a letter of mine to Mr. Pitt on this subject, I reminded him of a conversation, in which I had expressed to him ...

my apprehension that it would be necessary to remove that gentleman, and that he did not offer the slightest objection, or say a single word in favour of Mr. Beresford. This alone would have made me suppose that I should be exempt from every imputation of breach of agreement, if I determined to remove him; but when, on my arrival here, I found all those apprehensions of *his dangerous power,* which Mr. Pitt admits I had often represented to him, were fully justified, when *he was filling a situation greater than that of Lord Lieutenant,* and when I clearly saw, that if I had connected myself with a person *under universal heavy suspicions,* and subjecting my government to all the opprobrium and unpopularity attendant upon his mal-administration, I determined, while I meant to curtail him of his power, and to show to the nation, that he did not belong to my administration, to let him [and his friends] remain [unaffected] in point of income … in the enjoyment of *more emolument than was ever accumulated in any country upon any family.*[13]

Fitzwilliam was convinced that, when he accepted the Lord Lieutenancy, both Pitt and Portland would support Catholic emancipation, and that he had acted 'in perfect conformity with the original outline'.[14] He would not have accepted otherwise. Not for a second did he believe that there had been a misunderstanding. Pitt, in his earlier career, had strongly advocated emancipation. Fitzwilliam told Portland that he was not prepared to defer its implementation 'or to be the person to raise a flame in the country, that nothing short of arms would be able to keep down'.[15]

There has been much sympathy for Fitzwilliam in his predicament. He undoubtedly believed that Catholic emancipation could be achieved in a manner that would protect the interests of Protestant landowners, of which he was one. Yet the Coalition, probably including Portland, remained nervous of such a step. Fitzwilliam's own version of what had been agreed immediately following the meeting with Pitt on 15 November 1794 makes it clear that he had no authority to promote emancipation without further discussion. When he was later accused of acting without authority, there can be little doubt that he had.

Despite his earlier ambivalence about total Catholic emancipation, Grattan shared Fitzwilliam's indignation and saw him as a political martyr. They were both furious. Grattan wrote to Burke that Catholic relief 'cannot be resisted at this time with any effect short of ruin'. He feared that the Irish would turn to France for support, but he continued to advise Catholics to seek emancipation by citing:

> the justice of your cause, your attachment to His Majesty, your desire to preserve the connection with Great Britain, the firm but dutiful tone with which you apply for privileges and now the interposition of your Protestant brethren in your favour.[16]

With Camden as Lord Lieutenant, the Irish Whigs lost authority and Beresford was reinstated, forcing Ponsonby back into opposition. Catholic emancipation was left on one side, although Grattan's bill to establish a Catholic seminary at Maynooth received Royal assent. He also achieved a significant number of votes for the new Catholic Relief bill, which was only rejected by 155 votes to 84.

Whig opposition to the Irish Establishment was now in disarray. Although Grattan and other Government opponents attended a dinner, this only showed up the divided views of Catholic, United Irish and Whig attendees. They failed to agree to Grattan's call for a meeting to curb Defenderism. The United Irish present now concluded that it would take more than political agitation to achieve Catholic emancipation.

In Pitt's decision to protect Beresford, 'it is impossible to give any explanation of his conduct, creditable to his character as a statesman. The faction was not essential to his policy with regard to the union', and it left Ireland with a Parliament that remained corrupt.[17] He seems to have persuaded Portland, who was at best lukewarm about Catholic emancipation, to his point of view. The extent of Portland's support is not clear, but his failure to enunciate his views to Fitzwilliam with clarity probably contributed to the misunderstanding. He wrote privately to Fitzwilliam that he was 'too much hurt and grieved' at Fitzwilliam's ultimatum and begged him to be patient, believing that he could only recover his balance by escaping to England.[18] Yet the Cabinet accepted Fitzwilliam's resignation without more ado, and Portland wrote to him, claiming that recalling him:

> was the most painful task I ever undertook; [but it was] my opinion ... that the true interest of government ... requires that you should not continue to administer that of Ireland.

He claimed that Fitzwilliam was generally considered to be too much influenced by 'the prejudices of Grattan and the Ponsonbys'.[19]

Great efforts were made to persuade Fitzwilliam to remain in the English Cabinet, particularly by Portland, who wrote:

> I will retire, I will make any extirpation or atonement that can satisfy you – you are younger, more active, more able than I am, you can do more good. If my ... renunciation of the world will restore you to the public service, God forbid I should hesitate a moment.[20]

Yet, Fitzwilliam refused. On 28 February, he wrote to the Duke of Devonshire that his recall:

> is a subject of the greatest pain and mortification to me, because it must be the cause of the most complete separation between the Duke of Portland and myself. Either I have been the most wild, rash, unfaithful servant to the Crown and to England, or he has abandoned in the most shameful manner his friend, and his friend's character, for pursuing generally a system of measures that has been the perpetual theme of his conversation, and the subject of his recommendation for years back. It is painful, a trying task to submit to a separation from a man I have loved so long and so much; but I must submit to it, for I will not abandon my

character to the disgraceful imputations that must attach upon it if I do not justify it by charging him with the most shameful dereliction of his friend that ever was experienced by a faithful and a tried one.[21]

He did not stop there. On 3 April, he wrote to his friend, Thomas Grenville, that Portland:

has been bewildered, and in his confusion has been led into irretrievable error; but that error is of a nature never, I fear, to be got over: he has been induced to abandon his principles, and give up his friend, his firm, his steady his staunch supporter. ... [He] suffered himself to be the dupe of cunning and design, has been made the instrument of his own and my disgrace—a disgrace of a nature most gratifying to our common enemies. [I am resolved] to separate myself altogether from every sort of intercourse with the man with whom I have passed so many years of my life in the most intimate, cordial, unsuspecting friendship.[22]

It is generally accepted that Fitzwilliam was badly let down by both Pitt, whose immediate aim was to destroy the Whig party in Ireland, and Portland, who was 'seduced into altering "all his former opinions respecting the policy of this country"'. By their actions, they failed Ireland. When Fitzwilliam called for an investigation, it was refused. If he had had his way as Lord Lieutenant, Irish history might have been very different. Sectarian violence might have been brought under control, but would the Catholic hierarchy, on gaining emancipation, have remained loyal supporters of the English Crown, which had usurped their ancestral lands?

To the great disappointment of both Catholics and Presbyterians, Fitzwilliam's efforts had come to nothing. Grattan reported that, although they were silent and unhappy, there 'never was a time in which the opposition here were more completely backed by the nation, Protestant and Catholic united'.[23] An address sent to Fitzwilliam ended:

> We consider the day in which his Majesty entrusted the
> Irish Sceptre to your hand, as one of the brightest in the
> annals of our country; as we should that of your departure
> from us as a day of National mourning.[24]

There was great despondency in Belfast and riots in Dublin. Revolution
was now seen by many as the only way forward. The Great Strand Street
congregation voted not to welcome Camden as Lord Lieutenant. They
expected to be supported by its two most prominent members, Robert
Stewart, Lord Londonderry and his son, also Robert. Hitherto, both
had been liberal reformers and the congregation had assisted Robert Jr.
in his parliamentary campaign in co. Down. Yet Londonderry was
Camden's brother-in-law and, in expectation of preferment, father
and son 'gave in to the lure of ambition and changed their politics and
religion'.[25] In 1796, Londonderry became an Earl, with his son, Robert,
taking the courtesy title of Viscount Castlereagh. He was later British
Foreign Secretary and the principal British diplomat negotiating peace
at the Congress of Vienna after the battle of Waterloo. Londonderry's
volte face caused him to be lampooned in *The Northern Star* by the Rev.
James Porter of Greyabbey, who referred to him and his henchman,
the Rev. James Clelland, as 'Billy Bluff and the Squire'; in 1798, Porter
died on the gallows for this 'crime'.

While it was put about in Britain that threatened rebellion was
a spill-over from the agrarian rioting of Catholic Defenders, the
agitation arose from the republican aspirations of morally upright
Dissenters in the north. They had hoped to harness both the French
and leaderless Defenders to their cause. Their radical course was
strongly opposed by Irish Whigs, whose solution, which Fitzwilliam
would have endorsed, involved:

> Catholic emancipation, parliamentary reform, the promotion
> of Irish economic development and a severe scrutiny of the
> details and administration of the emergency legislation.[26]

To Government supporters in the Irish Parliament emancipation
remained an unwarranted gamble. Despite Grattan making brilliant

speeches, Parliament was now denuded of Whigs, and his oratory, 'hardened by twenty years of debate, was ill adapted to the exposition of consensus policies'.[27]

Fitzwilliam left Dublin on 28 March 1795. In Belfast 'there was not a Shop or Counting-House open during the whole day – all was one scene of sullen indignation'.[28] With Camden in office, Fitzwilliam wrote another letter to Carlisle admitting that he had accused Beresford of corruption. Beresford needed to clear his name and, on 22 June, wrote to Fitzwilliam that his character had been unjustly attacked:

> Direct and specific charges I could fairly have met and refuted, but crooked and undefined insinuations against private character, through the pretext of official discussion, your Lordship must allow, are the weapons of a libeller.[29]

This was a demand for satisfaction, and Fitzwilliam replied: 'I am ready to attend your call.'[30] Rumours of the impending duel leaked, and Fitzwilliam was 'obliged to quit the house ... hastily in the morning, for fear of arrest by the police'. They met at Paddington, but, as they took their marks, a magistrate ran onto the field to arrest Fitzwilliam, who said to Beresford 'that [as] we have been prevented from finishing this business in the manner I wished, I have no scruple to make an apology'. Beresford accepted it and they shook hands, with Fitzwilliam saying: 'Now, thank God, there is a complete end to my Irish administration'. He hoped that 'whenever they met it might be on the footing of friends'.[31] Burke wrote to Lord John Cavendish on 1 July that:

> it is happy, that a Virtuous man has escaped with Life and honour—and that his reputation for spirit and humanity, and true dignity must stand higher than ever, if higher it could stand.[32]

Part 6

The seeds of revolution to establish republicanism in Ireland

Chapter 18

The formation of the Society of United Irishmen 1783 – 1794

The Society of United Irishmen was established in 1791, four years before Fitzwilliam's Lord Lieutenancy. It should be said at the outset that the whole concept of uniting Catholics and Presbyterians into a single revolutionary body was doomed to failure. It was the tragedy of the republican movement in Ireland that it only exacerbated sectarian conflict. Uniting the two extremes of religious persuasion against the Establishment middle was always going to be difficult. 'There was no connection whatever between the republican spirit of the north and the insurrectionary spirit of the south.'[1]

For any rebellion to succeed, it would need to be properly armed and this would require assistance from France or America. Yet the Catholic hierarchy and senior churchmen in Ireland remained horrified by events in France, where the French peasantry had destroyed its monarchy, its aristocracy and its Catholic Church, and they deplored the massacres in Paris in September 1792. America, so newly freed from English rule, might have seemed a more acceptable ally, but the Americans were never going to support a revolt backed by the French. During the American Wars of Independence, the French had used opportunist tactics to pirate American shipping, even to the extent of 'an undeclared naval war'.[2] Although discontented and sometimes starving, Catholic peasantry in Ireland joined the United Irishmen in droves and 'cared not a jot for their plans of an ideal republic';[3] its sole objective was to use the Dissenter rebellion to dignify its petty insurgencies arising from its efforts to eke out a subsistence living on its over-priced tenancies. Although the United Irish made great efforts to harness disparate Dissenter bands, they were generally unarmed and proved unreliable as allies, not always prepared to fight when rival groups appeared on the same side.

The Catholic Church and aristocracy had no sympathy with republican ideals and were not about to ally with Presbyterians, who remained vociferously hostile to papal dogma despite the Dissenters' apparent show of tolerance. Notwithstanding its charm and charisma, the United Irish leadership lacked military experience or organising skills, and failed to attract well-established citizens, whether Presbyterian or Catholic, to its cause. It was easily infiltrated; 'when all their secrets were betrayed, all their measures known, and all their leaders seized, the United Irishmen allowed the Rebellion to begin.'[4] French support was at best lukewarm, and the Americans, who were focused only on building trading bridges with England, offered no assistance. This left the rebellion 'ill concerted' and 'worse directed'.[5] Worse still, the British Government was keen to encourage the appearance of an insurgency, so that it could implant sufficient fear into the Irish Parliament to support union with Westminster. In this respect, from a republican viewpoint, the rebellion was counter-productive.

It was Dickson, who, in March 1779 had first used one of his sermons in Belfast to call for Catholics to be admitted to the Volunteers. This 'was the first step in what eventually developed into a democratic project to modernise Irish society on a non-sectarian basis'.[6] 'This implied recognition that Roman Catholics could be trusted to play a full and virtuous role as free citizens in defending their country.'[7] Dickson 'urged the Volunteers to show that "it is only against the enemies of your country, liberty and peace, be their religion what it may be that your arms are pointed – and that whoever is a friend of these is your friend and the object of your protection"'.[8]

After their failure to progress Government reform, the Volunteers had had cold feet and were fearful of being suppressed. In the absence of Whig support, they pulled back from political agitation and, in doing so, lost much prestige with those working to achieve the Good Old Cause. At their convention at Dungannon in 1783, the Belfast Volunteers had at last concluded:

> We think it is a duty we owe to our country, to promote as
> far as our example can reach, an affectionate coalition of the
> inhabitants of Ireland. … This regiment affords a striking
> instance how far the divine spirit of toleration can unite men
> of all religious descriptions in one great object, the support
> of a free constitution.[9]

These first stirrings of United Irish sentiments were well received. It
took until the following year before they took into their ranks:

> persons of every religious persuasion, firmly convinced
> that a general Union of ALL the inhabitants of Ireland is
> necessary to the freedom and prosperity of this Kingdom,
> as it is congenial to the Constitution.[10]

This echoed pleas for a 'brotherhood of man'. It was not initially a call
for revolution nor was it particularly republican or anti-Royalist. It
was a moral crusade to encourage Presbyterians of all creeds to allow
the downtrodden Irish Catholics to live like other Irish citizens, to
participate in Government, in the judiciary, in education and in the
military and to have a vote. These sentiments mirrored the calls to
abolish slavery.

Matters needed careful handling. These were sensitive times;
America had achieved independence and Britain was at war with
revolutionary France. The British needed to avoid Ireland becoming
its Achilles heel by gaining either American or French support for an
Irish republican revolution. Dissenting theology became the catalyst
for those of a revolutionary frame of mind to justify their cause. It
was a small band of revolutionary idealists whose calls for an Irish
Republic eventually turned its leaders into folk-heroes.

The man who stepped forward to promote Dickson's call for the
Good Old Cause was William Drennan, the son of Thomas Drennan,
who had spent his early teaching career with Francis Hutcheson
in Dublin. Thomas Drennan had moved from Dublin after being
appointed minister at Rosemary Street, the principal Dissenter
meeting house in Belfast, and remained there until his death in 1768.

William was born in Belfast in 1754 and, as a young man, became an enthusiastic member of the Belfast Volunteers, strongly supporting American calls for independence. As a committed Unitarian, he admired Price and Priestley in England with their sympathy for the French Jacobins. They believed that they were living in an age of revolution, 'where unjust governments are falling in every quarter of Europe'. Yet Drennan was not initially a rebel. Certainly, he wanted to see Catholic emancipation, but hoped that it could be achieved through political persuasion.

In 1778, Drennan qualified as a physician in Glasgow and, on his return to Ireland, practiced at Newry where he took lodgings with the Rev. Boyle Moody, a cousin of William Bruce. He soon became 'disillusioned by the failure of the Volunteer movement and the Whigs to achieve parliamentary reform'.[11] With Moody's help, he tried, with limited success, to persuade the local Member of Parliament, Isaac Corry, to support the faltering Volunteers' progressive wing. Eventually, he concluded that it would take a more radical course to challenge the Establishment, and he drew on dissenting theology to justify his actions. In 1784, and again in 1785, he put forward an 'entire scheme for a secret inner circle of dedicated radical reformers', but his plans fell on deaf ears.[12]

By 1789, Drennan had realised that his medical practice in Newry was not attracting sufficient patients to provide him with an adequate living as a physician. He moved to Dublin, where his reputation as a writer on radical constitutional reform, Catholic emancipation and civil rights preceded him. He attended the two meeting houses in Dublin where his late father was still remembered, and these continued their links with Rosemary Street in Belfast. He befriended Dr William Bruce, the publisher's son, who had been educated at Priestley's Academy at Warrington and at Trinity College, Dublin. In about 1770, Bruce became minister of the Great Strand Street congregation, remaining there for twenty years. He became a well-established figure in Dublin, active in the Volunteers and a moderate Whig. In 1782, he joined James Napper Tandy and John Binns Sr. to form the Dublin Chamber of Commerce, which accepted Catholics among its membership. Yet many of the Chamber's members, the 'worthy and highly respected brethren, the merchants of Dublin', still feared that Catholics, once emancipated, would establish an inquisition to seek restitution of lands long since transferred to Protestants of all creeds.[13]

Tandy was the son of a Dublin ironmonger with a Quaker background. As a member of the Dublin Corporation, he denounced municipal corruption and later gained a seat in the Irish Parliament. He strongly supported the French Jacobins and, when the English protectionists arranged a boycott of Irish goods, he gained some notoriety by proposing an Irish boycott of English goods in retaliation. He joined the Whig Club founded by Grattan, against whose reforming objectives Clare had levelled 'abuse'. Drennan described Clare, with his strong opposition to Catholic emancipation, as 'that bouncing bully'.[14]

Theobald Wolfe Tone was another activist member of the Whig Club. He had published a pamphlet, *An Argument on behalf of the Catholics of Ireland*, aimed at discontented Presbyterians. Tone claimed 'that they would never attain the liberty they sought if they did not make common cause with their Roman Catholic fellow countrymen'.[15] The pamphlet was reprinted in Belfast, where it was greeted with delight. It hailed events in France, building on Dickson's earlier proposal in support of Catholic emancipation, saying: 'The Catholics of France put their duty as citizens above their religious inclinations, so Irish Catholics might do the same.'[16] The pamphlet's defence of the Whig Club:

> recommended him strongly to the Whigs, but they found him too warm an advocate, and he appears to have found them too little to his mind for their acquaintance to be of long duration.[17]

Tone had been born in Dublin in 1763, the eldest son of a successful coachbuilder, whose family were members of the Church of Ireland. He was academically brilliant and devastatingly attractive. Despite hankering after a military career, he had entered Trinity College, Dublin, where he eloped with and married Matilda Witherington, 'not yet sixteen, and as lovely as an angel'.[18] He then left for two years to study law at the Middle Temple in London, leaving Matilda with his father. Yet the law lacked the stimulus he craved. As he 'foresaw by this time I should never be Lord Chancellor', he focused on a hare-brained plan to colonise a south sea island.[19] In 1789, he returned to Ireland, where he was called to the Irish Bar, but failed to settle into a barrister's routine and spent hours in the visitors' gallery of the Irish House of Commons, contemplating a role in Parliament. It was here that he met Thomas Russell, a Cork-born Indian army officer, four years his junior. Although Russell was at Trinity College studying science, philosophy and politics, Tone harnessed his attention to radical political thought.

Mary Ann McCracken much later described Russell as:

> A model of manly beauty, he was one of those favoured individuals whom one cannot pass in the street without being guilty of the rudeness of staring in the face while passing, and turning round to look at the receding figure. Though more than six feet high, his majestic stature was scarcely observed owing to the exquisite symmetry of his form.[20]

Her admiration for this Adonis was not reciprocated. Russell had eyes only for the beautiful Bess Goddard. When Tone decided to spend a 'delicious' summer with his wife, Matilda, at a rented 'little box of a house' by the sea in Irishtown while she recovered her 'delicate' health, Russell was invited to join them in their 'frugal' existence to develop their friendship and political ideas.

In about 1790, Bruce moved from Dublin to Belfast to become the minister at Rosemary Street, where he befriended Henry Joy, owner of *The Belfast Newsletter* and probably the most influential Belfast business man at the time. Joy was descended from a Huguenot family, who had arrived at Lisburn in the 1690s. In 1783, he had joined with other Belfast merchants, including his father-in-law, John Holmes, one of the co-founders of the Belfast Bank, into following Bruce's Dublin example by forming a Belfast Chamber of Commerce. Despite

Joy maintaining a strong voice for moderation in calls for Catholic emancipation, his editorials in the *Newsletter* showed strong approval of the French revolutionaries. He wrote:

> The exultation, with which they [the people of Belfast] hailed the downfall of civil and spiritual despotism in France in the year 1789, affords a decisive proof of their disinterested solicitude for the universal diffusion of liberty and peace. Their joy was expressed by affectionate congratulations to the French patriots and by annual commemorations ...[21]

These sentiments were echoed in his support for the revival of the Belfast First Volunteers and the formation, in 1790, of a Whig Club in Belfast, made up of its more moderate citizens, who appointed him Secretary. At one of their first meetings, the club resolved:

> that considering the French revolution as one of the most important and universally interesting events which the world ever saw, and as particularly such to the inhabitants of these islands as it promises to lead the way to an orderly and gradual reform of these abuses which have maimed and disfigured the constitution we shall, as men, as Whigs – as citizens of this empire, meet on 14th of July next, to celebrate that astonishing event [the fall of the Bastille], which constitutes a glorious era in the history of man and of the world.[22]

This was followed by a procession through the streets with tableaux prepared by the Volunteers sporting green cockades as the national colour of Ireland. They carried a banner saying: 'Our Gallic brother was born July 14, 1789 – Alas! we are still in embryo and Superstitious galaxy – The Irish Bastille: let us unite to destroy it.'[23] They then sat down, 354 strong, to a banquet on a single long table at the White Linen Hall. This was a Volunteer attempt at reform by acting within the law.

In Dublin, Drennan, with support from Tandy, Tone and Russell, was taking a more radical approach. In 1791, after the fall of the Bastille and the publication of Paine's *Rights of Man*, he set out plans to form a secret society, a 'brotherhood of affection' based on the principles of Algernon Sidney. He proposed:

> a benevolent conspiracy – a plot of the people ... – the Brotherhood its name – the Rights of Man and the Greatest Happiness of the Greatest Number its end – its general end real independence to Ireland, and republicanism its particular purpose.[24]

He wrote to his brother-in-law, Sam McTier in Belfast, who was a member of a secret committee of democratic radicals, headed by Samuel Neilson. Neilson was a successful woollen draper and son of a Unitarian minister, who founded the radical *Northern Star* newspaper in the following year. Although McTier was, by inclination, a moderate, he confirmed his approval, replying that 'if your Brotherhood takes place we will immediately follow your example'.[25] The plan was to open the society to Catholics, Anglicans and freethinkers.

Despite an undercurrent of revolutionary intent among a few hard-line protestors, Joy and other influential Presbyterian members of the Belfast Whig Club and Belfast Chamber of Commerce encouraged Bruce to promote calls for moderation. Although Bruce saw the need for Catholic reform, he was concerned that a Catholic majority would restrain liberty of conscience. Despite his friendship with Drennan, he did not support Catholic emancipation, although Drennan may not have realised this. It was the nature of Unitarianism that different views were aired in a reasoned manner, and friendships papered over awkward ideological cracks.

A group of Belfast Whig Club members, including Neilson, Robert Simms, a paper mill owner, and William Sinclair became exasperated by the moderating influence of the club's senior members. They now began 'perfecting their schemes for uniting Irishmen of all creeds and classes in society pledged to more drastic action'.[26] In 1790, Russell moved to Belfast with the 64th Regiment of Foot. He 'found the people so much to his taste and in return rendered himself so agreeable to them ...'[27] When introduced by Tone to the Belfast Whig Club, he was admitted with enthusiasm. Having met Neilson, Russell helped him to develop plans for a Society of United Irishmen, knowing that Tone, who had remained in Dublin, would welcome their ideas.

On 12 October 1791, Tone made a two-day visit to Belfast to assist the group in remodelling certain of their resolutions. On his arrival at the Whig Club, he faced a conflict with Bruce, who still did not feel that the time was right for Catholic emancipation and universal male suffrage. This was 'an argument that was fuelled by alcohol'.[28] Tone described Bruce as 'an intolerant high priest'.[29] This split 'revolutionaries and moderate reformers'.[30] Bruce also found himself at odds with Drennan and members of his Rosemary Street congregation, but he held to his views and, in 1798, 'joined the yeomanry in defending Belfast to suppress the rebel threat'.[31]

Six days after his first visit, Tone returned to the Whig Club where, with twenty people present, the membership of the United Irishmen was at last opened up. In addition to Russell, Neilson and Tone, the meeting was attended by three freemasons, Henry Haslett and William Tennant, who were merchants and Thomas McCabe, a clockmaker. McTier, Gilbert McIlveen, William and Robert Simms and Thomas Pearce were among the others. They passed three resolutions:

1. that the weight of English influence in Government of this country is so great as to require a cordial union among all the people of Ireland, to maintain the balance which is essential to the preservation of our liberties and the extension of our commerce,
2. that the sole constitutional mode by which this influence can be opposed is by a complete and radical reform of the people in Parliament, and
3. that no reform is just which does not include Irishmen of every religious persuasion.

Members were required to subscribe to a test:

> I, A.B. in the presence of God do pledge myself to my
> country, that I will use all my abilities and influence in the
> attainment of an impartial and adequate representation of
> the Irish nation in Parliament; and as a means of absolute
> and immediate necessity, in the establishment of this the
> chief good of Ireland, I will endeavour, as much as lies in
> my ability, to forward a brotherhood of affection, an identity
> of interest, a communion of rights and an union of power
> among Irishmen of all religious persuasions, without which
> every reform of Parliament must be partial, not national,
> inadequate to the wants, delusive to the wishes, and
> insufficient for the freedom and happiness of the country.[32]

As Mary MacNeill puts it:

> The only fault of these United Irishmen lay, it would seem,
> in their being too far ahead of their times; the principles
> enunciated in this declaration are today accepted as the
> foundations on which democratic associations must be built.[33]

The new movement chose a badge of a harp over the motto: 'It is re-
strung and shall be heard.'

Tone's initial objectives were not revolutionary, and he never gained
the confidence of those in Belfast, like Neilson, who saw rebellion
as the only way forward. On 1 January 1792, Neilson launched his
newspaper, *The Northern Star*, propounding views which were more
radical than those of Joy's *Belfast Newsletter*. Tone was seeking political
reform by persuasion. Much later, he recorded:

> At this time, the establishment of a republic was not the
> immediate object of my speculations, my object was to
> secure the independence of my country under any form of
> government.[34]

The Society tried to separate religion from politics. It backed Grattan in his efforts to achieve change, but, with Grattan following Burke in seeking a 'gradual continuation of reform', it came to differ with him over his speed in progressing it.

Despite Bruce's scepticism, there was widespread support for the new Society. Its membership in Ulster grew spectacularly. Neilson reported:

> You can form no conception of the rapid progress of unions here; and I do assure you we are further forward than I ever expected we should have been in a twelve month. The universal question throughout the country is, when do we begin? Do we refuse hearth money or tythes first?[35]

Another member of the Whig Club supporting the United Irishmen was Henry Joy McCracken from a respectable Presbyterian merchant family, although he was away from Belfast during the initial formation of the Society. He was another extremely charismatic individual, tall, witty, charming and a leader of men, who became Russell's close friend. His father, John McCracken, had been a sea captain, and, on his retirement, had started a rope-walk in Belfast and manufactured sail cloth. His mother, Ann Joy was Henry Joy's aunt. This placed the McCrackens at the heart of genteel Belfast society. Ann owned a muslin business, which was now managed by her unmarried daughters, Margaret and Mary Ann. Mary Ann was an idealist and determined philanthropist like her brother, holding the well-being of the weavers in her family's employment close to her heart. She remained close to 'Harry' and their correspondence provides an insight into their hopes for reform. In 1789, Harry had joined a cotton printing mill, Joy, Holmes and McCracken at the Falls, which was some distance from Belfast and immediately went to Scotland to recruit skilled workers. He seems to have been more focused on their welfare than the mill's success, starting a Sunday school in Belfast, with his friends as teachers, to educate his workers.

> Writing as well as reading was taught. They did not presume
> to impart religious knowledge, but they taught their scholars
> how to obtain it for themselves, by which every sect might
> equally profit ... and then Mr. Bristow [the Sovereign of
> Belfast] came to the place of meeting with a number of
> Ladies, with rods in their hands as badges of authority,
> which put to flight the humble pioneers.[36]

Welfare was always close to the hearts of leading United Irishmen. In
1792, Russell wrote an impassioned letter against slavery, published
in *The Northern Star*. He swore never to eat products from the West
Indies until slavery was abolished, claiming: 'on every lump of sugar
I see a drop of human blood'.[37] Neilson pointed to the need to relieve
the three million slaves among the Irish peasantry. At about this time,
Russell had the misfortune to befriend a liberal-minded American,
Dr Thomas Digges, who had been working in England as an agent to
handle the exchange of American prisoners of war. Although Digges
had been received in Ireland with open arms, he was unable to pay his
way. He was arrested after Neilson was unable to recover a pair of silver
spurs which he had lent to him. Russell, who did not share the general
condemnation of Digges, agreed to stand surety of £200 for him.
Digges promptly went to Glasgow with a party on a shopping trip,
where he was arrested when some articles went missing without being
paid for. When he failed to return to Ireland, Russell was forced to sell
his commission with the 64th Regiment of Foot to meet the surety. His
sympathetic friends arranged his appointment to the lucrative post of
Senechal of the Manor Court in 'socially attractive' Dungannon. This
carried with it a seat on the magistrate's bench. Yet, Russell fell out with
his brother magistrates over their preferential treatment to Protestants,
and, within nine months, he resigned. Having returned to Belfast, in
1794 he became librarian of the Belfast Library at a salary of £30 per
year but spent most of his time with McCracken plotting rebellion. He
never regained financial security, and Bess Goddard chose elsewhere.

On Tone's return to Dublin after the formation of the Belfast
Society of United Irishmen, he consulted with Tandy, and Dublin

quickly followed suit. At its inauguration on 9 November 1791, the Dublin Society became 'the first avowedly non–sectarian democratic organisation in the country's history'.[38] At their first meeting at the Eagle Tavern in Eustace Street they appointed a barrister, Simon Butler, as chairman and Tandy as secretary. It was attended by Tone, Russell, Drennan, Archibald Hamilton Rowan, a giant of a man, who was a wealthy Unitarian with aristocratic connections, Henry Jackson, a successful Presbyterian businessman, Oliver Bond, his son-in-law, and Bagenal Beauchamp Harvey, a barrister. All were members of the Great Strand Street congregation. Although they were avowedly republican, supporting full political and religious rights for Catholics, the Society's objective was 'expressly to obtain a reform in parliament and the abolition of the penal code'.[39] Each member signed a test in the form prepared in Belfast. By his own admission: 'Tone quickly lost influence and "sunk into obscurity in the club, which, however, he had the satisfaction to see daily increasing in numbers and importance"'.[40]

Tandy was hot-headed. When Toler (later created Earl of Norbury), the Attorney General, referred to his indisputable ugliness, Tandy challenged him to a duel. With this breaching parliamentary privilege, a warrant was issued for his arrest. Having escaped to Philadelphia, he met Citizen Pierre-Auguste Adet, the Minister Plenipotentiary (Ambassador) for the French Republic, who recruited him to support future French action in Ireland. Adet described him as: 'An excellent republican, a man entirely devoted to France and hating England as much as he is attached to our cause.'[41]

Chapter 19

United Irish efforts to influence reform in the Irish Parliament 1792 – 1797

With England at war with France, the Irish Government's failure to enact political reform played into the hands of the United Irishmen. As Mary McNeill has so clearly explained:

> No one could blame the Parliament at Westminster for being preoccupied with measures for Britain's survival, but the folly of its tactics, as far as Ireland was concerned, was lamentable. Instead of a courageous policy of parliamentary reform, which, even at that hour, would have rallied all the elements of discontent to England's side, hastily conceived deterrents served only to enflame disaffection. Security measures were rushed though the Irish House of Commons; espionage was intensified, so that 'a perfect Inquisition reigns'; ... leaders of the United Irishmen in Dublin were arrested to lie in prison without indictment let alone trial; members of the rank and file, notably Defenders, were publicly executed with every display of cruelty and humiliation;[1] and, in order to avoid any possible disaffection of the landed interest, the ancient and all too successful remedy of bribery was once more produced. 'A new cargo of pensions is said to have come over to distribute as douceurs, like lottery tickets.'[2]

By late 1792, the United Irish membership had become more forthright, and their object was declared to be:

A national legislature, and its means a union of the people.
The government is called on, if it has a sincere regard for
the safety of the constitution, to coincide with the people
in its speedy reform of its abuses, and not by an obstinate
adherence to them to drive the people into republicanism.[3]

Both in Belfast and Dublin, great efforts were made to revive the
Volunteer movement. 'The principle that an armed citizenry provided
the best guarantee for liberty and freedom was a notion shared by both
reformers and revolutionary Irishmen.'[4] On 14 July 1792, the Belfast
Volunteers commemorated the anniversary of Bastille Day by holding
a review. *The Northern Star* reported that three battalions marched
through Belfast High Street carrying a portrait of Benjamin Franklin,
with Algernon Sidney's motto: 'Where liberty is, there is my country.'
Others:

carried slogans such as *Can the African Slave Trade, Though
Morally Wrong, Be Politically Right?* The flag of America,
the Asylum of Liberty, and the French tricolour hung from
many windows.[5]

The parade was followed by a meeting, which carried a motion
demanding immediate Catholic emancipation, after which the
participants retired for a convivial social evening at the Donegall
Arms, at which 104 people sat down to a dinner with thirty-three
toasts, generally in support of liberties achieved by both French and
American revolutionaries. These Volunteers enjoyed a good time; they
were not dour Calvinist Presbyterians, but men of the Enlightenment.

After their success in Belfast, they planned a similar review in
Dublin. In early 1793, buoyed up by their recruitment of Dublin
members, Rowan, Bond and Jackson formed their own radical
company of Volunteers, which they dubbed the National Guard,
displaying a harp without a crown on their banner. 'This identification
with the French Revolution alarmed the government', and calls for 'a
union of all Irishmen' resulted in a proclamation forbidding seditious

assemblies.[6] The Dublin United Irishmen then went a step too far. In February 1793, they declared that a secret committee of the House of Lords had acted illegally by forcing witnesses to recent disturbances to give evidence under oath 'in support of prosecutions already commenced'. This resulted in Butler, their Chairman, and Bond, the Secretary of the meeting, each being imprisoned for six months and fined £500. Drennan caused more trouble by preparing an anonymous pamphlet for distribution to the National Guard. This was headed: 'Citizen soldiers to arms.' He continued:

> Citizen soldiers you first took up arms to protect your country from foreign enemies and from domestic disturbance. For the same purpose it now becomes necessary that you should renew them ... We wish for Catholic emancipation without any modification; but still we consider this necessary enfranchisement as merely the portal to the temple of national freedom. The Catholic cause is subordinate to our cause ... for as United Irishmen we adhere to no sect but to society, to no creed but to Christianity, to no party but to the whole people ... Fourteen long years have elapsed since the rise of your associations [the Volunteers], and in 1782 did you imagine that in 1792 this nation would still remain unrepresented? How many nations in the interval have gotten the start of Ireland? How many of our countrymen have sank in the grave?[7]

This stirring appeal breathed no hint of disloyalty to the King and the Constitution, or any injury to the safety of the realm, but it was bitter in its opposition to:

> that faction or gang [the Irish Privy Council] that misrepresents the King to the people, and the people to the King, traduces one half of the nation to cajole the other, and by keeping up distrust and division, wished to continue the proud arbitrators of the fortune and fate of Ireland.[8]

Drennan was arrested on suspicion of writing the pamphlet, and Rowan was imprisoned for distributing it at an illegal gathering of Volunteers. Although Rowan was granted bail, the Government wanted to make an example of him. It delayed bringing him to trial until January 1794, when there was an attempt to pack the jury. Although the case for judicial murder against him failed, he was fined £500 and received a two-year prison sentence. The Working Manufacturers of Dublin sent him messages of support and hailed him as a martyr for liberty. Other opinion was divided, even among those anxious to achieve reform. Five months later, Drennan was tried for having written the pamphlet. This seems to have become well known, and he had already been branded a regicide. He certainly saw 30 January, the date of the execution of Charles I, as 'the day that makes tyrants tremble'.[9] If found guilty, he was likely to be executed, but he was ably defended by John Philpot Curran, the most highly regarded lawyer of his day, who managed to expose the false testimony of the chief prosecution witness, resulting in him being discharged on lack of evidence.

The Government immediately banned the Society of United Irishmen, whose sympathy for the French insurgents was well known, and it moved quickly to seize their funds. Although some members resigned, the more determined were forced underground. This made them more revolutionary and radical, but the leadership was divided between those preferring to await French support before starting their own rebellion and those prepared to press ahead regardless. When the authorities stamped harshly on a pre-emptive uprising in Leitrim, it was generally accepted that French support was essential.

In a further step to curtail insurgency, the Belfast Volunteers were forbidden from parading or appearing in 'military array'. They were disarmed, and the sale of arms and ammunition was prohibited. Even among the moderates, this caused great consternation. Drennan's sister, Martha McTier (Sam's wife) wrote copious letters, which expounded her undeniably 'moderate' stance. She expressed pity for:

> the Volrs. called on by the most respectable of their countrymen to continue those efforts from which nothing

but good was the consequence ... yet spurn'd & degraded,
by a base, cruel and powerful administration.[10]

All this played into the hands of the Presbyterian extremists. Efforts
to achieve the reforms that the Volunteers were seeking continued
underground with many members joining secret societies of United
Irishmen organised on a military basis. Every meeting now confirmed
their objective as: 'A republican government, and a separation from
England.'[11] The Dublin Government now infiltrated the United
Irish movement with a network of spies to forewarn them of future
disturbances. Their 'most secret proceedings' were now 'made known
to the government as soon as they were formed'.[12] It treated them like
'puppets, to be worked until they had produced' sufficient alarm 'to
be delivered over to the executioner ... having been at once dupes and
conspirators'.[13]

Grattan and the senior Irish Whigs never supported the United
Irishmen's republican objectives. In this period before Fitzwilliam's
Lord Lieutenancy, Grattan consistently backed the English
Government. Although he wanted Catholics to have the same rights
as Protestants in matters such as freedom of worship, ownership of
land and service in the professions, he continued to fear the impact
on Parliament of immediate Catholic emancipation. In 1793, Russell,
who sought an altogether more revolutionary approach, reported
in *The Northern Star*: 'He paddled and he pranced, he reviled the
government and the French republicans and levellers' but facilitated
'the perfect inquisition'.

In 1794, after an abortive French landing at Bantry Bay, the
authorities arrested Drennan and other key members of the United
Irish leadership. This left the remainder even more determined. In
1795, Tone, McCracken and Russell led a band of members to the top
of Cave Hill overlooking Belfast and swore 'never to desist in our effort
until we have subverted the authority of England over our country
and asserted our independence'.[14] Neilson had paid little attention to
the ban on United Irish activity, but he was not a leader of national
standing and his 'mass revolutionary movement' failed to gain much

support even in Belfast.[15] When he called for a petition to repeal 'the penal and restrictive statutes at present in existence against the Roman Catholics of Ireland', moderate Presbyterians moved to soften it. Joy and his supporters backed Grattan in wanting a progressive introduction of emancipation to give time for Catholic principles to be tested. Yet calls for full and immediate emancipation gained ground. Neilson's watered-down petition was signed by 600 Presbyterians and, within a fortnight, was presented to the Irish House of Commons. Joy did not support Neilson, writing in his *Newsletter*:

> At a period when Republicans are exhibited as models of perfection, I am persuaded it is consistent with the spirit of a free press, to recommend the principles of the British Constitution ... [Republicanism] is the fashion of the hour, and as ridiculous as most fashions are, to deprecate the Revolution of 1688 – and to despise the securities for our liberty, which that great transaction afforded.[16]

As moderates, Sam and Martha McTier agreed with Joy.

With its significant Catholic population, Dublin differed from Belfast in its attitude to rebellion. Its Society of United Irishmen had begun with about a hundred wealthy merchants, who published pamphlets and debated their radical views throughout Britain. Although Neilson tried to persuade them into a more revolutionary approach, the great majority of the membership, like the Belfast moderates, refused their support. Exceptions were Henry Jackson and Bond, who had become determined republicans. Jackson was 'a deep man slow in speech but much listened to', having served as an officer in the Volunteers and on the Dublin Corporation.[17] He had become wealthy and independent from his iron foundry business in Church Street, where he introduced a steam engine designed by Priestley's friend, James Watt, to pump the bellows. His business 'carried out major public contracts but also manufactured pikes', and was quite prepared to manufacture cannonballs of a calibre suitable to be fired from French cannon.[18] Bond was a prosperous wholesale woollen draper in Pill Lane with an income of £6,000 per year. He was charismatic and good looking 'with a shapely pair of legs of which he was just a little proud'.[19] He had been born at St Johnson near Londonderry in 1757, the son of a Presbyterian minister, but moved to Dublin in 1782. Nine years later, he married Jackson's pretty daughter, Eleanor, who became a sworn 'Unitedman'. She was a woman of 'sparkling courage', persuading other ladies to their cause.[20]

In 1793, in its attempt to break the Catholic–Presbyterian alliance, Parliament had passed a further relief measure to provide Catholics with 'all rights and liberties of citizenship' except admission to Parliament and appointment to the highest civil and judicial positions. In 1795, the hearth tax, through which Catholics had been forced to subscribe to the maintenance of Church of Ireland clergy, was at last abolished. Catholics were now expected to join the militia and to inform on United Irish activity. This caused sectarian hatred.

In September 1795, Catholic Defenders battled it out against gangs of Protestant subversives outside Loughgall, during which thirty Catholic Defenders lost their lives when the Protestants opened fire. The victorious Protestants marched into Loughgall, where they met up in a house to form a defensive association of lodges, to be known as the Orange Order. Its motive was to drive Catholics out of the area. Placards were placed on the doors of their houses 'to betake themselves to Hell or Connaught'.[21] Wreckers smashed looms, tore up linen webs and destroyed great numbers of homes. Within two months seven thousand Catholics were driven out of Armagh, with many going to Connaught. Yet many others flocked to join the United Irishmen.

Members of the Orange Order joined yeomanry regiments set up as an auxiliary military force to counteract the spread of the United Irishmen. Being strongly Protestant, its members were opposed to Catholic emancipation and any form of Catholic–Presbyterian alliance. The Government had judged concessions granted to Catholics well. Despite their support for Catholic emancipation, senior Catholics remained sceptical of United Irish attempts to establish closer links with the French. Drennan wrote:

> The Catholics are still more religionists than politicians, and the Presbyterians are more politicians than religionists. The one still cherish their creed as the first object; the creed of the other is in general Liberty and Equality.[22]

When British troops were withdrawn from Ireland to the continent to participate in the war with France, the Irish Government would not risk expanding the Volunteers with their United Irish sympathies. Despite the huge drain on the Exchequer, it now formed regiments of Yeomanry, which garrisoned towns to provide military protection. While the Volunteers had been funded privately, the Government had to contribute £500,000 in its first three months to fund the Yeomanry. Mary McNeill has been disparaging about this new military force:

> It attracted, for the most part, reactionaries and irresponsibles and was to perpetrate some of the gravest atrocities in '98 and '99. It is said that it was the recorded cruelties of the Yeomanry that, less than a hundred years later, did much to arouse the nationalist passion of Charles Stewart Parnell.[23]

'Licentious troops went about the streets creating trouble.'[24] 'In a country where female chastity was held in the highest respect, [it was] the licentiousness of a military rabble … [which made them] "terrible to all except the enemy".'[25] Martha McTier reported that they were '"booed" at the theatre and distrusted by everyone'.[26] Yet they did not divert her from her own genteel existence: 'We eat, drink, chat, sometimes a little warmly, just as during the American War – but not so as to interrupt good neighbourhood, or our Whist.'[27] When the magistrates at last arranged for the Yeomanry to be withdrawn, she recorded: 'In any town they would have been stoned to death – but there never was a Belfast mob, happy for us at present for I do believe it was ardently sought for.'[28] Martha McTier spoke too soon. A month later there was just such a mob and the man at its forefront was Harry McCracken. Sam McTier wrote to his wife:

I opened this letter to tell you that this evening there was all the appearance of a Riot and good reason to believe the Military intended one against the *Star* Office. Haslett [now working for *The Northern Star*] getting a hint of it went between 5 & 6 to Bristow [the Sovereign] who gave him a letter to Captain Barber requesting he would be particularly careful of his men. B. told him he had heard it was whispered and that he had picquets ready in the Barrack in case of any disturbance. Between eight and nine two recruits, drunk struck several people in the streets, they were beaten by the Mob. The Officers and some young men of the Town met in the croud [*sic*], where a Servt. of a young Officer swore he wd. defend his Master, and made several strokes at some of the croud on which he was knocked down, and his Master drew his sword & Barber laid his hand on his, when McCracken stepped forward and desired him not to draw it. Barber said he was Ringleader of the Mob and a Rascall. McCracken replied that he was his equal and would have satisfaction. B. said that was an improper place and he did not know him. McCracken said Mr. Bristow would tell him who he was, and his name was – and he was ready to speak to him anywhere. Whether it will end here no one can tell. Thro' the croud this Evg. I did not see a young Man that was not armed with a Stick or some good weapon.[29]

When matters settled down, McTier wrote again:

We have been since my last tolerably quiet, tho' not at all free from apprehension. Yesterday morning the Sovn. sent for Henry McCracken, to speak to him about what passed the night before between Capt. Barber; he wanted McCracken to make an apology to Barber; he refused. Col. French was present, who talked a great deal about his Soldiers being insulted in the Streets and that he would give them orders not to suffer it, and he swore by God if there was one Gun fired from any Window at any of his people he would immediately burn the Town, and he would now order three regiments more here and bring back the Dragoons.[30]

It was left to Joy to try to smooth thing out, but there were reports from the authorities of continuing scuffles, designed to discredit the townspeople. It was said 'that the Country will never know peace 'till Belfast is in ashes.'[31] Much to Drennan's distress, moderate opinion now became stifled. The Belfast extremists, led by 'Russell, Neilson, and perhaps Simms' were forced underground.

War in Europe caused a dislocation of business; the closure of many of its markets brought great economic problems for the Ulster linen trade. Matters were made worse when the English dumped surplus goods onto the Irish market at prices with which local manufacturers could not compete. There was widespread unemployment among weavers in both Dublin and Belfast, and farming and food shortages. Sectarian unrest developed, but Protestant suspects were invariably favoured by the judiciary (which had been the cause of Russell's resignation at Dungannon). Although bankruptcies were frequent, the Government did offer grants to merchants in financial difficulties.

Chapter 20

United Irish efforts to obtain French backing for a republican rebellion 1795 – 1798

Following Fitzwilliam's departure, threats of a French invasion undermined morale among moderate Presbyterians. John Holmes retired to Bath. He was 'just old and rich enough to be panic struck'.[1] Martha McTier was in fear of a call to arms. The real 'problem was the loss of public confidence [regardless of sect] in the Irish administration, controlled as it obviously was by the British ministry'.[2] In a letter to Fitzwilliam sent at the beginning of 1796, Grattan recorded the 'melancholy' state of the country, in which:

> a very general discontent has proceeded to treason, in some cases to plunder, in some to a hatred of British government and in all to a total lack of confidence in government. I don't speak of the higher orders or of the gentlemen of the House of Commons.[3]

For United Irishmen working underground, rebellion seemed the only way forward. With England's war against France going badly, there were justifiable fears of a French invasion to support the Irish rebels. Ships gathered in the French channel ports awaiting their opportunity. When, in April 1797, a section of the Royal Navy mutinied at the Nore, Camden placed the whole of Ulster under martial law, proving every bit as bloodthirsty as his ancestor, Judge Jeffreys. Yet the Irish authorities realised that they needed to tread carefully. Despite a careful watch being maintained on their activities, the revolutionary leaders were given:

every opportunity to escape, [with] the government fearing to bring them to justice, turning them thereby into martyrs and heroes. Of these, Wolfe Tone was the most notorious. He was the prime agent of the Catholic–Dissenter combination, which, in the view of Castle administrators, must be immediately broken, they being of the opinion that without Presbyterian stiffening the Catholics could be bribed and cajoled into docility.[4]

Harry McCracken was now bent on rebellion. He told his sister:

Whether we fail or succeed we expect to be the first to fall ... of what consequence are our lives and the lives of a few individuals, compared to the liberty and happiness of Ireland.[5]

In 1795, with Harry having failed to give it his full attention, the cotton printing mill business of Joy, Holmes and McCracken collapsed. Although he later started a printfield at Knockaird, this also seems to have closed.[6] His cousin, Henry Joy, was equally devastated by the impending conflict. He agreed to sell the *Newsletter*, which had been managed by his family for three generations and, on 15 May 1795, wrote his last editorial.

While Rowan was being held in prison, he received a visit from the Rev. William Jackson, an Anglican clergyman born in Ireland. Jackson was a maverick, who had become a vituperative political journalist in London. When London became too 'hot' for him, he escaped to Paris, where he associated with a group of radicals opposed to war against the French Jacobins. These included Thomas Muir, a Scottish lawyer, Paine and Lord Edward FitzGerald, the brother of the Duke of Leinster:

a young charismatic former army officer, [who] was a great-grandson of Charles II, [and] a first cousin of the leader of the opposition in the British House of Commons, Charles Fox.[7]

FitzGerald was a Member of the Irish Parliament, having been elected with Grattan for Dublin City, although Grattan never supported his United Irish affiliations. Despite his Establishment pedigree, he was a committed republican.

Jackson was sent by the Paris radicals to drum up support amongst Reformers in both England and Ireland for a French invasion of Ireland. After calling on Priestley in England, he arrived in Ireland with an offer of French assistance but revealed his objectives to a former associate spying on behalf of the British Government. Jackson visited Rowan in his prison cell to present the Paris radicals' proposal, after which Rowan asked Tone to go to Paris to explore it. As Tone was not permitted to travel, he prepared a written statement on the Irish situation for the French. Rowan gave a copy to Jackson, but, when Jackson was arrested, Tone's statement fell into the hands of the authorities.

Even now, the Irish authorities wanted to avoid bringing Tone and the other rebel leaders to trial. They still needed the semblance of a revolt to gain support for their vote on Parliamentary Union. They allowed Tone to escape to America, from where he became the hub for revolutionary propaganda through able lieutenants left behind in Ireland. He even spent a month in Belfast saying goodbye and held a large party at Cave Hill before his departure on 20 May 1795. Before leaving, he also met Thomas Addis Emmet and Russell at Emmet's home at Rathfarnham outside Dublin. Emmet was from Cork, a member of 'perhaps the pre-eminent republican family in Ireland in the era of the United Irishmen'.[8] He had been educated at Trinity College, Dublin, and at Edinburgh University. After abandoning a career in medicine, he was called to the Irish Bar in 1791, taking the Society's oath of allegiance in 1795. He became their legal adviser, drawing up their non-sectarian manifesto and later joining the executive as Secretary. He told them that, once in America, he would provide the French with details of the Irish situation through the French minister in Philadelphia. Having left his family in America, he hoped to obtain authority to travel to Paris to seek French support for Irish independence.

Meanwhile, Rowan managed to bribe his gaoler to let him visit his home, from where he escaped to France. Jackson was not so lucky.

He remained imprisoned while he tried to establish witnesses for his defence. He was determined to avoid having to reveal that he also held instructions to meet Sheridan, Pitt's political foe in the House of Commons, and he committed suicide by taking poison in the dock before having to do so. On Rowan's arrival in France he was arrested on suspicion of being a spy. When released, he was still suffering from fever contracted in his Irish prison. Although he met Robespierre, he was too unwell to hold a meaningful discussion. They agreed to reconvene as soon as he had recovered, but Robespierre had by then been overthrown and had gone to the guillotine. With French invasion plans now being deferred, Rowan met Mary Wollstonecraft, with whom he is thought to have conducted an affair. He then set off for America, where he held clandestine meetings with Tone and Tandy to avoid them being seen in public together.

Before moving to France, FitzGerald had developed a close friendship with Arthur O'Connor, another Whig member of the Irish House of Commons. O'Connor was born at Bandon in 1763, where he was probably a member of William Hazlitt's congregation. His mother brought him up as a follower of the Scottish Enlightenment, with its focus on the certainties of the laws of nature. After graduating from Trinity College, Dublin, he qualified as a barrister in London. On returning to Ireland, his wealthy place-chasing uncle, Richard Longfield, Lord (and later Viscount) Longueville, sponsored his seat in the Irish Parliament. O'Connor promptly attacked Camden's Government, saying: 'These are the men who oppose Catholic emancipation and why? Because it would be incompatible with their accursed monopoly.'[9] This infuriated Longueville, who disinherited him and forced him to resign his seat. O'Connor was now bent on revolution.

While in France, FitzGerald married the beautiful Pamela de Genlis, generally believed to be the illegitimate daughter of the Duke of Orléans. On 18 November 1792, he 'formally renounced his aristocratic title and became "Citizen Edward"'.[10] He now dressed in French republican fashion with cropped hair. On his return to Ireland with Pamela, his *croppy* hairstyle was copied by United Irishmen.

Despite their opposing faiths, he spent much time with O'Connor, who described him as 'the twin of my soul'.[11] Yet their views were too radical for the hierarchy of Dublin's United Irishmen, who still considered revolution abhorrent. They were received more favourably in Belfast, where O'Connor had already established a close affinity with Ulster Dissenters, who he described as:

> A population of the best-informed people in Europe and of the best public spirit and independence ... not a parish that has not a little library and all instruct and regale themselves with reading that excellent journal, *The Northern Star.*

With their Huguenot links, many Belfast residents could speak French.

O'Connor soon became a leading United Irishman. Being a friend of Sheridan and Fox, he travelled to London to contemplate a career as a Whig politician in England. On arrival, FitzGerald persuaded him to go on with him to Paris to promote the United Irish cause. With Britain at war with France, they were forced to detour to Hamburg, from where they travelled on to Basle to meet General Lazaire Hoche, the commander designated to lead the French incursion into Ireland. Hoche undertook to bring a French invasion force if O'Connor would return to lead a Presbyterian army from Belfast to Dublin, from where it was to march west to join up with him. O'Connor agreed, but confessed to Hoche 'that "if Ireland contained but the Papist population [he] never would have attempted the separation from England"'.[12] He was fighting for Catholic emancipation, despite his belief that 'Roman Catholicism was the death of mental liberty'.

Although FitzGerald attended the discussions with Hoche, he was refused entry to France because of his wife's connection to the Duke of Orléans (who had already gone to the guillotine). O'Connor travelled on to Paris alone to convince the French Directory to endorse Hoche's agreement. On arrival he met Tone, who had landed from America on 1 February 1796. Having briefed Tone on the plans, O'Connor returned to Hamburg to rejoin FitzGerald for their journey back to Ireland. Working entirely on his own, Tone now persuaded the Directory to increase Hoche's force from 2,000 to 8,000 men, and to provide 50,000 arms for the Irish insurgents. This was later increased by Hoche to 14,000 men with artillery, to be shipped on a fleet prepared at Brest.

In Dublin, the Committee of United Irishmen, based at Pill Lane, remained nervous of FitzGerald's revolutionary ambitions and lacked confidence in Tone. O'Connor went straight to see Neilson in Belfast to report the outcome of his successful discussions. He also gained an enthusiastic commitment from Bond and Henry Jackson, whose Dublin workforces had joined the growing ranks of United Irishmen. Neilson, Bond and Jackson now canvassed support among Belfast's enlightened Presbyterian merchants.

In 1796, O'Connor sent Jemmy Hope, a weaver with great organising skills, to Dublin 'to disseminate our views among the working classes'.[13] Hope was a farm labourer from Templepatrick in Antrim 'of stern Covenanting stock'. His father had arrived there after being 'forced from a Highland home by religious persecution'.[14] Recognising his abilities, his initial employer, William Bell, arranged for his education. At the age of fifteen, Hope was apprenticed as a linen weaver. He:

> represented the almost inarticulate aspirations of the strongly revolutionary element among the Presbyterian labourers both rural and urban; he was indeed the most radical of the United Irishmen – in some respects the greatest of them all.[15]

He became the precursor of the archetypal trade union leader, looking for a means to achieve peasant land ownership, saying:

> My concurrence shall not be given to the scheme of a delusive fixity of tenure, to enable the landlord to draw the last potatoe out of the warm ashes of the poor man's fire, and leave his children to beg a cold one from those who can ill afford to give it.[16]

He wrote: 'It was my settled opinion that the condition of the labouring class was the fundamental question at issue between the rulers and the people.'[17] He was concerned at the Irish radicals' lack of leadership, and cynically believed that it was 'merely between commercial and aristocratic interests, to determine which should have the people as its prey'[18] Despite his strong Presbyterianism, he was unimpressed with a 'clergy, puzzling its followers with speculations above human comprehension, and instigating them to hate each other for conscience sake, under the mask of religion'.[19] After joining the Volunteers, Hope became a United Irishmen. He was imbued with 'the republican spirit, inherent in the principles of the Presbyterian community' which 'kept resistance to arbitrary power alive.'[20] He was soon elected to the Belfast central committee, meeting Neilson, Russell and McCracken, with whom he built 'a bond of deep attachment and confidence'.[21] He helped McCracken establish himself 'amongst the Presbyterian tenants and farm labourers, organising them in Societies ...'[22] Yet McCracken's failing business commitments kept him away from the planning of the rebellion being organised by Neilson in Belfast. On arrival in Dublin, Hope helped to galvanise the workers 'to organise and agitate for the cause of United Irishmen'.[23] He settled in the Liberties (the rural area around the City), continuing his trade as a weaver, but also established connections in cos. Meath and Kildare to create a national organisation.

The Irish Government soon gained wind of the French invasion plans. Between August 1797 and September 1801, they distributed more than £38,000 to 'a well-paid army of spies', bent on 'detecting treasonable conspiracies'.[24] In 1796, they reported Tone's arrival in America. Camden appointed Castlereagh with his Dissenter background to assist Chief Secretary Pelham in seeking out Government opposition. Castlereagh drew a distinction between agitation for constitutional reform (with which he agreed) and treasonable dealing with Britain's enemies; he 'now viewed the Irish problem in the light of European events':

> He judged, and rightly, that the Presbyterian element in the North was the real centre of genuine Republican sympathy, and once and for all the North must be rendered ineffective.[25]

Above left: John Toland (1670 – 1722).
The original champion of the Dissenter
cause in Ireland.
Artist unknown.
(www.carboneria.it/Tolandfr.htm)

Above right: Rev. Thomas Emlyn
(1663 – 1741).
Minister at the Wood St. Congregational
Church in Dublin, who was dismissed
for his Dissenter views.
By Gerard Vandergucht after Joseph
Highmore.
(National Portrait Gallery, London)

Right: Francis Hutcheson (1694 – 1746).
Irish Presbyterian and teacher, who
became the father of the Scottish
Enlightenment as Professor of Moral
Philosophy at Glasgow University.
By Allan Ramsay.
(Hunterian Museum and Art Gallery)

Henry Grattan (1746 – 1820).
Achieved the abolition of Poynings' Law, making the Irish legislature independent of British Government supervision.
By Martin Archer Shee.
(National Gallery of Ireland)

Above left: Rev. William Steel Dickson (1744 – 1824). Moderator of the Synod of Ulster, called for Catholics to join the Volunteers and became a prominent member of the Society of United Irishmen.
(*Dictionary of Ulster Biography*)

Above right: James Napper Tandy (1739 – 1803).
Co – founder of the Dublin Chamber of Commerce and an Irish MP. An inaugural member of the Dublin Society of United Irishmen, who negotiated for French support for the 1798 rebellion, being appointed a French Brigadier-General.
(ScoreBoard Memories)

Right: Theobald Wolfe Tone (1763 – 1798).
An initiator of the Society of United Irishmen and rebel leader seeking Irish independence. He joined the French expedition to support the United Irish, travelling as 'Adjutant General Smith'.
(*Trinity News*)

Above left: Archibald Hamilton Rowan (1751 – 1834).
Wealthy unitarian with aristocratic connections. Imprisoned for distributing an illegal pamphlet in support of a United Irish rebellion. He escaped to France and then America, but continued to support United Irish aspirations.
(From Dr R. R. Madden, *Ireland in '98* – British Library copied by Flickr)

Above right: Thomas Russell (1767 – 1803).
Became a friend of Wolfe Tone and was described by Mary Ann McCracken as 'a model of manly beauty'. Until his arrest, he was one of the leaders of the 1798 rebellion, but returned to become involved again in 1803.
(newulsterbiography.co.uk)

Henry Joy McCracken (1767 – 1798). His Belfast linen weaving family was determined to improve its workers' lot. His charisma led to him taking charge of the 1798 rebellion when its leaders were arrested. Initially he evaded capture, but was eventually arrested and hanged.
(stairnaheireannblog.wordpress.com)

Above left: Lord Edward FitzGerald (1763 – 1798).
Brother of the Duke of Leinster, great-grandson of Charles II and MP for Dublin City, who gained French support for the 1798 rebellion. He led the planning for the 1798 rebellion, but was shot while being arrested before the uprising. (Today In Irish History)

Above right: Arthur O'Connor (1763 – 1852).
Whig MP and friend of FitzGerald, who initiated support for a United Irish rebellion in Belfast with French support. He was arrested in 1797 but was later acquitted for lack of evidence, returning to France as a Napoleonic general. By John Godefroy after François Pascal Simon, Baron Gérard c. 1804. (Wikipedia)

Robert Emmet (1778 – 1803). A patriotic dreamer, who, despite warnings from O'Connor, led the 1803 rebellion with very little chance of success. It was total and disorganized folly and he was arrested and executed. (Library of Congress, Washington, D. C. www.britannica.com)

Daniel O'Connell (1775 – 1847).
A Catholic barrister, known as 'the Liberator' for gaining approval for Catholics to sit in Parliament. He abhorred the use of force, but formed the Repeal Association, campaigning at 'Monster Meetings' for the repeal of tithes and the Act of Union. Drawn by Joseph P. Haverty.
(*Galway Advertiser*)

Above left: William Smith O'Brien (1803 – 1864).
Irish Liberal MP who led the Young Irelander Movement, having been educated in England. He was arrested having developed Fenian sentiments and was transferred to Tasmania. On his release, he founded *United Ireland* to promote land ownership reform.
(Wikimedia)

Above right: Charles Gavan Duffy (1816 – 1903).
Founded the *Nation* journal, which initially advocated violence against the Establishment. He became an MP standing for tenant rights. Despite failing to gain either Whig or Tory support, he was later knighted out of respect for his cause.
(Wikimedia)

Thomas Francis Meagher (1823 – 1867). Set up the Irish Confederation, which attracted support from the more militant members of the Repeal Association to form the Young Irelanders. After transportation to Tasmania, he escaped to the US, where he became a leading member of the Fenian movement.
(www.ricksteves.com)

Charles Stewart Parnell (1846 – 1891).
Came within a hair's breadth of achieving home rule for Ireland in alliance with
Gladstone, being determined to achieve concessions by political means after
having fostered Fenian affiliations. He was perhaps the greatest Irish politician
of any generation.
(Library of Congress – Wikipedia)

In September 1796, Castlereagh came to Belfast with warrants to arrest Neilson, Russell and six other prominent United Irishmen, despite lacking any evidence of involvement in treasonable activity. Neilson and Russell willingly gave themselves up and were held without trial as state prisoners in Newgate jail in Dublin. McCracken was arrested a few days later, as he had been away from Belfast on Castlereagh's arrival. This ended any 'light-hearted joyousness and gaiety'.[26] He was sent to the more modern Kilmainham jail outside Dublin, where Mary Ann and Margaret were permitted to visit him. They took the 'flying coach' to Dublin. Their cousin, the eminently respectable Councillor Henry Joy (a first cousin of the proprietor of the *Newsletter*), who lived in Temple Street in Dublin, wrote to Harry at Kilmainham to establish how he was. Harry replied on the bottom of the letter he had received:

> I am at present in excellent health but closely and indeed rigourously [*sic*] confined – denied the use of pen, ink and paper or the consolation of any living creature, the keeper and turnkeys excepted, who find me everything I wish for. I much fear the girls will be denied admission.

With Harry working his considerable charm on the guards, the sisters were permitted a visit. They remained in Dublin for about three weeks but, despite receiving generous entertainment, did not enjoy their experience, with their brother being incarcerated without prospect of trial. They rated the Dublin sights less favourably than familiar Belfast, 'the Athens of the North'. Although Harry suffered from rheumatism in the damp conditions, he made light of his discomfiture and was permitted to meet other State prisoners.

In March 1797, a second round-up of suspected insurgents in Belfast resulted in the arrest of Harry's eldest brother, William. He too was sent to Kilmainham to be held without trial. William was much more docile than Harry. Although married to Rose Ann McGlathery, they had no children. He was distressed on hearing that she had become unwell during his incarceration, although she soon recovered. Both William and Harry also fell ill, only adding to the McCracken family's worries. William was suffering a fever and Harry's rheumatism worsened. The family was soon complaining at the brothers' failure to write to say how they were. Eventually Rose Ann went to Dublin and was able to stay at the prison until William's release. Mary Ann and her sister Margaret returned to Belfast. They needed to manage their muslin business to keep their weavers employed and bring in a small amount of much needed income.

Although Neilson's wife continued to publish *The Northern Star* during his imprisonment in Dublin, the authorities considered it inflammatory and closed it down. In May 1797, the military ransacked its offices, wrecking the printing machinery. The Neilsons were left without a livelihood.

Despite many United Irish leaders being imprisoned, the French Government blindly went ahead with its invasion plan. In November 1796, an agent arrived in Ireland to confirm France's plan for assistance, but failed to say where its invasion force would land. Hoche had forty-three ships in Brest, including seventeen ships of the line, carrying 14,000 men, artillery and military equipment for distribution. Tone joined the expedition under the name of 'Adjutant General Smith'. After setting sail, the fleet became separated in bad weather, leaving Tone unimpressed with French seamanship. He was with a group of ten ships of the line, which, on 15 December 1796, arrived at the agreed rendezvous at Bantry Bay with 6,000 men and arms for their Irish supporters. Although they waited five days, Hoche and the remainder of the fleet failed to appear. Eventually their commander, Grouchy, lost his nerve and, to Tone's fury, set sail back to France. Their arrival had been a few weeks earlier than O'Connor was anticipating; he was completely immersed in his campaign for election to Parliament for Antrim, and the United Irishmen were not organised.

While the United Irish had hoped that news of the French arrival in the west would draw the British army to Galway, allowing O'Connor with the Belfast Presbyterians to march on Dublin, the British had no need to move. On 3 February 1797, O'Connor was arrested in Dublin. Without French support, the United Irish cause was hopeless. Yet the French continued to encourage insurrection 'as a means of distracting the British government, and preventing its interference in the Political changes which French ambition meditated on the Continent'.[27] The news of a French presence in Bantry Bay, however fleeting, had caused pandemonium in Dublin. A young Catholic barrister, Daniel O'Connell, wrote to warn his uncle of the alarm, claiming to be the last of his colleagues to join a volunteer corps for Dublin's protection.[28] 'Being young, active, healthy and single', he claimed to have no plausible excuse, and soon joined the Lawyers' Artillery Corps.[29] His biographer, Dennis Gwynn, has explained that he was placed in a quandary:

> He was enrolled as a liberator in defence of Government, yet the Government was intensifying its persecution of the Catholic people, of which he was one. ... He desired to enter parliament, yet every allowance that the Catholics had been led to anticipate two years previously [during Fitzwilliam's Lord Lieutenancy] was now flatly vetoed.[30]

O'Connell shared the United Irish mistrust for the British Government, recording:

> Vice reigns triumphant in the English court at this day. The spirit of liberty shrinks to protect property from the attacks of French innovators. The corrupt higher orders tremble for their vicious enjoyments. ... In Ireland the whole policy of the Government was to repress the people and to maintain the ascendancy of a privileged and corrupt minority.[31]

Despite these words, O'Connell was no rebel. In 1796, he wrote: 'The altar of liberty totters when it is cemented only with blood.'[32] He did not join the United Irish and awaited his opportunity to seek emancipation by negotiation.

In March 1797, the United Irish sent an agent to the French Government calling for a promised second invasion and asking for a loan of £500,000. Although a second agent was sent in June to confirm the urgency, he was held up in Hamburg before eventually reaching Paris. On his return to Ireland in October, he reassured his United Irish colleagues that a second French invasion force was being prepared. Meanwhile the original agent, who remained in Paris, reported that Dutch (Holland was by this time in alliance with the French) armaments were being readied on the Texel for shipment to Ireland. Tone joined the Dutch expedition, consisting of another 14,000 men carried on fifteen ships of the line, eleven frigates and several sloops. Again, bad weather intervened. The fleet was holed up in the Friesian Islands. When it was at last able to set out, it was crushed by Admiral Duncan at the Battle of Camperdown. Although Tone was able to return to France he arrived only to learn that Hoche had died from consumption. In January 1798, there was yet another United Irish application for French support, but nothing came of it. Tone's memoirs show that:

> there were moments when his enthusiasm was not able to conquer the lurking fear, that France might either take the opportunity of making Ireland a province tributary to herself, or of restoring it to England in exchange for the frontier of the Rhine, or the supremacy of Italy.[33]

Delays only heightened his concerns and caused desertions among United Irish ranks.

The Irish authorities were still having difficulty in establishing evidence against those they had arrested. No one would talk, and convictions depended on evidence provided by spies, most of which could not be corroborated. Without any case against O'Connor, they 'were delighted when he asked for permission to go to London'.[34] Yet he was now being watched. When he met up with radicals opposed to the war with France, he was shadowed by the Bow Street Runners. In early 1798, he was again arrested with fellow United Irishmen at Margate while trying to procure a passage to France. Tone learned of this from the French newspapers. One of those arrested with O'Connor was carrying documents being sent to France on behalf of London radicals. This led to a further thirty arrests. Although O'Connor was tried for treason, the extent of his plotting could not be established, and he was acquitted after Fox, Sheridan and Grattan (who had travelled from Ireland to act as a witness) gave character references on his behalf. He was immediately rearrested and escorted back to Ireland. To the embarrassment of his witnesses, he admitted his involvement in treasonable United Irish activities. He was imprisoned at Fort George near Inverness, where he faced a long incarceration with other United Irish leaders.

Grattan continued his strong opposition to United Irish plans for rebellion, despite unfounded reports of his involvement. In 1797, in 'a series of masterly speeches', he warned the Irish Government of Ireland's lawless condition. When these were not heeded, he did not re-contest his seat and retired from Parliament. He did not immediately return home from London, in part because there was widespread rioting near Tinnehinch in co. Wicklow, and in part because he was suffering from migraines. When his wife joined him, he recuperated for a period at an inn in Wales, before moving, until the end of 1799, to a rented house near Twickenham. When he at last returned to Ireland, the United Irish rebellion had failed, and FitzGerald was dead. He was still accused of sympathising with the rebels, resulting in his removal as a Privy Councillor and freeman of the City of Dublin. His portrait was taken down from the Public Theatre of Trinity College.

Chapter 21

The rebellion of 1798

Despite the United Irishmen's setback, everyone expected the French to return. FitzGerald was still free and the Dublin leadership, working underground, identified 500,000 members who had signed their test. Of these, 300,000 were thought able to bear arms and ready to rebel.[1] FitzGerald hoped that 100,000 men would rally to his call, in addition to 15,000 French. In February 1798, the leadership appointed a military committee, whose 'duty was to prepare a plan of co-operation with the French'.[2] With the authorities well aware of their prospect of French support, 'the rebellion never should have been permitted to arrive at that dangerous maturity'.[3] 'Had the rebels possessed arms, officers and discipline, their numbers would soon have rendered them masters of the Kingdom.'[4] Yet the Government was militarily prepared: it deployed 114,000 armed troops at an annual cost estimated at £4 million. Of these, 50,000 were members of the Yeomanry, which had scope to increase in numbers.

The authorities made a concerted effort to seek out weapons, even looking for cannon at several mills and factories, but nothing was found. The Dissenter prisoners in Dublin began to hope that they would avoid trial. There had been an understanding among them that none would accept release unless all were freed together. Yet the families of Neilson, Haslett and the seventeen-year-old Charles Teeling took steps to arrange for their exile in return for them revealing the Society's organisation and plans for rebellion. As a first step in this process, they were moved from Newgate prison to Kilmainham, where Harry met them. He was furious at their attempt to gain release without him. Mary Ann had much sympathy for Neilson, who was also in poor health. He had lost his livelihood as proprietor of *The Northern Star* and needed to support his five young children. She wrote most persuasively to seek Harry's reconciliation with him. This seems to have succeeded after her second visit to see Harry. With evidence against the rebel leaders being so sparse, efforts to gain their release were renewed, with bail being sought on grounds of ill-health. The McCracken family scratched around to find enough for the bail money, the settlement of the prisoners' other bills during their incarceration and the cost of medical certificates to confirm their illnesses. When at last the McCracken brothers wrote to confirm their release, they returned to Belfast to be nursed back to health. Harry was soon well enough to return to travelling on behalf of their businesses. When visiting Dublin, he showed a continuing concern for the welfare of weavers still in custody, but was never, intimately at least, involved in planning the coming insurrection.

Following Neilson's release three months later, he remained in Dublin as the close confidant of FitzGerald, now recognised as their leader. Senior officers were appointed to command insurgents in different counties, with Dickson becoming the 'general' for co. Down. They had great difficulty in preventing small groups from jumping the gun but remained crucially dependent on French assistance. To their great disappointment, a new French offer was limited to small raiding parties, and educated Catholics remained ambivalent about supporting their cause.

The authorities were fully aware of what was going on and continued their search for arms. The nemesis of the United Irishmen in Dublin was an unattractive but effective Government spy, Francis Higgins, known as 'the Sham Squire', a name given to him by a judge, when, in 1767, he was imprisoned for forgery and deception. Since then he had been a brothel keeper and was 'a person of evil name, fame and dishonest conversation and a common deceiver and cheat'.[5] He was now the outwardly respectable editor of the *Freeman's Journal*, which made its money from printing government propaganda. While watching 'the king-killers of Pill Lane', he provided Edward Cooke, the Under-Secretary for Ireland, with information. 'He also reported that their toast called for "all the kings of the earth be in hell".'[6] Cooke's network of spies kept him informed of meetings taking place 'almost every night', and 'that Oliver "Cromwell" Bond was holding a treasonable correspondence with Rev. William Steel Dickson of Portaferry, a well-known radical Unitarian clergyman'.[7] Higgins provided a description of the general membership of the United Irishmen:

> They are something above the common rabble. They were now reading newspapers and Paine's politics of Liberty and Equality [and are] talking of religious emancipation and [political] Union with England quitting their evocations and associating in numbers.[8]

With Bond actively seeking new members, it was almost inevitable that one would be an informer. On 12 March 1798, when he called a secret meeting of the Leinster directory, he invited a new member, Thomas Reynolds, who advised the authorities. Sixteen delegates, including Bond, were arrested, and, on Reynold's evidence, Bond was jailed in Newgate.

With Bond being imprisoned, O'Connor turned to Emmet, but he told O'Connor that he would not take part without French support on the ground. O'Connor considered him of 'extreme timidity of character', and they became bitter enemies.[9] Emmet remained doubtful whether the French support expected by FitzGerald would materialise and began to doubt his military skills. He realised that the insurgents were no match for disciplined English troops and was concerned at a lack of officer material to train them. Their disagreement 'damaged future relationships with the French, who had to deal with rival factions of disunited Irishmen, led by O'Connor and Emmet respectively'.[10] Yet Emmet remained involved, joining the directory from January to May 1797 and again in the following December until his arrest in March 1798. He was then imprisoned in Kilmainham Jail, from where, like the other leaders, he was moved to Fort George outside Inverness. It was not until 1802 that he was exiled to Amsterdam.

Up to this time, Drennan had been a senior figure in the United Irish hierarchy, but he continued to deplore violence and strongly disapproved of rebellion. He now withdrew his support, playing no part in the rising that was to follow. He recognised the potential difficulty for Catholic members when he said that the Presbyterians:

> love the French openly and the Catholics almost to a man hate the French secretly – and why? Because they have overturned the Catholic religion in that country and threaten to do it throughout the world.[11]

The United Irish leaders now formed a committee seeking to 'establish a democratic republic in Ireland with assistance from republican France'.[12] Until his arrest, Bond was at the heart of the plan 'and he travelled about as much as he could, transacting trade on one hand and administering the oath of allegiance to the brotherhood on the other'.[13] Realising that it had been infiltrated, the committee became extremely secretive, but informers reported that members addressed each other as 'Citizen' at meetings. Other revolutionary groups were co-ordinated by Dublin workers under the guise of reading clubs, Masonic and Defender lodges.

Despite the setbacks, FitzGerald planned the uprising for 23 May 1798. He established a new leadership committee consisting of Neilson and two lawyers from Cork, John and Henry Sheares, who had done much to extend the organisation while touring on legal circuits. They believed that 280,000 potential rebels were under their command but were arrested before the planned uprising date and ultimately hanged. To avoid arrest, FitzGerald moved from one hiding place to another, despite a reward of £1,000 placed on his head.

In May 1798, Higgins again assisted the authorities in preventing a Dublin insurrection. His Catholic contacts had recruited Francis Mangan, a young Catholic barrister, to infiltrate the United Irish committee. Although Mangan was lured with Government money, he was genuinely concerned at the consequences of a French invasion for the Irish Catholic Church.[14] When, by ill-fate, he was detailed to take Fitzgerald into his own home, he warned the authorities. When they attempted to arrest FitzGerald, he escaped after being protected by a bodyguard, which included Neilson. Mangan was not suspected of duplicity, and he was able to divulge the location of the new hiding place at the home of a Mr Nicholas Murphy in Thomas Street. On 17 May, after a desperate struggle, FitzGerald was arrested after being shot twice in the shoulder. He was taken in great agony to Newgate Prison, where he died on 4 June. Both Higgins and Mangan were handsomely rewarded. Although several loyal United Irishmen were accused by their colleagues, Mangan's involvement as the 'mole' was never revealed, leaving the leadership unsure who it could trust. It was only the evidence of Higgins's papers brought to light much later that revealed Mangan's involvement.

FitzGerald's arrest 'created utter confusion'.[15] Matters were made worse, when Neilson was caught outside Newgate prison by one of his former jailers, while reconnoitring an attempted rescue. On 23 May, the day on which the uprising was due to begin, Dickson was also arrested. It was too late to pull back, and Harry was proclaimed its leader. 'With amazing vigour and resourcefulness, he planned a campaign and rallied the men of Antrim, Down, Armagh and Tyrone.'[16] Many Dublin weavers were influenced to join him by Hope, with the more determined of them mustering in North Wicklow and south co. Dublin. Harry chose to make Antrim his key communication point, from where to coordinate the various local rebel groups attacking the military. On 6 June he proclaimed: 'Tomorrow we march on Antrim – drive the garrison of Randalstown before you and hasten to form a junction with the Commander-in-Chief.' The rebels approached Antrim on four sides. It was not strongly guarded, and within an hour United Irish pikemen had gained control. Yet Harry's plan had been leaked and, on 8 June, General Nugent with the military from nearby camps made an overwhelming counterattack, threatening to burn down the surrounding villages unless they surrendered. Hope wrote: 'When all our leaders deserted us, Henry Joy McCracken stood alone faithful to the last.'[17]

Despite a curfew in Belfast, floggings in the streets and soldiers billeted on the townspeople, Rose Ann and Mary Ann McCracken set out on foot in search of William and Harry. On reaching the village of

Whitehouse, they learned that William was with one of Rose Ann's relatives, so they went on together to look for Harry. After meeting rebels known to Mary Ann, they learned that he might be at the Black Bowhill. After trudging on over a moor they at last found him with Hope and five other companions. Despite being dejected, he was amazed and delighted to see them, and arranged for them to sleep in a nearby cottage before they set out back to Rosemary Street. Mary Ann could now send him money, which he acknowledged in a letter of 18 June.

Extraordinarily, Mary Ann obtained a forged pass and visited Harry for a second time near Cave Hill. She had arranged for a captain of a foreign vessel bound for America to take him on board at a secluded place in Belfast Lough. On 8 July, while approaching the rendezvous, Harry was spotted by a party of Yeomanry, who took him to Carrickfergus jail. Yet again, Mary Ann visited him, this time with her elderly father, and they had a few words with him, despite him being in strict isolation. Harry asked that a ring bearing a green shamrock should be given to his mother. It was inscribed with the words: 'To the sacred memory of Mr. William Orr who died for his country at the altar of British tyranny, 1797.' Orr had been a Belfast Dissenter, who was tried and executed while Harry was in Kilmainham.

With Harry being brought back to Belfast, Mary Ann appealed to the local colonel to be allowed to see him, but he slammed the door in her face. Yet, she tried again and was escorted to him by a young officer. His court martial was fixed for the following day, and Mary Ann again attended with her frail and elderly father, noting:

> The moment I set my eyes on him I was struck with the extraordinary serenity and composure of his look. This was no time to think of such things, but yet I could not help gazing on him, it seemed to me that I had never seen him look so well, so full of healthful bloom, so free from the slightest trace of care or trouble, as at that moment, when he was perfectly aware of his approaching fate.[18]

The prosecutor tried to persuade old John McCracken to talk Harry into revealing his accomplices in return for reducing Harry's sentence to exile, but the old man, who probably knew nothing of Harry's colleagues, refused. The evidence against Harry was perjured, and Mary Ann spoke out in his defence to point out its inconsistencies. Nevertheless, he was found guilty and was taken to the Artillery Barracks, where Mary Ann again saw him. Dickson came to comfort him, and she walked on her brother's arm to the place where gallows had been erected, after which she was led away. With fear of a public demonstration, a strong guard had been put in place, but General Nugent prevented 'the further ignominy of decapitation', in respect to Harry's extraordinary calmness and bravery.[19] When his body was cut down, it was quickly returned to the McCracken's home where vain attempts were made to revive him before his burial.

On the following day, Mary Ann wrote to Russell in Newgate Prison setting out all the circumstances. She mentioned:

> It was as impolitic as cruel to murder one who was the idol of the poor, he who was so patient of injuries, so benevolent of heart, hundreds now pant for revenge whom he had the power and benevolence to restrain, but this could neither restore him to life nor would it gratify him if he was sensible of it.[20]

Much later, she recorded: 'I never wished that my beloved brother had taken any other part than that which he did take.'[21] Her efforts were not completely in vain; she managed to arrange for William, when arrested, to be released on bail.

After Harry's execution, Dickson asked Mary Ann to visit him in prison. On arrival, he revealed to her that Harry had a four-year-old daughter, probably the child of Mary Bodel, whose father had often sheltered Harry on Cave Hill. Despite old Mr McCracken's reservations, Mary brought the child, Maria, to Rosemary Street, bringing her up as her 'only and affectionate daughter'.

Elsewhere, the rebels had some initial success. In Kildare, they rapidly gained control of a large area, but, in the face of concerted opposition they were defeated in Naas, Carlow and Tara, and failed to capture Athy. Pikemen at Ballyellis defeated 'a large column of government reinforcements', capturing their cannon.[22] Castlereagh 'heard from London that a French fleet had left Brest, and he pleaded for re-enforcements'.[23] Robert King, 2nd Earl of Kingston was captured by the United Irish 'Navy' off Wexford, and was not released until the rebellion was suppressed. Yet the United Irish were now leaderless and lacking discipline. With few arms or munitions, they were no match for Government troops and many were hung from bridges over the Liffey. On 13 June, the co. Down rebels, led by Dickson's successor, Henry Munroe from Lisburn, were overcome at Ballinahinch. In Wexford, with many armed only with stones, rebels courageously defeated the North Cork militia at Ouliart. With 100 Cork men lying dead, 'the rebels had one hundred extra muskets, swords, ammunition and bayonets'.[24] Thousands flocked to join them and they captured Enniscorthy and Wexford, to await a French landing. Shortly before the rising, Harvey was arrested after returning from Dublin to his Wexford home. He was placed in Wexford jail, but the insurgents gained control of the jail to free him. Despite lacking military experience, he was immediately appointed commander-in-chief and, on 5 June, led 20,000 rebels at the battle of New Ross. This proved a disaster, not least because on the evening beforehand Harvey:

> possessed not that calm intrepidity, which is necessary in the composition of a military officer, nor those rare talents by which an undisciplined multitude may be directed and controlled.[25]

His fellow leaders:

> being regaled with an excellent supper and exquisite wines, they were so well pleased with their cheer, and so far forgot their prudence as commanders, that they had scarcely time to have fallen asleep, when they were roused, according to the orders they had given in their sober moments, to commence the attack at the break of day.[26]

'Their example was followed by their troops the following day: and drunkenness alone was the cause of their defeat.'[27]

> After some hard fighting, they gained possession of the town [New Ross]; but instead of following up their advantage, 'they fell to plundering and drinking;' and after being some hours in possession of the town, the great body of the multitude was so inebriated as to be incapable of defending their new conquest. 'Such of the insurgents as were not too drunk to escape out of the town, of which they had been by this time some hours in possession, were driven out of the town;' but having recovered a little after their hasty retreat, which in a great measure made them sober, they again returned to their charge, and their intrepidity was more signally displayed than on any former occasion. They again got possession of the town; 'but even after this they soon fell into the same misconduct as before, crowning their bravery with drunkenness.'[28]

They were yet again driven out. With Harvey facing criticism, he resigned, but was immediately appointed president of the Wexford town committee.

Despite the rebels' shortcomings, there is no doubting the threat faced by the authorities. The early success in Wexford gave heart to the Wicklow and Kildare rebels, who acquitted themselves well at the battles of Prosperous and Ovidstown. It took 20,000 Government troops under General Lake finally to defeat them at Vinegar Hill on 21 June 1798. The authorities positioned seven other generals in Wexford. Their presence ended further outbreaks of insurgency and they turned a blind eye when the homes of those arrested were plundered. With the Government back in control, Harvey, who remained at large, was betrayed while trying to escape to France. After being arrested, he was hanged on 28 June from the bridge at Wexford.

All too late, Director Lazare Carnot in Paris ordered a small force of 1,200 French soldiers under General Jean Joseph Amable Humbert to sail to Ireland. Carnot had been pushed into providing support by Tandy, who had returned from America to Paris in the Spring of 1797 to assist Tone in promoting a French invasion. Although Humbert arrived at Killala in co. Mayo in August, he lacked any reputation as a general, and moved forward to Castlebar before the rebels had time to join up with him. His arrival 'struck terror through Ireland. [The Lord Lieutenant, General Charles] Lord Cornwallis advanced with the whole British army to meet him.'[29] When Humbert surrendered, the French were returned home leaving their insurgent allies to face massacre. In a separate expedition, Tandy, who was commissioned as a French brigadier-general, sailed under General Gabriel Venance Rey in a French corvette, the *Anacréon*, full of military equipment, to land at Rutland Island in co. Donegal on 16 September 1798. When news was received that Humbert's expedition had failed, they knew that adequate Irish support would not be forthcoming. To avoid the English fleet, Rey sailed his corvette round the north of Scotland. He captured an English ship *en route*, taking his prize to Bergen. From here, Tandy disembarked and made his way to Hamburg, which was then a neutral port, from where he hoped to return to France. On 2 October 1798, yet a third French expedition, led by Admiral Jean-Baptiste-François Bompart with 3,000 men, including Tone, encountered an English squadron in Lough Swilly. When the ship he was sailing in surrendered, Tone was arrested, but made an impassioned speech:

> From my earliest youth I have regarded the connection between Ireland and Great Britain as the curse of the Irish nation and felt convinced that, while it lasted, this country would never be happy. In consequence, I determined to apply all my powers, which my individual efforts could move in order to separate the two countries.

Much to the disgust of Clare, the Lord Chancellor, who believed he should have been hanged on arrest, Tone was brought to trial, but died in prison after cutting his own throat.

Tandy's arrival in Hamburg caused an international incident. The British Representative, Sir James Crawfurd, demanded his arrest pending extradition to Britain. Yet Tandy was a commissioned French officer. When the Hamburg authorities took no action, Crawfurd jumped the gun and took a party of marines to arrest him. Despite the French Consul's vigorous complaints, Crawfurd refused to release him. With Napoleon now in power in France, he threatened Hamburg with reprisals. Their authorities dithered over whether to back the English or French. In August they released Tandy to the English, who took him to London. Napoleon was furious. He threatened not to sign the Treaty of Amiens until Pitt returned Tandy. Although Tandy was sent on to Dublin, his trial, on 12 February 1800, was so arranged that he was acquitted. Yet he remained imprisoned and faced a retrial for having landed an enemy ship on Rutland Island. This time he was found guilty and, on 4 May 1801, was sentenced to death. With Napoleon continuing to delay signing the Treaty, on 14 March 1802 Tandy was quietly shipped to Bordeaux, where he was appointed a French general and handsomely rewarded. The Treaty of Amiens was signed ten days later, but Tandy died in Bordeaux on 24 August 1803.

Despite their former Dissenter associations, Londonderry and Castlereagh led the reprisals. They were particularly vehement against the Presbyterian clergy, 'unquestionably the great encouragers and promoters of sedition'.[30] Most of the thirty Presbyterian ministers in rebel ranks were Dissenters. Of these, three were hanged, five fled abroad, seven were imprisoned and four went into exile.[31] Despite this retribution meted out on Presbyterians, the rebellion was portrayed as a Catholic sectarian uprising. In his memoirs,[32] Tone recorded that they:

> asserted that, if emancipated, Catholics would set up an inquisition against all Protestants, that they would make retroactive land claims for all the property taken by the Protestant Ascendancy in the past two centuries, and that if given the chance to vote would instantly relinquish all power to the Pope, since Catholics were 'naturally slaves'.[33]

Although a few Protestants had been wilfully murdered by Catholic rebels, most of the leaders were Protestant. In Wexford they had fought for a 'perfect toleration for every creed and persuasion'.[34] The principal leaders, including O'Connor, Simms, Russell, Neilson, Tennant and Dickson were moved from Dublin to Fort George. Londonderry offered deals and bribes to prisoners to provide incriminating evidence against Dickson, but none was provided. Eventually, Dickson silenced the anti-Catholic propaganda by demonstrating that the State prisoners at Fort George were of every religious persuasion. On 6 October, Castlereagh declared that 'the dangerous and wicked rebellion' had been suppressed.[35] Yet martial law continued, and the prisons remained full. Many prisoners were sent to the newly established penal settlement at Botany Bay.

Extraordinarily, Hope evaded capture by keeping on the move between Dublin, Meath and Westmeath. Although Cornwallis called an amnesty, this did not include the rebel leaders, and Hope did not give himself up, as to do so was 'not only a recantation of one's principles, but a tacit acceptance in the justice of the punishment that had been inflicted on thousands of my unfortunate associates'.[36] He remained in the north until November 1798, but then went with his family to Dublin. In the summer of 1799, he was employed by his former United Irish colleague, Charles Teeling, 'who was then establishing a bleach green at the Nawl in the County Meath'.[37] On arrival, he was recognised and forced back onto the run for three more years, until ending up back in Antrim.

Despite his arrest prior to the rebellion, Bond only came to trial on 23 July 1798. He was found guilty of treason and condemned to be hanged, drawn and quartered. Nevertheless, O'Connor had arranged a pardon for State prisoners, if they made a full confession. Although Bond was included in this, on the day he was due to be reprieved, he was found dead outside his cell at Newgate reportedly after suffering an 'apoplectic seizure'.[38] It is thought that he was murdered on orders from Higgins acting on the Government's behalf. This injustice was not challenged by Bond's friends, who wanted to ensure that his wife Eleanor inherited his enormous £30,000 fortune. She duly did and, in 1809 relocated to America, where she joined her father, Henry Jackson, who had acquired property in Pennsylvania, although they eventually moved to Baltimore.

Rowan remained in America during the rebellion, where he met Priestley, who was continuing his scientific experiments there. Rowan's wife, Sarah, remained in Ireland to maintain their property. She did not share his political views and blamed Tone for his predicament. Yet it is more likely that Rowan had instigated Tone's involvement. Rowan remained steadfastly loyal to all his old colleagues and to Dissenting principles, refusing to shoot Indians or to hold slaves. When he eventually returned to Hamburg, Sarah managed to arrange a pardon for him, and in 1806 he returned to Ireland. Unlike most of his United Irish colleagues, he supported the Act of Union in 1800, seeing it as the means of ending corruption in the Irish Government. He lived on until 1834, remaining loyal, to the last, to his principles and his United Irish colleagues.

For rank and file United Irishmen, the punishment was torture, meted out to insurgents picked off the streets. The British authorities turned a blind eye to what was going on. Teeling reported the comments of 'a Country Gentleman':

> Thousands were tortured with the connivance of government, and multitudes condemned to death in defiance of every principle of law and justice. … It has often been asserted … that the Irish rebellion was fomented and encouraged by government for the purpose of carrying the Union into effect. … Many were suspected of being rebels who were perfectly innocent; multitudes were falsely accused, and not a few judicially murdered.[39]

The Establishment in Dublin hotly denied using torture. Although Castlereagh stood up in the English House of Commons to deny any knowledge of it, there is ample evidence that he condoned it as Ireland's Chief Secretary and 'that the screams of the sufferers might have been audible in the very offices where the ministers of government met to perform their functions'.[40]

Slow tortures were inflicted under the pretence of extorting confession; the people were driven to madness; ... Ireland was reduced to a state of anarchy and exposed to crime and cruelties to which no nation had ever been subject. The people could no longer bear their miseries. Mr. Pitt's object [to achieve the Union] was now effected. These sanguinary proceedings will, in the opinion of posterity, be placed to the account of those who might have prevented them.[41]

Regiments of soldiers vied in their ability to inflict pain. 'Tom the Devil', a sergeant in the North Cork Militia, was famed for 'his ingenuity and adroitness in devising torment'. With one prisoner, he:

cut off the hair of his head very closely, put the sign of the cross from the front to the back, and transversely from ear to ear closer still; and ... gunpowder was mixed through the hair, which was then set on fire, and the shocking process repeated, until every atom of hair that remained could be easily pulled out by the roots; and still a burning candle was continually applied, until the entire was completely singed away, and the head left totally and miserably blistered.[42]

'Pitch-cap' torture involved preparing caps of linen or strong brown paper smeared on the inside with pitch. These were then 'well heated' and placed on the head of anyone found with cropped hair (*a croppy*) until it stuck fast. Teeling summed up the situation:

The tortures practiced in those days of Ireland's misery, has not been equalled in the annals of the most barbarous nation, and the world has been astonished at the close of the eighteenth century, with acts, which the eye views with horror and the heart sickens to record – not only on the most trivial, but the most groundless occasions: it was inflicted without mercy on every age, and on every condition. In the centre of the city, the heart-rending exhibition was presented of a human being rushing from the eternal depôt of torture and death, his person besmeared with a burning preparation of turpentine and pitch, plunging, in his distraction, into the Liffey, and terminating at once, his sufferings and his life.[43]

To keep the evidence under wraps, troops of Hessian soldiers set fire to the hospital at Enniscorthy housing those who had suffered torture, burning all the patients to death. When the worst excesses and house burning could be hidden no longer, the Irish Parliament passed an 'Act of Indemnity for all errors committed by magistrates from supposed zeal for the public service.'[44] Some atrocities were on a large scale:

Every massacre of the people, at this period, was hailed as a great victory, and received with exultation. The slaughter of the unresisting capitulated people at the Gibbet Rath of Kildare was regarded as a measure which the emergencies of the time required. The rebels, according to Sir R. Musgrave, amounted to about 3,000 in number; they had entered into terms with General Dundas … on 26th of May, that general dispatched General Welford to receive their arms, and grant them protections. Before the arrival of the latter, however, on 3rd of June, the multitude of unsuspecting people were suddenly attacked by Sir James Duff, who, having gallopped into the plain, disposed his army in order of battle, and with the assistance of Lord Roden's Fencible Cavalry, fell upon the astonished multitude … 'pell mell'. Three hundred and fifty men under terms of capitulation, admitted into the king's peace and promised his protection, were mowed down in cold blood.[45]

The atrocities were not of course wholly one-sided. The rebels also played their part in the savagery. To the horror of their leadership, a group of United Irish insurgents locked a group of Government supporters into a barn at Scullabogue in Wexford. About 200 Protestants (and some Catholics) were held in an area thirty-four foot long, fifteen foot wide and with walls ten foot high. The barn was set alight, resulting in the deaths of at least 100 inside and a further thirty-seven, who were shot while trying to escape.

It is estimated that 70,000 people died as a direct result of the 1798 rebellion, 20,000 on the Government side and 50,000 rebels. Of the rebels, the great majority died in captivity, often under torture. Those United Irishmen who survived were deported. Anyone thought to have provided them with assistance risked having his house burned down. 'From the humble cot to the stately mansion, no property – no person was secure.'[46] Despite efforts by the authorities in Belfast to maintain a sense of gaiety, the poor faced great hardship. There was an acute shortage of foodstuffs in 1799 caused by heavy flooding and failed harvests. Charitable soup kitchens were opened to feed those arriving from the surrounding countryside. Fever spread in the overcrowded hospitals; even well-to-do families became infected.

Although America, the recipient of so many disenchanted United Irishmen, might have been expected to show sympathy for the Irish republican cause, it was concerned at the United Irish negotiations taking place with the French. Although Thomas Jefferson had shown support for the French revolution while Secretary of State under George Washington and continued to sympathise with United Irishmen in exile, his views did not carry any weight during the Presidency of John Adams from 1797 to 1801. Adams remained hostile to the French and to the rebellious nature of exiled United Irishmen. The United States Minister to Great Britain, Rufus King:

> refused to allow a number of Irish state prisoners, including Robert Emmet, to be exiled by the British government to the United States. 'I certainly do not think they will be a desirable acquisition to a Nation,' he wrote to the Duke of Portland, 'but in none would they be likely to prove more mischievous than in mine, where from the sameness of language and similarity of Laws and Institutions they have greater opportunities of propagating their [revolutionary French] principles than in any other country.'[47]

On 20 May 1796, America had appointed James Holmes (the author's great-great-great grandfather), and a younger brother of John Holmes, the Belfast banker, as its first US Consul in Belfast. James had been a Belfast merchant with a flourishing trade in American goods. Both brothers had become senior members of the Belfast Chamber of Commerce, and, in 1795, James was elected President. Yet he never took up this appointment and sailed to America, where his position as US Consul was confirmed by George Washington, and he only returned to Belfast about a year later. It is known that John Holmes, like most senior Belfast Presbyterians, supported Henry Joy in opposing the United Irishmen's calls for Catholic emancipation, and it is clear that James took a similar view. Despite opposing their cause, he had retained close associations with some of the senior United Irishmen. He had been a partner in a shipping group, The New Traders, led by Haslett, one of the United Irish founders. Its business suffered from financial difficulties in about 1795, perhaps the effect of bad weather and war on shipping movements, but also due to Haslett's prominent position with the banned Society. Certainly, James Holmes suffered serious financial losses at this time, resulting in him selling his substantial property, Ballymenoch House, at Holywood in co. Down. In his capacity as Consul, he described the uprising in his report to America, as a mildly embarrassing minor skirmish, causing the authorities to augment the Belfast garrison to deal with street riots. In 1805, he backed Castlereagh as Parliamentary candidate for co. Down. Someone with United Irish sympathies would never have done this.

It took until 1802 for the prisoners in Fort George to be released. Tennant, Simms and Dickson were able to return to Belfast, but Neilson, Russell and Thomas Addis Emmet faced exile as the price of their freedom. After a fleeting visit to his family in Ireland, Neilson went with Emmet to Amsterdam. In December 1802, he set sail for America, only to die there after a heart attack on 29 August 1803. Russell, who had been held without trial for nearly six years, went to Paris, where he joined up with a group of Irish exiles.

Part 7

Events leading to Union and emancipation

Chapter 22

The Act of Union 1789 – 1801

With Grattan's earlier achievement of removing Poynings' Law ending the requirement for Parliamentary decisions in Ireland to be ratified in London, Pitt needed other means to assure British authority. His initial concerns had arisen in November 1789, when George III's insanity meant that the absurdly extravagant Prince of Wales would be appointed Regent. With the Prince closely associated with Fox, he was likely to support the Whigs. To delay matters, Pitt called for his appointment to be ratified by Parliament to provide an opportunity to impose limitations on his prerogative. The Whigs, of course, thought this unnecessary, but the need for ratification was confirmed at Westminster with its Tory majority. Grattan irritated Pitt in the Irish House of Commons by calling for the Prince to assume the Regency of Ireland 'in plenitude of royal power'. Clare promptly contended that Ireland should follow the British example by ratifying his appointment with a bill in Parliament, but Grattan's proposal was approved, thereby passing parliamentary control to the Irish Whigs led by the Ponsonbys. Miraculously for Pitt, the King recovered, and, in February 1790, the temporary powers granted to the Prince were withdrawn, allowing Tories in both Britain and Ireland to recover their former parliamentary authority.

Pitt's solution had been to pack the Irish Parliament with 'place seekers' bribed to vote in accordance with Tory policy. The newly formed Irish Whigs, which Grattan had joined, were very critical of the new Lord Lieutenant, George Nugent-Temple-Grenville, 1st Marquess of Buckingham, and his successor, Westmoreland, who was Pitt's staunch ally. In his earlier years in politics, Pitt had supported Irish Catholic emancipation, but came to have concerns that a Catholic majority, already aggrieved at their ancestral lands being usurped by British settlers, would hand them free rein to redress their earlier mistreatment. He was also well-aware that the Protestant Establishment, being propped up to deliver Tory objectives, was corrupt. It abused its authority to protect its ascendancy, and there was a similar bias in the Courts.

Pitt also needed to counter the growing republican sentiment among Irish Presbyterians, particularly Dissenters, which had led to the rebellion in 1798. After being oppressed by the Establishment, they were using their dissenting dogma to justify opposition to monarchy and British rule. Their link with Catholic Defenders had made them a force to be reckoned with. While Fitzwilliam's approach had been to appease the Catholics with emancipation, which would root out corruption within the Establishment, Pitt feared that it would lead to Irish independence, just as in the American colonies. With Britain at war with revolutionary France, it was certain that the French would support any Irish insurgency when it arose. Nevertheless, with French revolutionaries disenfranchising the Catholic Church in addition to destroying the monarchy, he could rely on Irish Catholics being lukewarm to French offers of assistance.

Pitt needed a solution other than Catholic emancipation. Unlike in America, Britain maintained a dominant military presence in Ireland, which could be supplemented by British forces returning from the Continent. If he could dispense with the Irish Parliament completely and administer Ireland from London in a similar manner to Scotland, he could resolve all his perceived difficulties. He would end the corruption of the Protestant Ascendancy, he would be able to provide Catholic emancipation without handing out a majority vote in Parliament and he would be able to stamp out the republican aspirations of the United Irishmen.

It was probably Clare who planted the seeds of Parliamentary Union with Pitt. He had advocated it as early as 1793. When Pitt brought forward his proposals, they were opposed in the English House of Lords, unless they received approval of both houses of the Irish Parliament. Although Pitt retained a measure of control through his place seekers, the Irish

Whigs engineered sufficient initial opposition for parliamentary union to be rejected, 'an offence which Pitt never forgot or forgave'.[1] Both Pitt and Clare saw that the threatened republican insurgency, with its prospect of French Jacobin support, would strike fear into moderate members of the Irish hierarchy. This would encourage them to cede control to Westminster. Pitt's solution was to watch the United Irish scheming very closely, but to allow its revolutionary intentions to develop. Although he believed there was a sufficient military presence to sit on any rebellion when needed, he was lucky, because, if the French had landed an effective invasion force, he would have had a real fight on his hands. The result 'was to prove so destructive to the energies of the country as to enable [him] to accomplish his long-projected measure of the Union'.[2] His speeches showed:

> an inveterate hostility of opinion to the people of Ireland, which had represented them as 'irascable and quellable, devoted to superstition, deaf to law, and hostile to property'.[3]

Pitt's thoroughly underhand policy had been to leave the United Irish leaders at large to incite rebellion. A very clear example of this was allowing Jackson to travel between revolutionary cells in both England and Ireland without arrest, even though the authorities were well aware from the outset of his treacherous intent. Jackson was accompanied to meet Priestley and Rowan by an agent, Cockayne, who kept Pitt fully informed. Although Pitt's ostensible purpose was to gain information to incriminate the United Irish leadership, it was part of his plan to achieve parliamentary Union. He needed people to believe that the rebellion was more dangerous than it was, and the use of torture to demonstrate its gravity was another part of this strategy.

Neither the Irish Tories nor Grattan and senior Whigs wanted the political leadership of Ireland to pass out of the hands of its landed gentry, but Pitt did nothing to defend the Establishment from rumours of corruption and torture. When Grattan made a vehement and well received speech opposing the Union, Pitt saw to it that Grattan was lampooned as a rebel in the British press. Nothing was further from the truth. Although the Catholics backed the bill for Union in the hope of emancipation, they had no vote. In 1799, the Whigs mustered just sufficient support to defeat it in the Irish House of Commons. Yet, in May 1800, after a liberal distribution of pensions believed to have cost £1,500,000, and further offers of preferment for Establishment figures, the vote was carried, despite Grattan's impassioned speeches against it. Once passed, Grattan showed his stature with a call to make it 'as fruitful, as profitable and as advantageous as possible'. He now backed full Catholic emancipation and held a seat in the English Parliament until his death in 1820.

Clare differed from Pitt in one major respect. While Pitt had set his cap at delivering Catholic emancipation as part of the Act of Union, Clare was determined to protect the Protestant ascendency. Quite unscrupulously, he blamed the Catholics for the 1798 rebellion, reporting that 'in the North nothing will keep the rebels quiet but the conviction that where treason has broken out the rebellion is merely popish'. (Letter to the Privy Council, 4 June 1798) He managed to persuade George III that support for emancipation would be in violation of his coronation oath. The King even declared that it would cause 'the total change of the principles of government which have been followed by every administration in that Kingdom since the abdication of James II ... [it is] beyond the decision of any Cabinet of Ministers'.

When the Act was passed at Westminster, George III refused to ratify emancipation. He invoked the provisions of the Act of Settlement of 1701, under which the terms for the House of Hanover to accept a Protestant throne as heads of the Church of England were set out. Pitt resigned in protest. Henry Addington, who succeeded him as Prime Minister, was one of a significant number of English parliamentarians to support the King's viewpoint. From now on 103 Irish MPs sat in the House of Commons in London, and Irish peers elected twenty-eight of their number to sit in the House of Lords with four elected Irish Bishops.

Belfast merchants generally opposed the Act of Union believing it would worsen trade. 'Ireland, at this period, was regarded by England, not as a sister, but as a rival, whose clashing interests were constantly to be repressed.'[4] 'Her trade was impeded by prohibitory statutes which utterly sacrificed her interests to the aggrandisement of England.'[5] Although, in Dublin, Union was the 'burning topic', in Belfast, it was much more 'disregarded'.[6] Cornwallis realised the problem caused by protecting the Protestant Ascendancy. He reported: 'My occupation is now of the most unpleasant nature, negotiating and jobbing with the most corrupt people under heaven.'[7] On visiting Belfast to promote it, Cornwallis found some linen traders, former United Irishmen, were hoping for trading concessions in return for their support. The idealism that had led their leaders to seek both emancipation for Catholics and an Irish republic was suddenly less important than economic recovery. With the rebel leaders safely incarcerated at Fort George, they could be branded as 'extremists'. The muslin business of Mary Ann and Margaret McCracken was soon flourishing, with new patterns much in demand.

Chapter 23

The rebellion of 1803

Despite the Union, attempts to create a secular republic in Ireland did not end with the failure of the 1798 rebellion. There was no longer a perceived need to resolve corruption, but idealists within the Presbyterian community still hankered after an Irish republic independent of English control. Most saw this as justifiable revenge for the atrocities of 1798. Although Catholic emancipation had not been achieved, educated Catholics still lacked any revolutionary appetite. They sought reform through political negotiation. Even the Catholic peasantry were unenthusiastic.

Although Robert Emmet, the younger brother of Thomas Addis Emmet now in exile in Amsterdam, had enjoyed a brilliant academic career as a student at Trinity College, Dublin, he was expelled in 1798 after becoming the Secretary of the secret United Irish committee at the university, with plans to rekindle the United Irish cause. In April 1799, a warrant was issued for his arrest, but he escaped to France, where he met Tallyrand, gaining, so he believed, a pledge of French assistance for a second Irish republican uprising. He also met Russell, still directing the Irish in exile. Russell was closely in touch with both Napoleon and Tallyrand, who hoped to launch an English invasion. Russell had written:

> So far from seeing the cause of Ireland lost, or being weary of its pursuit, I am more than ever, if possible, inflexibly bent on it, for that, I stay (if I can stay) in Europe; all the faculties I possess shall be exercised for its advancement, for that I wished to go to Ireland not to reside, but to see how I shall be able to serve it, and this I can only do when at

large. Every motive exists to stimulate the generous mind –
the widows and orphans of my friends, the memories of the
heroes who fell, & the sufferings of the heroes who survive.
My very soul is on fire.[1]

From Paris, Robert Emmet went on to Amsterdam to see his brother,
Thomas Addis Emmet, but their request for the French to support a
new Irish rebellion was vetoed by Napoleon during the brief period
when France was at peace with England. In October 1802, Robert
returned to Ireland and, in March 1803, despite lacking any promise
of French support, began preparing for a new rising. He revitalised
the revolutionary movement, attracting many 1798 veterans, including
Hope, to his cause. Nevertheless, his decision to move Hope from his
powerbase among the Dublin weavers to raise the Ulster Presbyterians
proved a mistake. Without Hope in Dublin, he failed to attract Michael
Dwyer's Wicklow rebels, and the Kildare rebels were insufficiently
armed to become involved. In early 1803, Russell returned to Dublin,
in defiance of the terms of his banishment, to assist Emmet. When
Emmet sent him north to co-ordinate Belfast, he stayed with John
Rabb, one of Mary Ann McCracken's weavers, on the outskirts of the
city. Mary Ann had been determined to help Russell, both in respect of
his close friendship with Harry, and her own secret admiration for this
'Adonis of a man'. When the sisters visited him, they gave him a ring
containing a lock of Harry's hair and £10 to help his finances. Russell
was hopelessly short of funds and reliant on his friends' charity to
support both himself and his sister Margaret in Dublin. Although he
met William and Robert Simms and Francis McCracken, the Belfast
military had been strengthened, and they all tried to dissuade him
from a course that could only lead to disaster. Many former rebels had
been transported and little was to be hoped for from either France or
Irish Catholics. Russell accepted this and warned Emmet in 'bitter
anguish' that he should defer his plans.[2]

Unfortunately, the warning was too late. Emmet was manufacturing
weapons in *depôts* all over Dublin, but, when an explosion occurred at
one of them, he had to accelerate his plans. This was not a peasant

uprising along the lines of the French Revolution as in 1798, but the first call for Irish nationalism. It was total and disorganised folly, and quickly disintegrated into street fighting.[3] On 23 July 1803, workers with pikes 'briefly held their own against the 21st North British Fusiliers'; they pulled the Lord Chief Justice, Lord Kilwarden, from his carriage and hacked him to death. Twenty members of the military and fifty rebels died. Although Emmet fled, on 25 August, he was apprehended while trying to visit his sweetheart, Sarah Curran, in Dublin.

A reward of £1,000 was offered for Russell's arrest, half of which was raised by Belfast merchants, but his hiding-place was never revealed. With Emmet imprisoned, Russell was determined to assist his escape. Mary Ann paid two fishermen to take him in an open boat to Drogheda, from where he managed to reach Dublin. On 9 September, he too was arrested and taken to Kilmainham jail. Ten days later, Emmet was tried for high treason and, with his defence attorney being bribed by the authorities not to represent him, was found guilty. During the proceedings, he was asked by Clare: 'Did you not think the government very foolish to let you proceed as long as you did?' Emmet replied: 'No, my Lord, whatever I imputed to Government, I did not accuse them of folly; I knew we were very attentively watched.'[4] The rebels had already been infiltrated at a senior level when they applied to France for assistance. (Infiltration worked both ways. During O'Connor's examination, he stated 'that "minute information of every act of the Irish government" was obtained by' the United Irish leadership.)[5] Towards the end of his trial, Emmet made an impassioned speech. Although there is no transcript, one version of his concluding words records:

> I am here ready to die. I am not allowed to vindicate my character; and when I am prevented from vindicating myself; let no man dare to calumniate. Let my motives repose in obscurity and peace, till other times and other men can do them justice. Then shall my character be vindicated; then shall my epitaph be written.[6]

He was hung on the following day and then decapitated after death. Although 3,000 rebels were arrested and incarcerated, only twenty were executed. Hope never faced trial; he was sheltered by a sympathetic English friend who offered him employment. In later years he wrote a poem to symbolise his philosophy:

> These are my thoughts, nor do I think I need
> Perplex my mind with any other creed
> I wish to let my neighbour's creed alone
> And think it quite enough to mind my own[7]

Mary Ann stepped in once more to assist Russell to escape, providing £200, of which £100 was to bribe the turnkey. Unfortunately, Russell was moved to Downpatrick, where he faced a similar trial to Emmet. The McCracken family arranged for James Ramsey, a young Belfast attorney, to defend him without charge. Mary Ann plundered the resources of her muslin business to employ Counsellors Joy and Bell at a cost of 100 guineas each. Although she wanted to attend the trial, she risked being arrested as an accomplice. Much to her annoyance, old Mr Teeling persuaded her mother to prevent her from going. Her brother, Frank, sent one of his clerks, Tom Hughes, who knew the jailers well, to try to arrange Russell's escape, but to no avail. Despite an impassioned defence by Counsellor Joy, who admitted afterwards 'that he never in his life felt so interested in any man', Russell was found guilty.[8] He was now aged thirty-five. When sentenced, the judge refused his request to be allowed three days' grace to complete his translation from the Greek of the Revelation of St John, the Divine. Prior to his execution, Mary Ann wrote to him, but with no hint of her unrequited love. He would not read her letter, fearing the emotion it would cause. Like Emmet, he was hanged and decapitated. Mary Ann arranged his burial at Downpatrick church and continued to provide for his sister Margaret, who was earning a pittance as a teacher, until her death in 1834. Mary Ann never married but became one of Belfast's great philanthropists and a driving force among anti-slavery campaigners.

In his Consular report to Pickering in America, James Holmes affirmed the rebellion's very limited support. He wrote that 'the late rising in Dublin' had been more of 'a Riot than a regular System of Rebellion having been begun and ended in less than an hour'. Despite being the source of great worry, the public was now 'orderly and well disposed & and ready to enrol in the different Yeomanry Corps'.[9] This does not suggest any personal or American sympathy for Emmet, although James's cousin, Robert Holmes, was married to Emmet's sister, Mary Emma. There was little Catholic sympathy. O'Connell wrote: 'A man, who could coolly prepare so much bloodshed, so many murders and such horrors of every kind, has ceased to be an object of compassion.'[10] This is a damning indictment from the type of educated Catholic that Emmet hoped to attract.

Despite failing to attract Irish backing, Emmet had hoped to be 'supported by an uprising of British and Irish radicals in London led by Colonel Edward Marcus Despard'.[11] Despard was an Irishman of Cromwellian stock, born in co. Laois in 1751. He had fought with distinction as an English army officer alongside Nelson in the Caribbean and was appointed Governor of British Honduras. On arrival, he made himself unpopular by demanding fair treatment for the local natives. He then scandalised local landowners by taking a native girl, Catherine, as his wife. By 1792, he was so unpopular that he returned with Catherine to London. When his expenses as Governor were withheld, he spent two years in debtors' prison. On his release, he joined the United Irishmen and was one of those apprehended with O'Connor at Margate. In 1797, Higgins reported that he was spying for the French and arranged his arrest. He was held for three years without trial in appalling conditions at Coldbath Fields in Clerkenwell, 'the English Bastille'. In 1801, his friends were able to arrange his release, but he remained closely watched.

In 1802, Despard was once more arrested in a Lambeth public house with a group of Irish workers. He was attempting to arrange a London diversion to deflect attention from a proposed French landing in support of Emmet. He was tried on a trumped-up charge of planning to assassinate the King. He was convicted of treason, despite Nelson appearing on his behalf as a character witness. On 21 February 1803, he affirmed his innocence before 20,000 workers, who appeared in silent protest at his execution. He was hanged, drawn and quartered, being the last person in England to face this gruesome ritual.

Thomas Addis Emmet moved on from Amsterdam to New York where he was established as 'the favourite counsellor' at the New York bar, even becoming State Attorney General from August 1812 to February 1813. He died in Court in 1827 while conducting a case. Drennan also pulled back from revolution. In 1800, he married Sarah Swanwick of a well-to-do dissenting family in Shropshire but returned with her to live at Cabin Hill to the east of Belfast. In 1807, he became the founding editor of *The Belfast Monthly Magazine.* Together with John Templeton and John Hancock, he set up the Belfast Academical Institution as a non-sectarian place of learning, although it failed to attract many Catholic pupils. He died in 1820.

Chapter 24

The Liberator 1806 – 1841

With Grattan now sixty years of age, there was growing acceptance that he had played no part in supporting the 1798 rebellion. In 1806, he was persuaded by Fitzwilliam to stand for Parliament in London and he accepted Fitzwilliam's seat at Malton, making a powerful speech in support of Catholic emancipation. After Pitt's unexpected death in 1806, he was tipped to become the Irish Chancellor of the Exchequer as part of the Ministry of all the Talents. As always, he declined this opportunity, preferring his backbench position as an 'influential supporter of the new government'. The new coalition tried to promote a Tithe Commutation bill. It did not involve Grattan in its process, as this could have been emotive, but he persuaded Catholics not to embarrass the Government by making immediate calls for emancipation. He then stood as the member for Dublin and, after winning the seat by a narrow majority, continued to hold it unopposed until his death in 1820.

Irish Nationalism was now 'fractured along sectarian fault lines'[1] The republican cause was now equated with Catholicism. There was no longer a place for Dissenters, but 'the values they held dear, such as the right to individual conscience and opinion, the right of people to choose or change their government, the rights of man and civil and religious liberty are the foundation stones of modern secular democracy'.[2]

The man who stepped forward to promote Catholic emancipation was Daniel O'Connell. He had been born in 1775 of a well-to-do Catholic family in co. Kerry. After being sent for his education to Douai in France, he moved on to London to be admitted, in 1794, as a barrister at Lincoln's Inn. Two years later, he returned to Dublin to practice at King's Inn. While he approved of United Irish objectives to achieve Catholic emancipation and to eliminate corruption within the Protestant Ascendancy, he strongly disapproved of inciting rebellion. He wanted change by negotiation and played no part in the rebellions of 1798 and 1803. Instead he spent ten years engrossed in his legal practice on the Munster circuit.

In 1811, O'Connell established the Catholic Board, making speeches to promote Catholic emancipation. In 1815, he described the Dublin Corporation, now a stronghold of Protestant ascendancy, as a 'beggarly corporation', and its membership branded him as 'worse than a public nuisance'.[3] One of them, John d'Esterre, challenged him to a duel. D'Esterre was a noted duellist, and Protestants welcomed this opportunity for O'Connell's removal. The protagonists met at Oughterard, Kildare, where to almost universal disbelief, O'Connell shot d'Esterre in the hip (the bullet lodged in his stomach), and mortally wounded him. He was not only mortified at killing a man, but at leaving d'Esterre's wife and daughter destitute. He offered half of his income to them, which d'Esterre's wife refused, but she accepted an allowance for her daughter. This was dutifully paid by O'Connell, who remained haunted by his actions until his death thirty years later.[4] He attended mass and took Holy Communion every day, and always wore a black glove on his right hand to condone the shedding of d'Esterre's blood.[5]

In 1823, O'Connell set up a Catholic Association with the objective of achieving electoral reform, reform of the Church of Ireland, tenant rights and economic development.[6] This became a pressure group for Catholic emancipation. The Association was funded out of a Catholic 'rent', collected in conjunction with the Catholic Church.

In 1828, O'Connell stood for parliament in a bye election in co. Clare, and even though, as a Catholic, he was refusing to swear the Oath of Supremacy to allow him to take his seat, he won the election. On his arrival in London, both the Prime Minister, the Duke of Wellington, and the Home Secretary, Sir Robert Peel, were opposed to Catholic participation in Parliament, but recognised that it would cause an outrage if he were banned. Wanting to avoid a new outbreak of rebellion and 'in the face of defiant opposition' from George IV, Wellington threatened to resign if he did not permit members of all Christian faiths to sit in Parliament. In 1829, Wellington, with Whig support, guided the Roman Catholic Relief Act (10 George IV. Cap. 7) through Parliament. A new Oath of Allegiance permitted Roman Catholics to enter Parliament, to belong to Corporations and to be eligible for senior military and civil positions.[7]

'Catholic emancipation seemed to herald a new era for the Irish, with Catholic Bishops expressing thanks to the British Government and calling on priests to avoid future political activity.'[8] Yet, the Act was not made retrospective, which meant that O'Connell had either to swear the Oath of Supremacy or to seek re-election. When he tried to take his seat without taking the oath, the Solicitor-General declared his seat vacant and called a new election. O'Connell was re-elected unopposed and at last took his place at Westminster. 'O'Connell, by the sheer force of his intellect, and with no other weapon than his voice, had succeeded.'[9] He had become the 'Liberator'.

O'Connell was supported by an Irish Liberal MP, William Smith O'Brien, who led the Young Irelander movement, another association, initially at least, determined to avoid the use of physical force. O'Brien was the second son of an Irish baronet, Sir Edward O'Brien, having been educated at Harrow School and Trinity College, Cambridge. Despite his Protestantism, he supported O'Connell's calls for Catholic emancipation. Yet the outcome did not prove the hoped-for panacea:

> It was not long before O'Connell and the nation found that the glories of Catholic Emancipation were but a mockery and an illusion. ... The material condition of Ireland was worse in the years succeeding, than it had been for several years before the Act of Emancipation.[10]

O'Connell focused on the repeal of tithes, which was not covered by the Catholic Relief Act. Although their purpose was to fund the Anglican Church of Ireland, their main burden still fell on subsistence tenant farmers, both Catholic and Presbyterian, who did not attend its services. Nevertheless, they were required to pay out 10 per cent of the value of their production.

> The clergymen of the opulent Protestant Establishment gathered their dues of wheat from a poverty-stricken Catholic peasantry, backed by soldiers and police and guns, and sometimes amid scenes of mad passion and much bloodshed.[11]

It was no help that the Anglican clergy were very often non-resident. The Catholic Church, to which the great majority of the population belonged, received no such funding, leaving its finances in dire straits, particularly after the British ended support for the Catholic seminary at Maynooth in about 1830.

The Catholic Church now encouraged a plan for the peaceful non-payment of tithes. The Government immediately compiled a list of defaulters, and the newly formed Irish Constabulary was ordered to confiscate stock and other agricultural produce to meet tax commitments. It often tried to enforce collection when people were congregated for market fairs, resulting in sporadic outbreaks of violence. In 1831, Patrick Lalor, a farmer from Tenakill, proposed passive resistance without breaking the law. He did not oppose the confiscation of his livestock but asked his fellow countrymen to leave it unsold by refusing to bid for it at auction. In another incident in co. Kilkenny, a Catholic priest was encouraged by his bishop to take local farmers' stock into his ownership prior to sale. When 120 Yeomanry attempted to enforce seizure, there was a riot. The revolt spread to co. Wexford, where the Irish constabulary killed twelve farmers by firing on them while resisting seizure. Objectors rang their church bells to warn communities to round up their stock as the constabulary approached. In more concerted opposition, farmers ambushed a detachment of forty police at Carrickshock, killing the chief constable and eleven others. O'Connell successfully defended the rebels in the Courts. In 1832, the president of the Catholic Carlow College was imprisoned for failing to pay tithes. Army barracks had to be reinforced to handle the clashes. In 1834, when the constabulary, supported by British soldiers, tried to enforce a tithe order, fighting continued for several hours. Violence, deaths and criminal unrest continued. The Roman Catholic Bishop of Kildare, Dr James Doyle, wrote to the Chancellor of the Exchequer, the Anglo-Irish Thomas Spring-Rice (soon to become Lord Monteagle):

> There are many noble traits in the Irish character mixed with failings, which have always raised obstacles to their own well-being, but an innate love of justice, and an indomitable hatred of oppression is like a gem upon the front of our nation, which no darkness can obscure. To this fine quality I trace their hatred of tithes, may it be as lasting as their love of justice.[12]

Eventually the Government suspended collections after an official complained: 'It costs a shilling to collect tuppence.'[13]

O'Connell strongly supported efforts to abate the tithe system but found himself in a political difficulty. In 1835, Irish MPs had made a compact with the Whigs and other radicals at Lichfield House seeking to repeal the Act of Union of 1800. O'Connell did not want to jeopardise this relationship by seeking the complete removal of tithes. Yet the British Government heeded concerns at the Church of Ireland's extravagance by promoting The Church Temporalities (Ireland) Act of 1833 (3 and 4 William IV. Cap. 37). This suppressed ten bishoprics and appointed ecclesiastical commissioners with powers to divide livings and to build and repair churches.[14]

Nevertheless, local Anglican incumbents depended on tithes for income. Some sold their future rights to 'tithe farmers' for a fee. The Irish Tithe Arrears Act of 1833 (3 and 4 William IV. Cap. 100) advanced £1,000,000 to relieve clergy no longer able to collect tithes.[15] In 1838, Parliament introduced the Tithe Commutation Act, which reduced the charge by about a quarter and made the remainder payable in rent to landlords. This helped to eliminate confrontation, but it was not until 1869, when William Gladstone disestablished the Church of

Ireland under the Irish Church Act, that tithes were finally abolished.

Having achieved Catholic emancipation in London, O'Connell was elected in 1841 as the first Catholic Lord Mayor of Dublin since James II's time. This was of itself extraordinary, as 'the Corporation was the great home of Orange Conservatism'.[16] He now arranged an Act to open all municipal councils to Catholics. This achievement was not all that it seemed. It was the High Sheriff, not the Lord Mayor, who appointed jurors on behalf of the Crown. He was not helped when Roman Catholic bishops opposed education systems that were non-sectarian 'on the grounds that they endangered the faith and morals of Roman Catholic students'.[17] This only reinforced segregation between differing faiths.[18]

O'Connell continued to campaign to repeal the Act of Union, hoping to revert to a separate Irish Government as achieved by Grattan in 1782, but with full Catholic emancipation and with Queen Victoria retained as Ireland's head of state. He made a brilliant speech in the Dublin Corporation, which endorsed repeal by forty-five votes to fifteen. Demands for home rule 'gripped the country';[19] nevertheless, on 23 April 1834, his motion at Westminster 'was laughed at on both sides of the House; and, when he went into the lobby, he was supported by but 40 votes'.[20] It was Peel, now Tory Prime Minister, who had become 'the bitter and uncompromising enemy of all Irish Reform.'[21]

O'Connell now formed the Repeal Association, a mass membership political movement, which called a series of 'Monster Meetings' throughout Ireland attended by more than 100,000 people. A meeting at Tara attended by 500,000 people, engendered a national frenzy in favour of repeal. There is no doubt that his meetings were intended as military training exercises, although O'Connell always denied it. This lost him Whig support, and Peel became extremely nervous over the extent of his backing. When O'Connell arranged a Monster Meeting at Clontarf outside Dublin (emotively the scene of the Irish victory over the Vikings in 1014), Peel banned it as seditious. He threatened war if the agitation did not stop, sending 35,000 troops to Ireland backed by naval ships. O'Connell accused Peel of hypocrisy and cowardice but wanted the Irish to remain loyal to the Crown and 'would not purchase freedom by shedding one drop of Irish blood. ... We will violate no law, we will assail no enemy.'[22] Yet, he seemed to be going a step further than this, as he continued:

> But you are much mistaken if you think others will not assail you. ... What are Irishmen that they should be denied an equal privilege? Have we the ordinary courage of Englishmen? Are we to be called slaves? Are we to be trampled underfoot? Oh, they shall never trample me – at least, I can say they may trample me, but it will be my dead body they will trample on, not the living man!'[23]

These words implied that O'Connell had contemplated insurrection but had pulled back. Charles Gavan Duffy, the founder of *The Nation*, believed that O'Connell missed an opportunity to push the masses into an unstoppable attack on Dublin Castle armed only with pikes. It was even suggested that the Establishment was provoking 'violence, in order to make the bloodshed inevitable'.[24] *The Nation* now represented a new phase in Irish Politics as the voice of O'Brien's Young Irelanders, bringing vigour to O'Connell's Repeal Association: 'It convinced; it inspired; it roused loftiest hopes and fiercest passions.'[25]

A strong influence for taking a harder line was John Mitchel, an early contributor to *The Nation*, who was rapidly establishing himself as a Young Irelander leader. He was the son of an Ulster Unitarian clergyman, but later split from Duffy to start another radical paper, *The United Irishman*, in which 'insurrection was openly preached'.[26] He also split with O'Connell. He advocated force to seek lower rents from landlords to allow tenants to subsist on the food that they were producing. This was probably unrealistic, as many smaller tenants could not subsist at any level of rents.

O'Connell's objective had been to lead the Repeal Association back into league with the Whigs, but he was heavily reliant 'on the good intentions and promises' of Lord John Russell, the Whig leader.[27] The Whigs would not support repeal. This left Repeal Association members without 'the fate of elections in their hands'.[28] They also differed over tenant rights in the face of wholesale evictions of small tenants. In 1826 and 1827, new laws had facilitated tenant evictions to reduce rural over-population. A further 500,000 evictions were brought about by the Poor Law legislation in 1838. When a motion was introduced in the House of Commons to ensure that 'a tenant in possession has a right to occupation of the land, provided he pay his rent punctually', Russell considered it subversive.[29] He favoured 'a better mutual understanding' between landlords and tenants so that voluntary agreements were 'carried out for the benefit of both'.

Despite O'Connell's determination to achieve change by peaceful negotiation, he was arrested. At his trial, the jury was packed with Orange Conservatives. The judiciary showed its bias when Chief Justice Pennefather described his defence as 'the other side'.[30] He was found guilty of conspiracy and was sentenced to a one-year prison sentence with a £2,000 fine. He never recovered from this shock, and 'both he and his policy had lost their prestige'.[31] When he appealed after three months, the sentence was reversed. Chief Justice Denman in the House of Lords called his trial by jury 'a mockery, a delusion and a snare'. Yet he was now physically and mentally broken and had lost his appetite for future action.

Although O'Brien had not initially supported O'Connell's efforts to break the Union, he was shocked at his imprisonment and re-established his support for the Repeal Association. Yet O'Connell's continued determination to avoid rebellion fragmented his supporters, causing O'Brien to resign with other Young Irelander group members. When Peel made a large grant to the Catholic Maynooth College, even the Vatican's support for O'Connell came under pressure and his authority melted away.

It was only in January 1847, in conjunction with Thomas Francis Meagher, a Catholic with powerful speaking skills and similar objectives for repeal of the Union to his own, that O'Connell was at last more confrontational. He set up the *Irish Confederation*, which attracted more militant members of the Repeal Association to its banner. Although there were no calls for rebellion, there were no pledges of peace. Yet O'Connell was depressed and died in Genoa in

1847 while on a pilgrimage to Italy, with his reputation for peaceful agitation intact. Gladstone described him as 'the greatest popular leader, the world has ever seen'. Despite popular support, O'Connell had failed to gain a following in Parliament.

It was a condition of Parliamentary membership that candidates should have an income of £300 per annum to sit for a borough seat and £600 per annum as a county member. Most Irish members were landlords, and, whether Protestant or Catholic, they condoned existing abuses. Even Catholic place seekers with theoretical support for the Repeal Association accepted the deepening misery. They saw no advantage in a return to home rule, benefitting as they did from State patronage. Following O'Connell's death, Young Irelanders called on Irish Members of Parliament to refuse Government office until abuses were resolved, but O'Connell's son, John, who now led the Repeal Association, 'refused to accede to any such pledge'.[32] Young Irelander candidates were left isolated, failing to win the seats they contested.

Part 8

Famine, destitution and agitation for independence

Chapter 25

Famine c. 1800 – c. 1870

With British legislation having imposed restrictions on Irish manufacturing, the cause of much of Ireland's political, religious and social unrest lay in economic hardship. Although it remained at peace, the rural population faced growing destitution. A principal problem was the population increase, particularly among Catholics. Ireland was essentially an agricultural economy, totally reliant on farm produce to feed its rising population in an uncertain climate. Following the arrival of British settlers, the native Irish had been left with smaller tenancies. With the population growing, parcels of land had to be divided among numerous children until these parcels became too small to support the occupiers. Unlike in England there was no industrial revolution to offer employment to the surplus rural population. With fears that low Irish wages would enable Irish manufacture to undercut British prices, protectionist interests in the British Parliament discouraged Irish industrial production.

With the native Irish traditionally being:

> cattle farmers, and, with the English propensity for eating beef, much Irish produce was destined for the English market. As land confiscations had increased in the 17th Century, the more fertile grazing pastures had been transferred to English and Scottish settlers, leaving the Irish peasantry as tenants on less fertile soil, often covered in a layer of peat. This needed to be cut out before grazing could be established or crops planted.[1]

Estates were generally owned by absentee landlords, often the proprietors of substantial areas. (The estates of George Bingham,

3rd Earl of Lucan, amounted to more than 60,000 acres.) Unlike in Scotland, landlords fostered no hereditary loyalty or bond of kinship with their tenantry, and, being 'separated from the tenant by creed, race and caste, aggravated all the evils of the system'.[2] Only rarely did they co-operate with tenants to develop the productivity of their land. 'Behind [their failure to provide support] there stood at least a century of extravagance.'[3] The Irish squire was 'a spendthrift, a gambler, often a drunkard', and suffered from the sins of the father.[4]

> He spent his money on his Dublin town house, generally built on a more lavish scale than those of English landlords in London. Although he had expected the Irish Government to remain in Dublin, the Act of Union had obliged him to build a London residence. He fell into debt and pawned his Irish estates to money lenders, whose only interest was in collecting the rents when due. He was still in debt at the time of the Great Famine.[5]

With tenants 'brooding over their discontent in sullen indignation', Ireland, according to Clare, was a hostile place for landlords to live. They rarely, if ever, visited their estates, which were managed by 'middlemen', often described as 'land sharks' or 'bloodsuckers', who took long leases for subletting in small parcels to subsistence farmers.[6] The landlords simply milked estates from afar for as much as they could take. With many living in England, the rental moneys they received no longer circulated round the Irish economy. As the Irish population started to grow, the increasing shortage of farmland resulted in great competition for tenancies, forcing up rents to levels that were not affordable, so that parcels of inferior land were broken down into ever smaller plots for let. Most farmers were left with insufficient areas for pasture; 'industry and enterprise were extinguished, and a peasantry created, which was one of the most destitute in Europe'.[7]

Poverty reached such a point that the only way for peasants to produce sufficient nourishment to subsist on their meagre lands was to grow potatoes. These had been introduced into Ireland as a garden crop during the seventeenth century, but by the early part of the eighteenth century were already the staple diet of the poor, also providing fodder for cattle. The potato provided larger yields per acre than any other crop and was suited to both soil and climate. It could support life without any other supplement and 'was the thin partition between famine and the millions of the Irish people.'[8] Despite its nutritional benefits, the native Irish were often forced to supplement their income with seasonal trips to England and Scotland to provide cheap labour at harvest time. Even larger tenancies faced acute difficulty in generating sufficient income to pay rents, often resulting in them being settled in wheat, oats and livestock, while the farmer was left to subsist on his potato crop. If this was large, the landlord received the surplus, 'returning nothing to the soil. [He received] its whole produce minus the potatoes strictly necessary to keep the inhabitants from dying of famine.'[9]

Food shortage was not a new problem for Ireland. During the 1720s, a series of harvest failures caused by poor weather led to relief efforts to provide corn for the poor. In 1739, a wet summer again reduced the grain harvest, and cut turf would not dry. In the exceptionally cold winter that followed, Ireland, like the rest of Europe, faced an unprecedented cold spell lasting for two successive winters, causing many deaths and much distress. It was so cold that mill wheels became frozen, lamps were snuffed out in the Dublin streets, winter sown grain crops failed, and potatoes became inedible after being frozen in their clamps after harvest. The cold winter of 1739 was followed by a drought in the spring of 1740 that destroyed newly sown crops, causing acute food shortages. Dogs ate the dead in the fields 'for want of people to bury them'.[10] Violence broke out in Drogheda, where a ship loaded with oatmeal destined for Scotland was boarded by the starving local citizenry, who removed the sails and rudder to retain the cargo. In May 1740, rioters in Dublin, where food prices had soared, broke into bakers' shops to obtain bread. The Lord Mayor of Dublin, Samuel Cooke, looked for ways to stop hoarding and bring prices down. Archbishop Boulter launched a feeding program at his own expense. War in Europe exacerbated the problems, with Spanish privateers attacking vessels with grain destined for Irish ports. In the following winter, chunks of ice floating down the River Liffey at Dublin overturned smaller vessels. With the weather at last improving and prices starting to fall, hoarding ceased, and food prices returned to normal. In 1744, both potato and oat crops again failed after a wet and cold summer, so more relief was needed. Some 400,000 are estimated to have died in this period, causing a 20 per cent fall in the Irish population, a greater proportion than those dying during the six years of the Great Famine in the 1840s.

The potato crop had always depended on reasonable weather, and it failed in many seasons. In 1816, famine, after another crop failure, reinforced the urgent need for agricultural reform. It was followed by a typhus epidemic in the autumn. This was so virulent that, in 1818, hospitals and dispensaries were established under the Fever Hospitals Act (58 George II. Cap. 47). In 1817, Parliament passed the Poor Employment Act (57 George III. Cap. 34) to empower the authorities to employ the destitute on public works. This was to be financed by a mortgage on the rates.

'In 1822, "half-starved" wretches appeared in Galway from fifty miles away, while 100,000 subsisted on charity in co. Clare and a further 122,000 in co. Cork, despite a successful grain crop in both 1821 and 1822.'[11] In 1824, a Government report stated: 'A very considerable proportion of the population, variously estimated at a fourth and a fifth of the whole, is considered to be out of employment.'[12] When a Select Committee enquired into conditions faced by the Irish poor, £50,000 was provided to employ the destitute in road-building. 'In 1831, The Public Works (Ireland) Act reorganised the Board of Works and laid the foundation for major schemes, including piers and harbours.'[13]

It was recognised that rural over-population had to be halted; farms needed to be of a size to allow the poor to be fed and prosperity to increase. A policy of assisted emigration to remove the surplus peasantry was adopted. Yet, with the Irish being 'a breeding people', the population continued to grow. 'The 1831 census recorded a population of 7,767,401, but, ten years later, it was 8,175,124' despite subsidised emigration. 'The increase caused both disease and food shortages.'[14] Inevitable unrest needed to be brought under control, and, in 1822, the Irish Constabulary Act (3 George IV. Cap. 103) required local magistrates to establish and direct police forces in every county. This was to be regulated by central Government.

With public hygiene being poor ('night soil' was left piled up outside people's doors), fever reached epidemic proportions and famine continued. In 1832, a cholera outbreak in Belfast spread rapidly into co. Londonderry, but the abolition of window and hearth taxes allowed homes to be properly ventilated and warmed. 'In 1838, the Poor Law in England was extended to Ireland by the Poor Relief (Ireland) Act (1 and 2 Victoria. Cap. 56), and Robert Peel set up a commission to augment the relief effort.'[15] Despite these efforts, an undercurrent of unrest persisted.

In Ulster, it was an Anglican clergyman, the 'wise and humane' Rev. George Vaughan Sampson, who pointed out the peasantry's problems.[16] In 1802, he reported 'that the poor lived in dens of indescribable wretchedness, without hope or incentive' to improve matters;[17] that absentee landlords were a curse, 'uninterested in their lands or their tenants other than to squeeze as much cash out of them as possible'; that 'the County [Londonderry], once so well-wooded, had been stripped of its trees'; and that something should be done to remedy this.[18] He noted that enormous areas of slob- [salt-marsh] and bog-land could be reclaimed for use and in any case the bogs ought to be better managed or they would be ruined as a resource.

> Holdings were far too small to support the families living on them, as, if any part of the system (making linen, growing potatoes for food etc.) broke down, rents could not be paid, and eviction and starvation would follow. ... Cash collected from tenants should be ploughed back into the estates to improve them, build houses and other structures, and transform the economy, rather than be squandered on dissipations in London or Bath. ... He concluded that a huge transformation and much effort was needed to bring prosperity, civilisation, peace and other benefits to a land ruined by a century of exploitation and neglect.[19]

The London Livery Companies, still the principal landlords in co. Londonderry, woke up to Sampson's criticisms and heeded his recommendations. As soon as the war with France had ended in 1815, they organised 'an era of great reform', with the replanting of trees and hedges, and land reclamation. Sampson advocated:

> a stop to the excessive sub-divisions of farms and to the process of rack-renting; the reduction of all rents to reasonable levels; the resumption of [estates] under the direct control of the [Livery] Companies; the planting of boglands and the establishment of nurseries for trees; programmes of draining and enclosing lands by means of fences and hedges to improve and protect it; a scheme of reclamation of slob-lands by the banks of Lough Foyle; planting of all thin soil with rape to provide food for sheep and to produce oil; the amalgamation of small farms to form establishments of 20 to 200 acres apiece; the creation of small townships on each Proportion to facilitate trade; reclamation of all wastelands; a programme of building of model farm-houses; encouragement of the industrious to stay put rather than to emigrate, and the encouragement of the surplus population to emigrate; the building of mills; improvement of all roads, bridges, and infrastructure; and the establishment of model schools in decent buildings, with properly trained schoolteachers, books, and other equipment provided and paid for by the Companies.[20]

This was a faultless list of proposals, to which the Londoners paid full attention. After regaining control of their estates from their head tenants, some of the Companies:

> built model farms, schools, churches (for all denominations), exemplary dwellings, mills and other structures, and began a major programme of improvement on the land (including draining, planting with trees and thorns, and reclaiming slob-lands).[21]

Co. Londonderry was transformed by establishing neat towns and villages, good countryside management and the development of trade.[22] Those dispossessed were granted compensation for improvements they had made to land they were renting. This would otherwise have discouraged tenants, who generally lacked longer term security of tenure, from carrying out remedial works. The result was 'superior prosperity and tranquillity in Ulster compared to the rest of Ireland'.[23]

During this time, there were more general signs of economic improvement:

> Wars with France and America increased demand for linen and other goods, bringing an appreciable rise in prosperity. In 1824, duty on goods moved between England and Ireland was abolished. Excise licences were brought into line with those of Britain. The merging of British and Irish currencies under the 1825 Currency Act (6 George IV. Cap. 79) also facilitated trade. In 1815, the first steamship travelled from Dublin to London, and the completion, in 1826, of the road bridge across the Menai Strait provided access to Holyhead and a ferry service to Dublin. In 1824, Thomas Colby was directed by the Board of Ordnance to provide the first Ordnance Survey maps of Ireland.[24]

During the 1830s, railways started to arrive, and harbours and wharves were improved.

Elsewhere in Ireland, landlords failed to follow the Livery Companies' lead, and tenants, who were dispossessed, considered that they had been robbed. The problems did not go unrecognised by the British Government. Numerous commissions:

> without exception professed disaster; Ireland was on the verge of starvation, her population rapidly increasing, three-quarters of her labourers unemployed, housing conditions appalling and the standard of living unbelievably low.[25]

In November 1830, the Irish Solicitor General 'described the houses of the tenantry as such as the lower animals in England would scarcely, and as a matter of fact did not, endure'.[26]

Even the Duke of Wellington denounced absentee landlordism. In 1831, Lord Stanley reported 'a crisis of awful distress in Mayo' resulting in a subscription being called from landlords, which raised £60 between two of them, when their total annual rental income was £10,400.[27]

A succession of Government committees reported on the parlous state of Irish agriculture. In 1819, a lack of employment was blamed on a shortage of capital, caused by landlord absenteeism and the consumption of tenants' capital on farm improvements. In 1823, rack-renting was denounced. In 1829, a bill was tabled to promote bog drainage and wasteland reclamation. In 1830, a Select Committee recorded:

> The situation of the ejected tenantry, or those, who are obliged to give up their small holdings, in order to promote the consolidation of farms, is necessarily most deplorable. ... They have increased the stock of labour, they have rendered the habitations of those who have received them more crowded, they have given occasion to the dissemination of disease, they have been obliged to resort to theft and all manner of vice and iniquity to procure subsistence; but what is perhaps the most painful of all, a vast number of them have perished of want.[28]

Ejection of tenants caused inevitable unrest. Although this was blamed on poor relationships with their landlords, a principal cause of the difficulty was the need for plots to be shared between expanding family groups. Measures to relieve the smaller tenants' position came to nothing.

> Unprotected by the law from robbery, and face to face with starvation, the tenants formed secret and murderous organisations, and assassination and eviction accompanied each other in almost arithmetical proportion'.[29]

It was unrest which attracted the British Government's attention, not its cause. As early as 1800, immediately after the Union, Parliament had passed a Coercion Act, empowering military tribunals to try those accused of involvement in violence. In 1812, Peel became Chief Secretary in Dublin, 'an office [according to Cates Dictionary of General Biography], which he held with much advantage to the country till 1818'. Yet T. P. O'Connor has cynically seen the 'advantage' as 'the preparation of the famine'.[30]

Peel was probably correct in believing that the only way to bring unrest under control was to reduce the agricultural tenantry, but his methods were heavy-handed and inhumane.[31]

> He formed a constabulary, the 'Peelers' and abolished trial by jury. He established martial law, under which 'no act shall be questioned in a court of law'.[32] In 1817, he permitted landlords to hold their own tribunals, after forming themselves into bodies of 'justices' accompanied by a Sergeant-at-Arms or a Queen's Counsel. These could impose sentences of up to one year's imprisonment or seven year's transportation with no right of appeal. To reduce agitation, political meetings for 'seditious purposes' were suppressed. In most years from 1802 to 1834, Habeas Corpus (the right to trial) was suspended, and, although there were regular acts relating to coercion, eviction, insurrection and importation of arms, eight attempts to gain approval for relief bills were dropped.[33]

The Poor Law Inquiry of 1835 reported 2,235,000 people out of work and in distress for thirty weeks in a year.[34] There were calls for differences between landlord and tenant to be settled on 'rational and useful principles' as 'no language could describe the poverty'.[35] It was held that 'Irish property must support Irish poverty'. After the enactment of the Poor Laws in 1837, a rate was imposed on landlords to fund a system of work houses. This obliged landlords to make a contribution:

for each tenant paying less than four pounds annually in rent. Landlords with large numbers of small tenancies faced crippling bills. They immediately evicted smaller tenants and amalgamated plots to lift them above the four-pound rental threshold. Tenants were given small sums to induce them to leave and were 'cheated into believing the workhouse would take them in'.[36]

The Poor Relief (Ireland) Act of 1838 set up a Poor Law Commission to establish workhouses administered by boards of guardians. 'With an estimated 500,000 evictions, the workhouses were overwhelmed.'[37]

'Although soup kitchens were opened, the laws forbade anyone with as much as one quarter of an acre from receiving relief.'[38] This had been a Tory amendment, which became an estate clearing mechanism. Impoverished farmers were forced to hand back their tenancies to their landlords to enable their families to be fed. Even in Parliament it was recognised as 'indirectly a death dealing instrument'. About 200,000 tenants returned their meagre holdings, and seven landlords were shot in revenge.

In 1844 (before the Great Potato Famine), Benjamin Disraeli described Ireland as 'a starving population, an absentee aristocracy, and an alien church, and in addition the weakest executive in the world'.[39] 'By 1845, 24 per cent of plots outside co. Londonderry were between one and five acres, with a further 40 per cent between five and fifteen acres.'[40]

In February 1845, William Courtenay, 10th Earl of Devon chaired a commission, which explained 'that the famine was inevitable without land reform; and that its advent could fail to be foreseen only by invincibly ignorant Ministers and Parliaments.'[41] His report continued:

It would be impossible adequately to describe the privations which [the Irish peasantry] habitually and silently endure ... in many districts their only food is the potato, their only beverage water ... their cabins are seldom protected against the weather ... a bed or a blanket is a rare luxury ... and nearly in all, their pig and a manure heap constitute their only property.[42]

It cited the evidence of a well-known engineer, Alexander Nimmo:

> I have seen a great deal of the peasantry, ... I conceive [them] to be in the lowest possible state of existence; their cabins are in the most miserable condition, and their food is potatoes, with water, very often without anything else, frequently without salt, and I have frequently had occasion to meet persons who begged me on their knees, for the love of God, to give them some promise of employment, that from the credit, they might get the means of supporting themselves for a few months until I could employ them.[43]

'In the autumn of 1845, the people had staked their all on the success of the potato crop.'[44] There were reports in Roscommon of people selling 'their only cow to procure seed potatoes, and of persons having sold their beds for the same purpose'.[45] Yet difficulties were 'borne with patient endurance' in the face of 'greater sufferings' than anywhere else in Europe.[46]

> Despite all the forewarning, the arrival in Europe of potato blight *(Phytophthora Infestans)* from America in about 1844 was devastating. It spread rapidly, and there was no known cure. It reached Ireland in September 1845 causing the loss of about 40 per cent of the cultivated acreage, rising to 75 per cent in the following year. A crop could be sound one day and rotten the next. Even potatoes already harvested rotted in their pits (clamps). By 1847, there was such a shortage of seed potatoes that few could be planted.[47]
>
> It was only in co. Londonderry that blight did not cause insuperable problems. A principal reason was that local farmers were still growing flax. Quite apart from the linen industry bringing in some much-needed income,

flax required a rotation of crops. Thus, unlike in the rest of Ireland, potato planting was rotated and not placed continuously in the same soil. This greatly reduced the blight's effect.

Co. Londonderry received a huge influx of destitute poor, who arrived:

> from their miserable smallholdings in County Donegal, [and] had to be supported, housed and given food, all of which strained the resources of the county and its inhabitants.[48]

Disease was as much of a problem as starvation, with dysentery and scurvy being the principal outcomes, but problems were exacerbated by cholera and smallpox. Starvation even caused blindness. With hospitals and workhouses rapidly becoming over-filled, 'road fever' spread among those struggling to find medical help.

> Before accommodation for patients approached anything like the necessity of the time, most mournful and piteous scenes were presented in the vicinity of fever hospitals and workhouses in Dublin, Cork, Waterford, Galway and other large towns. There, day after day, numbers of people, wasted by famine and consumed by fever, could be seen lying on the footpaths and roads waiting for the chance of admission; and when they were fortunate enough to be received, their places were soon filled by other victims of suffering and disease.[49]

'Those who were not admitted – and they were, of course, the great majority – having no homes to return to, lay down and died.'[50] There was not space in hospitals and workhouses for 'a tithe of the applicants' and overcrowding made it 'impossible to separate the sick and the healthy', so that 'the epidemic was spread and intensified, instead of being alleviated and diminished'.[51] Prisons were now regarded as a refuge, and became full to overflowing, with petty crimes being committed to gain entry, and it became 'good fortune' to be committed to transportation. 'Botany Bay was transformed in the peasant imagination from the Inferno of the hopeless to the Paradise of sufficient food and a great future.'[52] Yet disease was such that few survived even a week in prison, with the inmates generally 'in a state of nudity, filth and starvation' while awaiting transportation.[53] It is estimated that about 1,600,000 people, one in four of the Irish population, suffered from fever. Deaths from fever alone totalled more than 250,000 between 1841 and 1851 and included medical staff. The volume of deaths led to the development of a hinged coffin, used extensively in Cork. This:

> was made with a movable bottom; the body was placed in it, the bottom unhinged, the body thrown into the grave, and then the coffin was sent back to the workhouse to receive another body.[54]

At Skibbereen, two large pits provided coffin-less graves for hundreds of bodies.

Although Irish Members of Parliament and commentators called for food exports to be banned, they were powerless without British Government support. 'O'Connell, speaking at the Dublin Corporation, warned of wholesale starvation and complained at the export of wheat and oats, both of which crops were abundant.'[55] He also asked for the treatment of tenant improvements adopted in Ulster to be extended throughout Ireland. He argued that, if the Act of Union were repealed, a Government in Dublin would be better able to deal with the crisis. He could see that 'if a [tenant] worked harder he was more likely to enrich his landlord than himself'.[56] He was a lone voice calling for suspension of the Corn Laws to allow imports from other countries, but no remedial steps were taken. 'The Irish land system [approved by Parliament] necessitated the export of food from a starving nation.'[57]

> Peel, now Tory Prime Minister, was preoccupied with a serious political struggle to retain office. He seemed to believe that initial reports of hardship in Ireland were exaggerated. When, at last, he realised the danger, he was

impotent to provide assistance. Although he proposed the opening of Irish ports to free trade, his colleagues would not agree. To do so would conflict with the Corn Laws, which, since 1815, had provided protection for the price of English grain by setting a duty on imports.[58]

It was Disraeli who led concerted opposition to repeal of the Corn Laws on behalf of the landed classes. With most members of parliament being landowners, they benefitted from this protection for British produce provided by law.[59] Protectionists and landlords united to dismiss as 'unreal and exaggerated' the reports of the distress caused by the famine.[60]

On 3 November 1845, the *Evening Mail* reported: 'The potato crop of this year far exceeded an average one.' Some days later it stated: 'The apprehensions of a famine are unfounded, and are merely made the pretence for withholding the payment of rent.' And yet again: 'There was a sufficiency and abundance of sound potatoes in the country for the wants of the people.'[61] Lord George Bentinck claimed: 'The potato famine was a gross delusion – a more gross delusion had never been practised upon any country by any Government.'[62, 63]

'Peel made the potato famine a major plank in his call to repeal the Corn Laws.'[64]

> With his personal fortune based on mill owning, [he] had support from other factory owners, who complained that they kept bread prices artificially high. With bread forming the British workers' staple food, factory owners had to offer higher wages to attract employees, thus making their products less competitive.[65]

He also:

> had parliamentary backing from O'Connell and the Whigs led by Russell. Such was the realisation of the famine's horrendous impact that, in early 1846, Peel carried the

repeal through Parliament, despite opposition from more
than two-thirds of his Tory [party members].[66]

'Although duties on imported corn were now removed, Ireland was
on its knees.'[67] 'Despite worrying that it would act as a disincentive
to local relief efforts, Peel purchased £100,000 worth of maize from
America.'[68] On its arrival in Ireland in November 1845, it needed to be
milled, but there was no local equipment able to undertake the double
milling process required. Without a lot of cooking, it was indigestible,
causing bowel complaints. With its yellow colour, it was soon known
as 'Peel's brimstone'.[69]

Peel was only too aware that repeal of the Corn Laws would not
of itself resolve Ireland's problems. He recognised that the farming
population had grown to a level which was unsustainable. Small
farmers were totally reliant on the potato for food, and there was no
urban employment for surplus agricultural workers.[70]

The Highlands of Scotland faced a similar problem, causing
landlords to clear out their tenants and to utilise poorer land for grazing
sheep. The Highland clearances in Scotland resulted in the wholesale
emigration of its Gaelic-speaking peasantry to America, Canada and
Australasia. Peel saw emigration as Ireland's best solution, but with no
landlords in occupation, he had no mechanism to bring it into effect.

Despite the famine, landlords continued to dispossess their tenants.
At Ballinglass one landlord turned out 270 people, taking the roofs off
their sixty homes. Without a properly formulated emigration plan, the
dispossessed had nowhere to go. Ousted tenants hid in ditches but
were again driven out. The roads were full of the homeless, starving
and dying. In the face of horrendous provocation, several landlords
were murdered. Although those evicted were encouraged to turn to
the workhouses, these had become the objects of 'dread and loathing'
having become a refuge for 'the rustic victims of vice and the outcasts
of the towns'. Entrance to the workhouse meant 'social ruin' and
'moral degradation'; people preferred death than to enter 'those hated
walls'. When they were left with no choice, the workhouses were full.
At Westport, 3,000 people needing relief arrived in a single day, but

its workhouse could accommodate only 1,000 and was already full beyond capacity.

With unrest growing, Peel tabled a new Coercion bill to allow the arrest without trial of people causing disturbance. If passed, it would have empowered the Lord Lieutenant to proclaim a curfew. 'No person could with safety visit a public house, or a tea or coffee shop, or the house of a friend'.[71] The penalty was transportation. Although the bill gave the Lord Lieutenant authority to tax any proclaimed district to pay for additional police and magistrates to maintain order, the landlords were to be exempted, while even the poorest tenants were subject to it. Peel might have expected protectionist support for his bill, but, after the abolition of the Corn Laws, protectionists wanted him out of office. They combined with the Whigs and O'Connell to oppose it. In June 1846, when his bill failed, Peel resigned.[72]

'The Tory party was split; the Peelite faction, including Gladstone, joined the Whigs to form a new Government under Russell, the Whig leader.'[73] Russell had been one of the strongest critics of the Coercion bill as he wanted to put in place remedial measures to the landlord and tenant legislation.[74] He had no doubt of the land's fertility, which 'had been the theme of admiration with writers and travellers of all nations'.[75] He proposed a grant for the reclamation of wastelands and a scheme for tenant rights. He commented:

> If you wish to maintain the Union ... [as] a source of increased strength to the United Empire, beware lest you in any way weaken the link which connects the two countries. Do not let the people of Ireland believe that you have no sympathy with their afflictions, no care for their wrongs, that you are intent only upon other measures [the Coercion bill] in which they have no interest.[76]

Earl Grey was another eminent Whig who supported Russell in opposing Peel's Coercion bill, claiming that 'the state of the law and the habits of the people, *in respect to the occupation of the land,* are almost at the roots of the disorder'. He later admitted: 'Ireland would never have got into its present state if the landlords, as a body, had done their duty to the population under them …'[77]

Although Russell seemed to have his heart in the right place and did not believe that a lack of strength or industry of the Irish was at fault, he proved completely two-faced. In 1848, he pronounced:

> While I admit that, with respect to the franchise and other subjects, the people of Ireland have just grounds of complaint, I, nevertheless, totally deny that their grievances are any sufficient reason why they should not make very good progress in wealth and prosperity, if, using the intelligence which they possess to a remarkable degree, they should fix their minds on the advantages which they might enjoy rather than upon the evils which they suppose themselves to suffer under.[78]

He was completely unable to cope with the disaster as it unfolded.

During his three-month interregnum, it became clear that the 1846 Irish potato crop would again fail. What had been great hardship during the winter of 1845 had become a catastrophe. Hoarding of foodstuffs forced up prices. Famine advanced 'with giant strides'.[79] '[The] Government should have placed an embargo on Irish food exports to Britain (a relief measure imposed, despite the lobbying of merchants, after the earlier crop failure in 1782 – 83). This would have reduced prices in Ireland, although tenant farmers had no money with which to buy anything.'[80]

Ireland remained a net exporter of food throughout the famine, and livestock exports actually increased [with 933,000 animals being sent abroad in 1846]. Cattle and sheep were escorted to the ports under armed guard from even the most famine-stricken areas.[81] It is estimated that the value of cattle and crops exported significantly exceeded the cost of providing soup kitchens.[82] In 1845, there was an abundant wheat harvest; 779,000 quarters of wheat and wheat flour were exported to Britain, compared to an average of 318,000 quarters over the previous four years. Although exports fell in 1846 and thereafter, they still accounted for a significant proportion of the crop. Mitchel called it 'an artificial famine – starvation in the midst of food'.[83]

> Although grain sent to Britain was eventually returned, unscrupulous Irish merchants retained it on arrival, hoping for yet higher returns. They refused to release it even when offered generous prices, until it eventually rotted in store.[84]

At least the speculators were ruined in the process. Maize from America:

> bought for £9 or £10 per ton was selling for £17 5s. in Cork; was not to be had for any price in Limerick, but in the shape of meal was fetching from £18 10s. to £19 a ton.[85]

Russell's inept efforts proved counter-productive:

> He was wedded to the concept of free trade, which had led to his support for the abolition of the Corn Laws. He was determined not to restrict the regular operation of merchants by supplementing grain imports. After the Achill potato crop failed, a deputation went to Sir R. Routh, head of its Commissary Department, with money to purchase food from Government stores. They were turned away on arrival as 'nothing was more essential to the welfare of the country than strict adherence to free trade'.[86]

'People died with money in their hands.'[87]

Relief organisation proved shambolic. No provision was made to care for the sick and dying. 'Charities did not know what was required. Some sent books, believing that they would be helpful.' Although Peel's Government had employed 97,900 relief workers to handle distribution, Russell dismissed them, adding a 'vast army' to the unemployed.[88] The Poor Employment Ireland Act of 1846 encouraged public works to provide employment, financed out of Treasury loans.

Peel had allocated £100,000 to employ the destitute, expecting them to become involved in extending railways and roads or in bog clearance. Russell's Government called on Sir Charles Trevelyan to supervise projects, but he limited amounts advanced, believing that 'the judgement of God [had] sent the calamity to teach the Irish a lesson'. Outside co. Londonderry, proposals to spend the money on useful works 'met with flat refusal, and a lecture on political economy'.[89] Russell was determined [not to] interfere with private enterprise, and devoted the money exclusively to 'unproductive works'; building new monuments, roads to nowhere, digging holes and then filling them up again. 'Miles of grass grown earthworks throughout the country now make their course and commemorate for posterity one of the gigantic blunders of the famine time.'[90, 91]

Without generating income, costs could not be defrayed. Yet:

> there were railways demanding extension; millions of acres of wasteland demanding reclamation; miles of marsh waiting to be drained – all such work was forbidden.[92]

Government projects stopped people from farming. The prospect of paid work was 'more enticing than the uncertainty of a remote and fickle harvest', so that fields were left deserted and nothing was grown.[93]

With the famine worsening, people became distraught.

The few remaining dogs ceased to bark. Merriment disappeared, and children looked like old men and women, 'with parents willingly dying the slow death of starvation to save a small store of food' for them. By the end of August 1846, calamity was universal. People 'grasped on everything that promised sustenance; they plucked turnips from the fields; many were glad to live for weeks on a single meal of cabbage a day'.[94] 'In some cases people feasted on the dead bodies of horses and asses and dogs',[95] 'There is at least one horrible story of a mother eating the limbs of her dead child'.[96] 'Seaweed was greedily devoured, so also were diseased cattle'.[97] 'Corpses lay strewn by the side of once frequented roads'.[98] The dead and dying lay together in their cabins.

There were no funerals, and bodies lay for days unburied, allowing ravenous dogs to make a meal of the corpses. When disease broke out, the Irish Public Health Act of 1846 authorised the Lord Lieutenant to appoint a Central Board of Health. This had powers to direct Poor Law Guardians to provide fever hospitals, dispensaries, medicines and food.[99, 100]

Eventually Russell was forced to resort to coercion. In 1846, he tabled a bill, 'which in all essentials was the Coercion Bill of Sir Robert Peel'.[101] Despite his earlier humanitarian approach, it was not accompanied by measures to provide relief or to stop the removal of tenants from their lands. The police were urged into 'unusual activity' and large bodies of the military were pressed into service. They:

> seized the produce of the fields, carrying them to Dublin for sale – acted in every respect as the collectors of the rent of the landlord, and thus shared with the landlord the honour of starving the tenants.[102]

In October 1846, Parliament would no longer tolerate Russell's inconsistency. Peel was returned to office, although Russell remained in Government. Valuable time had been lost, and, even now, efforts to end the famine proved totally inadequate.[103] The Labour-Rate (Ireland) Act of February 1847 turned famine relief into an orgy of red tape, with every action needing approval. 'Ten thousand officials, often corruptly appointed, were involved in 'the maddening preliminaries of vexatious and imbecile official delays'.[104] All this stifled independent initiative.

> Over the whole Island, for the next few months, was a scene of confused and wasteful attempts at relief ... striving to understand the voluminous directions, schedules, and specifications, under which alone [donors] could vote their own money to relieve the poor at their own doors.[105]

When Government projects were at last organised, the starving people were 'too wasted and emaciated to work and those that did fainted away or died on the roadside'.[106] 'O'Connell complained with justification that, if the Act of Union were repealed, a Dublin Government would be better able to deal with the crisis.'[107]

More action was needed. In February 1847, at Russell's instigation, a Temporary Relief Act, better known as the 'Soup Kitchen Act' was also passed. Committees were set up to list those deserving of relief. 'Food was to be given – at reasonable prices to some, gratuitously to the absolutely destitute.'[108] Numbers involved in the relief effort rose from 20,000 in October 1846 to 734,000 in March 1847. Meanwhile, other support was reduced, regardless of local circumstance, in the expectation that soup kitchens would solve the problems. Yet, during the time they took to put in place, famine recurred. When at last they began operating, the famine came temporarily to an end. 'Fever grew less intense in the hospitals; and the fields were fairly well tilled.'[109]

With the potato crop failing in 1848 and 1849, starvation and plague broke out again. 'In 1848, 2,043,505 persons received poor-law relief – 610,463 being in the workhouse, and 1,433,042 receiving outdoor relief.'[110] Fever and dysentery again became prevalent in institutions and in parts of the west coast 'as to almost entirely depopulate them'.[111] Although blight was less severe in 1848, more than 200,000 died, half from 'famine-produced diseases'; a further 178,000 emigrated.[112] With a poorer crop in 1849, there were more than 240,000 deaths, of which 123,000 were from disease. Blight continued 'with varying virulence until 1851'.[113] By then, taxes had been imposed to pay for the relief effort. The census of 1861 showed that during the previous ten years, the Irish population had fallen by 11.5 per cent to 5,798,967. It is estimated that it fell by between 20 and 25 per cent directly as a result of famine.

Outbreaks of revolt led to the Treason Felony Act, for which the penalty was transportation. Habeas Corpus was suspended by an almost unanimous vote in the House of Commons. With Mitchel having written a series of critical articles in the *United Irishman*, Russell brought him to trial for sedition, promising to the House of Commons that both the trial and the composition of the jury would be fair. The jury contained no Catholics and was packed with Orangemen; Mitchel was convicted and sentenced to fourteen years' transportation. 'It was the British Parliament and the British Ministers that worked the wholesale slaughter of Irishmen and produced the murderous hatred of so many of the Irish race for England.'[114] O'Connell was right: repeal of the Union would have done much to alleviate the suffering and mitigate discord between Britain and Ireland. It was not just a problem of Government. Few trainee Irish barristers could afford to join one of the Inns of Court in London, as the law required.

In November 1845, Peel had warned his Cabinet that Irish agitation would disincline the charitable from making 'any great exertions for Irish relief'.[115] This proved wrong. Although:

> the Irish were too proud to ask for help and too bitter to seek it from Britain. British fund raisers collected massive sums and arranged its distribution, resulting in probably unfair criticism that 'it took the profit of it'. Queen Victoria contributed £2,000 and signed a letter which raised a further £172,000. Irish soldiers and civil servants in India sent £14,000; The British Relief Association raised £263,000.[116]

Money came from as far afield as Turkey and from American Indians. Yet bureaucracy slowed the release of food supplies, so that they 'arrived too late to prevent the deaths of about a million people'.[117] Although dispensaries were re-established on a wide scale, just as many died from disease as from starvation.

Without doubt, the Irish rural population needed to be reduced. Far too many peasant farmers lived below subsistence level. Yet landlords were immune to tenants' suffering. 'It was eviction rather than famine and fever, which was accountable for the horrible conditions of the people.'[118]

> A series of cold and wet seasons in 1860, 1861 and 1862, followed by severe drought in 1863 and 1864 extended the 'disastrous agricultural depression', leading to the need for further remedial legislation.[119]

Landlords 'tumbled' cabins on small holdings, even where tenants were up to date with rental payments, leaving them without shelter. Those taken into the overcrowded cabins of their neighbours scattered 'disease and dismay in all directions'.[120] 'Ireland was once more in a state of chronic disorder and economic disaster.'[121]

At last, the British Government was forced into action. The Eviction (Ireland) Act of 1848 required landlords to provide forty-eight hours' notice of impending eviction to the Poor Law Guardians, to give them time to provide food and shelter for those evicted. Eviction in the two hours before sunrise and sunset or on Christmas Day or Good Friday was forbidden. Demolishing or unroofing cabins was prohibited. Yet landlords' agents circumvented these requirements. They often arrested tenants, but would discharge them if they agreed to their dwellings being thrown down and handed over. This totally defeated Government objectives. T. P. O'Connor has concluded:

> I have proved the Irish landlords to have used their powers
> – amid a national calamity of almost unprecedented extent –
> with a cruelty more atrocious than that of any other class of
> men in the modern history of civilised countries.[122]

It was the Irish peasantry, not their landlords, who were seen in Britain to have caused the problem. On 22 February 1847, *The Times* wrote:

> Remove Irishmen to the banks of the Ganges or the Indus,
> to Delhi, Benares, or Trincomalee, and they would be far
> more in their element there than in a country to which *an*
> *inexorable fate has confined them.*[123]

The 'Government's main objective was to stop riot and assassination'.[124] 'Towns with more than 1,500 residents were required to elect commissioners for their supervision.'[125] *The Nation* reported: 'The only notice vouchsafed to this country is a hint that more gaols, more transportations and more gibbets might be useful to us.'[126] George William Hyde, 4th Earl of Clarendon, the new Lord Lieutenant, called for more troops. At least he understood the hardship, reporting:

It is quite true that Landlords in England would not like to be shot like hares and partridges ... but neither does any landlord in England turn out fifty persons at once and burn their houses over their heads, giving them no provision for the future.[127]

Peel also understood the problem. He was far more energetic in denouncing the atrocities than Russell had been. He reported:

It would appear from the evidence recorded that the forcible ejectments were illegal, that previous notices had not been served, and that ejectments were perpetrated under circumstances of great cruelty. The time chosen for the greater part nightfall on the eve of the New Year. The occupiers were forced out of their houses with their helpless children and were left exposed to the cold on a bleak western shore in a stormy winter's night; that some of the children were sick; that their parents implored that they might not be exposed, and their houses left till morning; that their prayers for mercy were in vain, and that many of them have since died.[128]

With the Government failing to take action, it was not let off lightly by the Press. On 13 February 1847, *The Illustrated London News* reported: 'There was no laws it would not pass at [Irish Landlords'] request and no abuse it would not defend for them.' On 24 March, *The Times* claimed that the Government had caused 'a mass poverty, disaffection and degradation without parallel in the world. It allowed proprietors to suck the very life-blood of that wretched race'.[129]

At last, The Encumbered Estates Act of 1848 authorised the sale of estates of bankrupt landlords, both Irish and British. This drove many ancient families from their properties. Yet, at the height of the famine, they fetched nothing like their true value. The buyers were generally local shopkeepers seeking to better themselves, who simply took the opportunity to increase rents, and to evict tenants who failed to pay, regardless of any improvements made. Irish landlords very often proved the worst offenders in the abuses occurring. To mitigate this problem, a scheme was developed for a new plantation of English and Scottish landlords to replace those dispossessed. The Irish race was not considered fit for Ireland.[130]

> There can be no doubt that the British objective had been to reduce the Irish peasant population, and famine conveniently achieved this for them.
>
> Although potato crops failed all over Europe, it was only in Ireland that this led to famine. If the Government had taken prompt action to prevent Irish exports and to provide humane assistance, hardship could have been averted.[131]

Yet it did very little. It set up an Irish Committee, made up of six peers and twelve commoners, to examine the wholesale emigration of the Irish peasantry from Ireland. The Committee formulated a plan to transfer 1,500,000 to Canada at a cost of £9,000,000 levied out of income tax. Paupers in work houses were granted assistance to emigrate. Husbands, who went first, sent back money to enable other members of the family to join them. A million left for a new life abroad. 'One-fifth of those journeying to Canada in "coffin ships" died in transit', and others died on arrival.[132]

> Crowded and filthy, carrying double the legal number of passengers, who were ill-fed and imperfectly clothed, and having no doctor on board, the holds were like the Black Hole of Calcutta and deaths in myriads.[133]

'By 1850, about 25 per cent of the populations of New York, Boston, Philadelphia, Baltimore and the principal cities of Eastern Canada were Irish.'[134] 'In the United States, the 1860 census showed that its Irish-born population amounted to 1,611,304, about forty per cent of its foreign-born total. Toronto, then a township of 20,000 people, was engulfed by 38,000 Irish famine victims.'[135] Many new arrivals were 'aged people unfit for labour'.[136] The Irish:

population fell from 8 million in 1845 to 4.4 million in 1911. During the 18th Century, emigrants had been mainly Protestant (resulting in many presidents of the United States being of Ulster stock). While Protestants continued to move to Canada, Catholics now went in their thousands to the United States and the growing cities of Britain, particularly London, Liverpool, Manchester and Glasgow.[137]

They brought their fever with them, accounting for 750 of the 1,150 patients in the Glasgow fever hospital. Many of those coming to Britain were employed in the back-breaking work of building the railways and as 'navvies' working on the navigation canal systems. 'It was only later in the nineteenth century that emigration from Ireland to Australia and New Zealand began to develop.'[138]

Ireland was changed for ever, almost causing the loss of the Gaelic language, and happiness was destroyed.

> Their ancient sports and pastimes everywhere disappeared, and in many parts of Ireland have never returned. The outdoor games, the hurling-match, and the village dance are seen no more.[139]

All stores containing sustenance now needed padlocks to prevent pilferage:

> This state of things struck a fatal blow at some of the most beautiful traits of Irish life. It destroyed the simple confidence that bolted no door; it banished forever a custom which throughout the island was of almost universal obligation – the housing for the night, with cheerful welcome, of any poor wayfarer who claimed hospitality. Fear of 'the fever', even where no apprehension of robbery was entertained, closed every door, and the custom once killed off has never revived.[140]

'The temperance reformation, the political training of a generation, the self-respect, the purity and generosity which distinguished Irish peasants, were sorely wasted.'[141] Begging among the children and the maimed now became commonplace.

1846 proved a watershed for Ireland's agricultural economy. The countryside lost large numbers to industry, to England, to Scotland, and to America. With larger plot sizes, pasture replaced tillage as the most usual mode of farming. In 1858, a new Act facilitated the sale and transfer of land.[142] It took until 1860 for:

> The Society for Improving the Condition of the Labouring Classes to encourage relief work and to call for better quality housing. This resulted in the Land Improvement Act of 1860, which authorised loans to build [new rural dwellings].[143]

Within a further ten years, land reforms were gradually resulting in the break-up of large estates.

Chapter 26

Continuing evictions despite calls for tenant rights 1850 – 1870

The eviction of the peasantry from their tenancies brought renewed calls for tenant rights. Presbyterians again joined Catholics to agitate for reform. Although Ulster farmers enjoyed a measure of protection with their right to compensation for improvements they had made, they were not protected from rack-renting. Duffy, the editor of *The Nation,* stood as a Member of Parliament on a Tenant Rights ticket. A Tenant Rights Convention on 6 August 1850 at the City Assembly House in Dublin had called for the three Fs, fixity of tenure, free sale and fair rents for tenants. It also asked that rental arrears arising during the famine 'should be subjected to inspection by a valuator', with agreed arrears to be paid in instalments.[1] This caused an anti-Catholic clamour in Britain. It was unfortunate that the request arose while the Pope was seeking to call Catholic Bishops in Britain and Ireland by the name of the see for which they were the incumbents, so that, for example, Cardinal Wiseman would be named Archbishop of Westminster. This 'innocent step called forth a tempest of indignation among' fanatical Protestants.[2] Russell denounced it as 'Papal aggression'. He tabled an Ecclesiastical Titles bill, enacted in 1851, to prevent the Pope's request. The Irish were up in arms, fearing that Russell would seek to renew the Penal Code.

Although Duffy tried to organise Tenant Rights activists in Parliament, he was unable to link with either the Tories or Whigs, both of whom retained strong protectionist lobbies favouring landlords. The land question was now at the heart of the debate for repeal of the Union. Although *The Nation* continued its campaigning, Tenant

Rights activists lacked representation in Government. With most Irish members benefiting from bribes as place seekers from either Tories or Whigs, they were at their beck and call, and firmly upheld the Union and landlords' rights. It was unfortunate that two undesirable Irish place seekers, John Sadleir and William Keogh, were seeking to defray the cost of bribing their way into parliament on Tenant Rights tickets by gaining Government preferment. It was Keogh who had persuaded Tenant Rights activists to stand aloof from Government offers, so as not to queer his pitch. This undermined the activists' potential influence.

Sadleir was the unscrupulous owner of the Tipperary Bank, while Keogh was a gambler with rudimentary legal training, but with oratory skills able to whip up support for any cause. By forming a group known as the Catholic Association (and later the Catholic Defence Association), Sadleir and Keogh ingratiated themselves with Irish Catholic clergy and Irish agitators by speaking out strongly in favour of tenant rights and the repeal of the Ecclesiastical Titles Act. They were mistrusted by Duffy, who recognised that their motives were solely designed to gain office.

Sadleir and Keogh were just two examples of Irish candidates who used Parliament for the purpose of personal advancement, finding it the only way to achieve professional promotion.[3] By this means, Irish barristers, regardless of legal competence, could be appointed as judges. T. P. O'Connor expressed it this way:

> The difference between the judicial benches of the two countries may be summed up as this: that in England the bench consists of the best of men, and in Ireland it is largely recruited from the worst.[4]

The mechanism for appointing Irish judges since the Union had been entirely political. Although Gladstone called for their appointment by the Irish executive, this was an anathema to Palmerston and his Liberal Government, who needed British control of the Irish judiciary as a means of retaining landlords' rights.

By 1852, Parliament was split between the Whigs under Russell, the Protectionist Conservatives under Disraeli, and Peelites under George Hamilton-Gordon, 4th Earl of Aberdeen. When Disraeli's budget was rejected in December 1852, Aberdeen invited the Catholic Defence Association to join him in forming a Government. Sadleir became Lord of the Irish Treasury and Keogh was made Irish Solicitor-General (a role for which he was completely unqualified). Other Catholic Defence Association members also gaining office included Edmund O'Flaherty, who became the Commissioner for Income Tax. Tenant Rights activists remained out in the cold, leaving the cause of the Irish farming community unrepresented. To take office, Sadleir and Keogh needed to be re-elected to Parliament. When Tenant Rights members opposed them, Sadleir was defeated by six votes, but soon bribed his way into re-election for Sligo. Keogh also used bribes to regain his seat, dashing the hopes of Tenant Rights reformers.

Despite being hopelessly in debt, Keogh even persuaded a committee of the House of Commons that he had the requisite income of £300 per annum to sit as a member. In a vitriolic attack, *The Nation* described him as 'the greatest political scamp of his country, and the type *par excellence* of Irish demagogue rascality'.[5] Although he faced criticism in Parliament, he avoided the worst of it by lying.

In 1855, when Aberdeen was replaced as Prime Minister by Palmerston, Keogh became Irish Attorney-General. By then, O'Flaherty had fled from London leaving unpaid bills of £15,000. When Sadleir was caught trying to raise loans on fraudulent securities, he committed suicide by taking prussic acid on Hampstead Heath. His Tipperary Bank was left with a shortfall of £1,250,000, causing losses for all its mainly tenant farmer depositors. Yet Keogh nimbly sidestepped his colleagues' difficulties. When rumours arose that he was to become a judge on the Bench, *The Nation* reported:

> Mr William Keogh a judge! With life and death on his hands; with the peace, and honour, and property of the community hanging on the breath of his lips; with the liberties and the safeguards of society under his direct control. Mr. William

> Keogh, with the antecedents of his unprincipled political career, his mediocre professional character, his false pledges, his disreputable associates; this gentleman a judge!

Despite this, in April 1856, when a vacancy appeared, Keogh was appointed. It was he who would be responsible for the sentencing of many of the Fenian rebels.

From 1855 to 1865, a large body of Irish place seekers gave the Whigs, led by Henry George Temple, 3rd Viscount Palmerston, unassailable power. Proposals to reform Irish land tenure were contemptuously rejected. 'Lord Palmerston could not tolerate such an interference with the rights of property.'[6] Between 1856 and 1858, several new attempts to extend the Ulster custom of tenant compensation across the rest of Ireland were defeated, 'mainly through the influence of Lord Palmerston'.[7] Even calls for tenants to receive compensation for improvements expressly approved by his landlord were rejected. This allowed landlords to foreclose and to re-let with the benefit of improvements already made. Irish farmers also tried to prevent rack-renting, by calling for rents to be set by the Courts. Nevertheless, Archbishop Whately wrote:

> If you were to make a law for lowering rents, so that the land should still remain the property of those to whom it now belongs, but that they should not be allowed to receive more than so much an acre for it, the only effect would be that the landlord would no longer let his land to the farmer, but would take it into his own hands, and employ a bailiff to look after it for him.[8]

This, of course, would only have applied where the bailiff could generate sufficient income to cover the lost rental income.

Palmerston exclaimed: 'Tenant right is landlord wrong!'[9] Others argued: 'Compulsory compensation for improvements effected against the will of the landlord is not a principle which is consistent with the rights of property.'[10] Yet in England, landlords generally involved themselves in improvements for farm buildings and land reclamation. Furthermore, English leases often extended for sixty years, so tenant improvements could be amortised over a longer period. Yet a Parliament dominated by landowners believed in the landlord's right to do as he pleased with his own land. He could farm it or let it to a tenant. If he wanted it back at a lease's expiry, the tenant faced eviction. This left the landlord unchallenged. He continued to raise rents to fund a lifestyle that was often profligate. Even when he sold, the purchaser carried on as before.

Tenants faced 'office rules', under which grasping landlords imposed fines for minor misdemeanours to add a further source of income.[11] Lucan fined a tenant 14s. 8d. for receiving his daughter into his house to be with his wife while he was in England. John, 3rd Lord Plunket, evicted Catholic tenants for refusing to send their children to church mission schools designed to seek their conversion to Protestantism. Some families were bribed with food if their children attended, making them known derogatorily as 'Soupers'. Yet, when food shortages became less pressing, they reverted to their Catholic faith. Landlords also sought to replace Catholics with Protestant tenants. Henry Petty-Fitzmaurice, 4th Marquis of Lansdowne, regulated tenant marriages. William Sydney Clements, 3rd Earl of Leitrim, evicted the widowed mother of the Rev. Mr Lavelle, a well-known Catholic priest, because she had taken in her daughter and son-in-law for companionship. Leitrim threatened a family with eviction and consequent starvation in an attempt to force one of their daughters to become his mistress.[12] After taking advantage of her, she was transported to America, only to be replaced by another estate girl on a similar basis. These abuses led to a wholesale clearance of Catholics. George John Browne, 3rd Marquess of Sligo, moved 2,000 families out of a two hundred square mile area (128,000 acres), so that it could be let to a single tenant. Lucan removed all his tenants at Aughadrina, even though most of them were up-to-date with rents and had been occupying plots of between five and forty acres. Dispossessed tenants had nowhere to go and lacked the resources to travel to America; many died on the roadside. With much land reverting to pasture, cabins were demolished or unroofed, leaving rural areas deserted. Towns lost their rural market, which had provided the principal source of their commerce, and faced an influx of beggars. Prosperous towns soon became struggling villages, extending poverty for many years.[13]

There is no doubt that landlords considered Irish tenants to be inefficient. A good example is a report on the 3rd Duke of Leinster's estate in Kildare. During the famine most of his tenants 'threw up their holdings' amounting to 2,000 acres in all. His former Agent, Francis Trench:

> cleared the land by an extensive emigration and advertised widely in the Scotch papers for tenants. In time, the estate was re-let. The rental, which had been £35,000 a year, was, by improved management and by the falling in of very old leases, raised to £45,000; and the tenants (especially the Scotch) are doing well.[14]

T. P. O'Connor has explained the reason for this uplift, using the example of a 70,000 acre estate at Farney in co. Monaghan. This had originally been seized from the M'Mahon for granting to the Earl of Essex. He let it to Evor M'Mahon for £250 per annum. In 1633, there were thirty-eight tenants and some under-tenants, but the total must have been small. As the population grew, the land became more valuable. In 1729, it was producing £2,000 per annum and in 1769, it was valued at £8,000 per annum divided between two sisters. By 1843 there were 8,000 tenants and a total population of 44,107. In 1867, the rent had increased to £54,833.

> No doubt … the rise in the price of produce and the value of land had done much to cause this increase. But the main cause, beyond all question, is that the barony had increased enormously and rapidly in population, … [who had] gradually converted, by their labour, the lands of the barony from being a waste unenclosed alder plain, into one of the most cultivated districts in Ireland, well enclosed

arable land, while scarcely an acre of reclaimable land now lies unreclaimed. ... [This was thanks] to the energetic and unrelaxed toil of the tenant farmers who lived upon it, but, who, when they had made the barren plain fruitful, and when there remained no more land to be reclaimed for the landlord's benefit, were felt to be an intolerable burden upon the landlord's hands.[15]

Landlords undoubtedly raised rents on the back of tenant improvements, but population growth left land increasingly scarce. The British Government believed that 'the sooner Ireland becomes a grazing country, with the comparatively thin population that a grazing country requires, the better for all classes'.[16] George Howard, 7th Earl of Carlisle, the Lord Lieutenant, shared this view. During the following eight years, the agent at Farney levelled 2,009 houses, reducing the population to 31,519. He moved out 12,588, mainly to America and Australia, but 'some to the pauper's grave'.

Although Government handling had been deplorable, eviction was condoned by the Irish judiciary. Between 1849 and 1860, 1,551,000 emigrants left Ireland, with a further 867,000 from 1861 to 1870. About 90 per cent of those leaving were aged under thirty-five. With the additional ravages of starvation and plague, the Irish population was reduced by nearly one-half between 1845 and 1885. It was 'the ailing, the weak and the aged', who were left behind. Even the British press was unsympathetic. An Irish priest 'lamenting the wrongs of Ireland' was described in the *Daily Telegraph* as 'a surpliced ruffian'. The *Saturday Review* described emigrants as 'the demons of assassination and murder'.[17]

Emigration was a tragedy for the Irish populace. 'Aged parents never more knew a bright or happy hour.' 'Family ties were peculiarly close and strong.'[18] Those departing remained attached to their homeland; vast sums 'were sent over out of hard-earned wages by the Irish in America to the Irish at home'.[19] 'It is one of the saddest and most dreadful stories of all history,' but they were determined that emigration would not be the end of their struggle.[20]

Chapter 27

The Fenian movement 1848 – 1879

Without O'Connell's moderating influence, *The Nation* newspaper gathered round it a group of young men with 'a constant feeling that enough was not being done to save the people'.[1] In 1848, there had been a whimper of an uprising at Ballingarry in co. Tipperary by Young Irelanders led by O'Brien and Meagher, who were becoming progressively more militant. One of those involved was James Stephens, who at the age of twenty-three had become O'Brien's *aide-de-camp*. When the authorities demanded that the locality should hand over their arms, Stephens spoke against this at a public meeting. Although Young Irelanders advocated force to help dispossessed tenants, the peasantry was too starved and demoralised to offer meaningful support, and unrest became confused and disorganised.

When Stephens heard that a party of Dragoons was planning O'Brien's arrest, he erected barricades at Killenaule and manned them with his rifle, supported by thirty Young Irelanders with pikes and a few muskets. When the Dragoons appeared, they did not have a warrant for O'Brien's arrest, so Stephens escorted them on their way through the barricades. At this point, Meagher called a 'council of war' at Ballingarry. He was joined by John O'Mahony, a distinguished Gaelic scholar, and Terence Bellew MacManus, both of whom, in 1843, had supported O'Connell's efforts for repeal of the Union. Although most of them wanted to defer further rebellion until the harvest was in, O'Brien was determined to continue their agitation. When a party of forty-six police tried to arrest them, Stephens again erected a barricade, occupying a house overlooking it with several armed supporters. When the police saw them, they took refuge in an isolated building occupied by a widow and her children, who were taken hostage. In an almost bloodless affray, the rebels failed to oust them.

With unrest petering out, most of the Young Irelander leaders, other than Stephens, were arrested. This gained them cult status. They were brought to trial, but, despite a plea for clemency with 70,000 Irish and 10,000 English signatures, a jury packed with Orangemen made it a 'mockery, a delusion and a snare'.[2] O'Brien, Meagher, MacManus and other fellow ringleaders were sentenced to death for treason, although this was commuted to transportation to Van Diemen's Land (Tasmania). On arriving there, Meagher and MacManus met Mitchel, with whom they escaped to America to rekindle Ireland's republican movement among Irish-Americans. In 1854, O'Brien, who had not escaped with them, was permitted to return to Belgium; two years later he was granted an unconditional pardon to return home. By then the Young Irelanders had ceased to exist, but their former supporters were backing Duffy and his Tenant Rights activists in Parliament.

Although Stephens had been followed, his pursuers were put off the scent by false reports of his death in the *Kilkenny Monitor*. On reaching Paris, he met up with O'Mahony, who had also evaded the authorities, but was now living in great poverty. For several years they undertook teaching and translation work, but were determined to avenge the Ballingarry fiasco. They joined revolutionary societies and planned 'the fight to overthrow British rule in Ireland'. In 1854, O'Mahony left Paris to join Mitchel in New York, where, in 1860, he founded the Emmet Monument Association, a body loosely organised for revolution. It was this that developed into the Fenian Brotherhood (from the *Fianna* – a group of young Gaelic warriors), through which Irish-Americans planned to create an Irish republic.

On MacManus's death in San Francisco, his remains were returned to Ireland for burial. His body was carried across America and shipped to Queenstown in Ireland, where it arrived on 30 October 1861. On 10 November, 50,000 people followed his coffin at his funeral in Dublin, with at least as many lining the streets. The procession paused 'at every spot sacred to the memory of those who had fought and died in the good fight against English tyranny'.[3] At nightfall, the body was deposited in Glasnevin Cemetery. This was a trigger for a rapid growth in Fenian membership.

At the outbreak of the American Civil War in 1861, many Irish republicans joined the 69th Regiment of the New York State Militia. Although O'Mahony was appointed its colonel, he gave up command when the growth in Fenian support required his full attention. The Militia became closely affiliated with the 'Corcoran legion', a group of Irish regiments commanded by a charismatic Irishman, Michael Corcoran. When he was killed in a riding accident in 1863, Meagher became its brigadier-general.

In 1856, Stephens left Paris for London, and, two years later, he returned to Ireland. While still on his travels, members of the Emmet Monument Association had asked him to set up a revolutionary organisation at home. Although he was warned by O'Mahony that the American association was little more than loosely affiliated groups, on arriving in Ireland he set to work. He began what he called a '3,000 mile walk' to meet former Young Irelanders and, on St. Patrick's Day 1858, he formed the Irish Republican Brotherhood (IRB), a secret society aimed at converting Ireland into an independent democratic republic. On reaching Skibbereen, he met Jeremiah O'Donovan (better known as Rossa), the leading light in the half-literary, half-political Phoenix National and Literary Society, formed in 1856. Its members now joined the IRB. Although Stephens took charge, there was only lukewarm support for an Irish rebellion. In October 1858, he visited America, where, despite falling out with O'Mahony, he had better success in combining Fenian groupings with the IRB to create 'a formidable political and revolutionary force'.[4]

Although Stephens reported back to O'Donovan in Ireland that Irish-Americans would supply arms for a revolutionary conspiracy, support for him never spread beyond Ireland's south-west. When the Government learned what was going on, the Irish ring-leaders, including O'Donovan, were rounded up for trial. Although they were convicted, the Crown considered their threat insignificant and did not inflict heavy punishment. Although Stephens returned to Ireland to galvanise support, he realised that a social revolution would be needed to achieve an Irish republic. Ireland was still being governed by an executive at Dublin Castle under a Lord Lieutenant who was directly responsible to the British Cabinet. Irish Members of Parliament had established no authority at Westminster. When Stephens rejoined O'Mahony in America, he was able to persuade the various action groups that 'the Irish had a natural right to independence' and 'that right could only be won in armed revolution'. In 1863, he again returned to Ireland, where he launched a newspaper *The Irish People,* financed with American money. Although Fenian cells were formed in Canada, Australia, South America, London, Manchester, Liverpool and Glasgow, they were quickly infiltrated, and the British Government was kept well-informed.

With the American Civil War ending in the spring of 1865, Irish-American soldiers were available to serve elsewhere. They gave great impetus to Fenian calls for rebellion. Irish-American officers arrived in Ireland in their hundreds, causing Fenian membership to rise rapidly. There were now widespread rumours of an impending rising. Between 1860 and 1867, $500,000 was raised in America to support Ireland's liberation. Fenians joined the British army and, by 1865, it is estimated that 15,000 serving soldiers had been recruited to the Fenian ranks, organised along military lines, and bent on a 'wholly and unequivocally' democratic republic in Ireland 'for the weal of the toiler'.

The Government authorities remained well-aware of what was going on. Documents outlining Fenian plans initiated in America fell into their hands. A mole in the office of *The Irish People* leaked more information, and, on 15 September 1865, a raid on its offices resulted in the paper being closed-down. O'Donovan and two other editors were taken into custody. Parliament suspended Habeas Corpus allowing leading Fenians to be arrested throughout Ireland and sentenced to penal servitude. When Stephens returned to Ireland in November, he too was arrested. Although he was held in Richmond jail, he managed to escape with the connivance of two prison officials and made his way back to France.

With agitation continuing in America, Stephens openly pledged that an Irish rising would take place in 1866, but there were conflicting views on how to proceed. 1866 came and went. Fenians in Ireland became desperate and wanted to rebel with or without Irish-American assistance. Although they assembled at various meeting points, arms from America failed to arrive and they were easily dispersed. Irish-Americans, who arrived at Cork to co-ordinate them, were quickly arrested. Other Fenian leaders were transported.

In America, the leadership faced criticism. Although Stephens was resupplied with Irish-American money, he was losing authority. O'Mahony's presidency was challenged by William Randall Roberts, who was backed by battle-hardened veterans of the American Civil War to take a more militant stance. After raising large sums from the Irish immigrant population, Roberts organised a bizarre military raid into Canada attempting to gain control of the Canadian transportation system. After crossing the Niagara River, Roberts's associate, Colonel John O'Neill, captured Fort Erie and defeated a Canadian force at Ridgeway. Initially the US authorities, still smarting at Britain's failure to support them during the American Civil War, turned a blind eye to their actions, but wanted to avoid them escalating into war. They interrupted Fenian supply lines and arrested O'Neill's reinforcements, confiscating their weapons. Although O'Neill was forced to retreat, the weapons were later returned after assurances that they would not be used to invade foreign territories. When other incursions into Canada were contemplated, there was little Canadian sympathy for Irish republicanism and Britain moved quickly to establish the Canadian provinces into a Confederation.

Meanwhile, in 1867, Richard O'Sullivan Burke planned an uprising of Fenians in England. Although he raised money to purchase arms in Birmingham, he was arrested and imprisoned at Clerkenwell. When a group of his colleagues attempted to free him by wheeling a large bomb into a narrow street next to the prison walls, the explosion left twelve dead and 120 wounded in adjacent tenements. Although the prison wall was blown apart, no prisoners escaped. This resulted in a backlash of hostility against Irish republican sympathisers. Barrett, the ringleader, was convicted and hanged in front of Newgate prison.

The secret leader of the Fenians in England was a Colonel Kelly. In the autumn of 1867 he attended a meeting in Manchester, where Fenian sympathies were running high. While returning home with a companion, Captain Deasy, the two were arrested on suspicion of loitering to commit a burglary. Although they gave false names, it was soon realised that they were the two formidable Fenian leaders. On 18 September, a party of thirty men with revolvers attempted to rescue them at a railway bridge from the prison van carrying them to Salford jail. One of the horses was shot and the unarmed police fled. Although the party attacked the van door with hatchets, hammers and crowbars, they failed to open it. They then opened a ventilator and called on the policeman inside to give up the keys. When he refused, they mortally wounded him by firing a pistol through the keyhole in an attempt to blow open the lock. One of the female prisoners inside took the keys from his pocket and passed them out through the ventilator to allow the van door to be opened. Kelly and Deasy escaped and were never recaptured. Meanwhile police reinforcements had returned accompanied by a large crowd. Four of the Fenian rescuers were seized and the crowd threatened to lynch them. When charged with the policeman's murder, one could demonstrate that he had not been involved, but the other three were hanged. On the day of the execution, crowds walked in funeral processions all over Ireland 'to testify the terrible depths of their grief'.[5]

'Fenian outrages throughout this period, and a deteriorating relationship between Roman Catholics and Protestants led to sectarian rioting and murders.'[6] The abandonment of 'constitutional and tranquil agitation' attracted great concern.[7] Outbreaks of rebellion on both sides of the Atlantic were condemned by Pope Pius IX, but, in 1867, a group of priests in Limerick issued a declaration calling for repeal of the Union. Protestant opinion was dismayed, but agitation continued. During the late 1860s, there were raids for arms on police barracks and other places in co. Cork. In one of these, O'Brien's son, William, was arrested with a Captain Mackay, who was accused of leading revolutionary cliques, and held without trial. While they were incarcerated, William's two brothers and a sister died, probably from consumption. On his release, he too was suffering from tuberculosis and was sent to Egypt to recover. When he returned, he joined the *Cork Daily Herald.* In 1876 he transferred to the *Freeman's Journal,* where, during 1879, he published articles about the impending calamity in co. Mayo arising from rural poverty. When he tried to combat coercion by joining the Land League, his friends warned him that his health would not survive another period in prison. Instead, Parnell invited him 'to found *United Ireland* and to become its editor'.[8] He found his *métier* writing political editorials of 'feverish and bewildering force' against the terms of the Land Acts.[8] (See chapter 28) With insufficient mainstream support for rebellion, Fenian agitation petered out. The door was now open for a more conventional approach to achieve Irish home rule through parliamentary debate, in what became known as the New Departure initiative.

With Fenianism awakening Irish concerns at the quality of its parliamentary members, calls for Irish nationalism became progressively more vocal. With anti-Unionists determined to be heard, they became a perennial thorn in the side of successive governments. The execution of 'the Manchester martyrs' was the trigger for Charles Stewart Parnell to begin political agitation. Parliament now became the battleground for seeking Irish self-government and the disestablishment of the Anglican Church of Ireland. It was Irish land ownership that was now seen as the principal grievance.

Part 9

Parliamentary agitation for Irish Home Rule

Chapter 28

Gladstone's initial approach to reform in Ireland 1867 – 1874

In 1859, Peelites merged with Whigs and Radicals to form the Liberal party. Following Palmerston's death in 1865, Lord John Russell returned as their leader. On his retirement in 1867, he was replaced by William Ewart Gladstone, who had been Palmerston's Chancellor of the Exchequer. Gladstone quickly realised that, to win the next election, he would need to harness Irish members to the Liberal cause, and he courted them with promises of legislation to appease Nationalist opinion.

The problem for Gladstone was not just in seeking land reform for Ireland. With the protectionist lobby among landowners dominating parliament and particularly the House of Lords, hopes of gaining reform required the British electoral system to be updated. In 1867 the second Reform bill was passed; this extended the voting franchise to many working men in towns and cities, adding 938,000 new electors, who almost doubled the voting register. Forty-five new urban seats were created by taking a similar number away from the small rural towns.[1] The reforms also limited the power of the Crown to that of ratifying the results of General Elections. Although Queen Victoria detested Gladstone, and greatly preferred the more sycophantic Disraeli, she faced criticism herself, following the death of Prince Albert, for living as a recluse and losing influence with her political leaders.

There is no doubt that Gladstone was sincere in his desires for Irish reform. He wrote to the Duke of Argyll:

> To this great country, the state of Ireland after seven hundred years of our tutelage is, in my opinion, so long as it

continues, an intolerable disgrace, and a danger so absolutely transcending all others that I call it the only real danger of the noble empire of the Queen.[2]

He was not initially in favour of Irish home rule but hoped to woo Irish Nationalists with a series of other legislative reforms.

Electoral reform had been supported by Disraeli and the Tories, who had reorganised themselves to gain support from the new electorate, but it was the Liberals who won the 1868 election with Gladstone becoming Prime Minister. 'The popular vote was not Liberal by divine right'.[3] In the industrial north, particularly in Lancashire, there was strong Tory support. In part, this was out of deference to the wealthy industrial employers of the burgeoning cotton industry, and, in part, out of antipathy for Irish immigrants. Their arrival had caused a surprising backlash of support for Church, State and Protestantism.[4]

The 1860s were a period of growing nationalism throughout Europe, and Fenian sentiment in Ireland was no exception. In 1869, Gladstone combatted this by carrying major enactments through Parliament 'to weaken and finally dismantle the fabric of the Protestant Ascendancy'.[5] The first of these, the Irish Church Act (32 and 33 Victoria. Cap. 42), disestablished and partly dis-endowed the Anglican Episcopal Church despite House of Lords opposition. A synod was provided for its government with a Representative Church Body to administer its finances. Capital sums were to be paid to the Presbyterian and Roman Catholic churches in place of the *Regium Donum* and Maynooth College grant. The Act permitted the sale of Church lands to its tenants and vested ruined churches in a Commission of Public Works to preserve them as national monuments. Its effect was to alarm English churchmen without placating the Irish.

The burning issue was land reform. With Irish rental income received by absentee landlords being repatriated to England, it was not available for circulation within the local economy. It was the tenant, not the landlord, who was expected to provide better buildings and undertake land improvement. Yet, except in Ulster, he received no compensation for improvements to the infrastructure at the end of his lease. Thus, landlords were free to increase rents on renewal to reflect improvements that previous tenants had paid for. With agricultural land in increasingly short supply, rack-renting forced up rents, with tenants desperate to retain sufficient land to remain economically viable. The only safety-valve was emigration.

Gladstone was sincere in his desire to settle agricultural unrest in Ireland by providing a fair system of land ownership. In 1869, he introduced a bill to Parliament, which was to become The Landlord & Tenant (Ireland) Act 1870 (33 and 34 Victoria. Cap. 46). The bill required landlords to pay compensation to outgoing tenants for all improvements that they had made and called for evicted tenants to be compensated for 'disturbance'. Yet efforts to control rack-renting proved contentious with senior Liberal parliamentarian landowners, as there had been considerable economic improvement since the Great Famine. Gladstone did not personally favour financing individual tenants to purchase their freeholds, as he saw the economic advantage of land being held in larger units. Yet, John Bright, President of the Board of Trade, had proposed that tenants should be offered State-funded grants and this view prevailed. Gladstone's focus was on discouraging landlord absenteeism. He wanted a landlord 'to have a position marked by residence, by personal familiarity and by sympathy among the people among whom they live'. The bill was not an attack on the rights of property, and it only applied in Ireland, but property owners in the House of Lords turned it into an unworkable compromise. Its resultant terms called for:

1. The Custom of Ulster (to grant compensation for tenant improvements on eviction – although this was not defined in the act) to be given the force of law where it already existed,
2. Tenants, who did not enjoy this protection, (the great majority) to receive:
   a. Compensation for improvements on eviction, unless they were being evicted for non-payment of rent, and
   b. Compensation for 'disturbance' for tenants being evicted for reasons other than non-payment of rent

(These were to be based on a scale of charges,) and

3. Tenants to be able to borrow from Government two-thirds of the cost of acquiring their holding at 5% interest, repayable over thirty-five years, but only if the landlord was a willing seller.

To stop eviction by rack-renting, 'excessive' rents (as defined by the Courts) were to be prohibited. Yet the House of Lords changed 'excessive' to 'exorbitant'. The effect of this change was to allow landlords to raise rents to levels which tenants could not afford and then to evict them for non-payment without compensation. Fewer than 1,000 tenants could fund the purchase of their freeholds even with the benefit of Government loans, and few landlords were willing sellers. Legal disputes over the definition of 'exorbitant' rents only worsened landlord/tenant relations. With the Act's concessions falling far short of the three Fs (fixity of tenure, free sale and fair rents for tenants), as sought by Tenant Rights activists, agitators remained dissatisfied. Poor drafting also had the effect of making tillage uneconomical, which had the opposite effect to what was intended, as land returned to pasture only increased rural poverty.

In 1870, the Liberal William Edward Forster introduced his Education bill, which, for the first time, offered primary education for all throughout Britain and Ireland. Although it passed into law, it faced bitter opposition from non-conformists, who objected to the Anglican church's continued control over primary education.[6] In 1871, the Trade Union Act legalised unions, providing them with court protection. In 1872, Gladstone again tried to appease moderates by tabling the Ballot Act to introduce secret voting. This allowed Irish tenants to vote as they wished, and not at the bidding of their landlord. At last the real voice of Ireland could make itself heard, but it reduced Liberal party influence there.

Irish Nationalist agitation was not just focused on Irish land reform, but it sought home rule. With so few supporters in Parliament, it was difficult for Nationalists to follow a constitutional approach. This left the Fenians sceptical of Parliament as a means of achieving their objectives. In 1869, the Supreme Council of the IRB adopted its 'Constitution of the Irish Republic'. This gave birth to the Irish Home Rule movement and marked the beginnings of modern Irish Nationalism. Its calls to break with monarchy and with Britain gained the support of Tenant Rights reformers.

Again, Gladstone offered concessions to the Nationalists. Agitation was now almost exclusively Catholic and was associated with 'the ideal of reviving Gaelic culture', romantic, backward-looking and deeply conservative.[7] Growing Fenian fanaticism alienated the Anglo-Irish, despite their desire to preserve the Irish language, culture and antiquities. This led to nationalism being denounced by Cardinal Paul Cullen, Roman Catholic Archbishop of Dublin. Furthermore, unlike in the rebellions in 1798 and 1803, it had no appeal for Presbyterians.

Moderates aired their support for home rule with considerable trepidation. At a meeting in Dublin on 19 May 1870, a group, led by the Tory Lord Mayor, Edward Purton, which included Major Lawrence Knox, proprietor of the *Irish Times*, and Isaac Butt, a Member of Parliament and their chief speaker, passed a resolution: 'That it is the opinion of this meeting that the true remedy for the evils of Ireland is the establishment of an Irish Parliament with full control over its domestic affairs.'[8] This gave birth to the 'The Home Government Association of Ireland'. Support spread rapidly, and the Irish became wedded to its cause.

Butt was the natural leader of this new movement. He was the son of a Protestant minister from Ulster, educated at Trinity College, Dublin. He had studied for the Bar and was a well-respected Queen's Counsel and lecturer in Political Economy. As a young man, he had sat on the Dublin Corporation as a vocal advocate for maintenance of the Union and stood firmly for the principles of Orange Toryism. In 1852, at the age of thirty-nine, he became Member of Parliament for Youghal and later for Harwich in England. Yet his involvement in London politics curtailed his Dublin legal practice, causing him financial difficulties. This was principally because he borrowed heavily to lend to others, until left with insurmountable debts. This led to appearances at police courts and a period in debtors' prison. Despite these shortcomings, Butt was 'a supreme political genius … [but] the irregularities of his life shut him out from official employment'.[9] This left his 'inferiors to reach to position and wealth while he remained poor and neglected'.[10] Yet he later returned to his Dublin legal practice and resumed the political struggle for home rule.

Butt was caught by surprise when Gladstone dissolved Parliament in 1874 to call a general election. With his party having almost universal Irish support, Butt had hoped to promote a Nationalist candidate in every Irish constituency. Yet he had insufficient resources with which to run a national campaign. On the day after Parliament's dissolution, he was arrested for debt. Instead of supervising his party's election campaign, he was required to return to England. He could only fight seats where Home Rule candidates would bear the election expenses themselves. Although he attracted names like Alexander Martin Sullivan, editor of *The Nation,* many candidates were 'time-worn Whigs and Tories', prepared to swallow 'the Home Rule pledge', but with no real enthusiasm for Irish Nationalism.[11] Butt attracted younger lawyers, just as ready as Keogh had been to sell themselves to the highest bidder as soon as they reached Westminster, and many went on to gain political office. (In 1878, Keogh 'developed symptoms of insanity' and was removed to Belgium. After attempting to kill both his attendant and himself, he died on 30 September 1878. No one requested the return of his body to Ireland for burial.)

Butt and sixty others gained seats at Westminster, pledged to achieve legislative change between the two countries, but, with Disraeli and the Tories now in power, calls for Irish Nationalism were not promoted with cohesion. By displaying charm and leadership qualities, Butt became, next to Gladstone, the finest Parliamentarian of his day 'with the modesty and simplicity of real greatness'.[12] Yet his spendthrift nature still presented huge problems, and he faced a dilemma on whether to neglect his Dublin legal practice or his role as leader of the National party in London. He failed to demonstrate that, without concessions, the Irish would call for revolution. He could not persuade a sceptical House of Commons of the serious impact of further rack-renting and hunger on increasingly demoralised Irish farmers. Despite his repeated efforts to achieve land or any other reforms, the Tories overwhelmingly rejected them. At sixty-one, he was losing heart and failed to conjoin his Nationalist members to focus on issues where the two larger parties disagreed. He preferred a more comfortable approach, seeking office in one or other of them. A 'period of dry rot had set in'.[13]

Butt was joined in Parliament in 1874 by Joseph Biggar, the member for West Cavan. With Butt's approach being seen as sycophantic, Biggar initiated a practice of 'obstruction' (or filibustering) to delay the process of Government legislation. He spoke for nearly four hours against a coercion bill 'in a manner which rendered him totally unintelligible'.[14] Although this made him extremely unpopular in the House of Commons, he gained cult status among the Irish, with toasts being made to him at National party dinners, followed by long spontaneous cheering. His approach was soon to be adopted by Charles Stewart Parnell.

Chapter 29

The rise of Charles Stewart Parnell 1874 – 1882

Another candidate in the 1874 election was Charles Stewart Parnell, from a well-to-do landed family in co. Wicklow. He had been brought up isolated from politics on his Wicklow estate and gave every impression of shyness. At the time of the dissolution of Parliament, he had just become High Sheriff, a role debarring him from standing as a member for Wicklow, which he was not permitted to resign. He was completely unknown to the Nationalists and, as a landlord, was treated with suspicion. Although a nomination was available for the co. Dublin constituency, it was against a strong sitting Tory member, leaving only forlorn hopes of winning the seat. Nevertheless, his willingness to fight it at his own expense (which was likely to be considerable) assured him of a hearing with the Nationalists.[1] As he gave the appearance of seeking the seat out of social ambition, his adherence to Nationalist ideals seemed half-hearted.

When he met with the Council of the Home Rule league, Parnell made a favourable impression and Sullivan undertook to propose his adoption. When accepted with acclamation, he attempted to address the assemblage, but broke down in nervous anxiety. Although the audience cheered him on, it was feared that, if he ever reached Westminster, he would be unable to open his mouth. With the Tory candidate winning the election comfortably, it was generally accepted that he had been a very poor candidate, lacking the qualities to be expected of a successful Irish leader. Yet, he was difficult to judge, always diffident about himself and about speaking in public. As Parliament soon discovered, when he did speak, he said exactly what he meant to say.[2]

Parnell's family background positioned him as a Nationalist. He hated injustice and was brought up with stories of British atrocities. The Parnells were Protestants who had arrived in Ireland from Congleton in Cheshire. His antecedents had joined the legal profession and served in Parliament, where they opposed the Union. Parnell was born in June 1846 at Avondale in rural co. Wicklow. His mother, Delia Tudor Stewart, was the daughter of a respected American admiral. She was strongly Nationalist and is known to have sheltered Fenians on the run, enabling them to make their way to America. His father, John Henry Parnell, had travelled to America as a young man, meeting Delia in Washington. They divorced when Charles, their third son, was six, but he seems to have inherited the 'evenness of temper and coolness of judgment' of his American grandfather.[3] Charles was educated in England, and attended Cambridge University, but financial difficulties forced his return to Wicklow. He did not sit for his degree, despite a keen interest in mechanics. After travelling to America, he returned in 1871, setting up a saw mill and brush factory.

After his failure to be elected to Parliament in 1874, Parnell had a second opportunity in the following year at a by-election in co. Meath, caused by the death of the veteran Young Irelander, John Martin. On 21 April 1875, he won the seat with strong Fenian support. He spent a year in the House biding his time, while cultivating Fenian sentiments and holding numerous discussions with Biggar. They were both concerned at Butt's growing lethargy, and Parnell joined in on Biggar's 'obstructionist' tactics, with which Butt disapproved. They took on 'the boldest, most difficult, and most hopeless [projects] that two individuals ever proposed to themselves to work out'.[4] This made them extremely unpopular on all sides. With many of their Nationalist colleagues being 'false' men, with no real concern for their party's reforming objectives, they gained little parliamentary support for their approach. As T. P. O'Connor has said: 'The House of Commons loves and respects only those who love and respect it.'[5] They showed complete indifference to its opinions. Their tactics required their 'incessant attendance in the House' and 'considerable preparation'.[6]

It was later said: 'Parnell has done mighty things, but he had to go through fire and water to do them.'[7]

Biggar was oblivious to criticism, using a range of extremely unpopular tactics. He would call out 'I espy strangers', which required the public galleries (except for the Ladies' Gallery) and the Press to be cleared. He chose to do this when the Prince of Wales was sitting there. Both Disraeli, the Prime Minister, and William Cavendish, Marquess of Hartington (later 8th Duke of Devonshire), the leader of the opposition, stood to denounce this 'outrage upon its [the House's] dignity'. Biggar was held to be 'wanting the instincts of a gentleman'. Even a Nationalist member joined the assault, saying: 'A man should be a gentleman first and a patriot afterwards.' Biggar was described derogatorily as a member who had 'made his money in the wholesale pork trade', but he retained his self-control and Parnell continued his support.[8] Butt, who had been a Tory before becoming the Nationalist leader, remained under Tory influence. He 'attacked his two subordinates with fierce anger and reproach'.[9] He seemed to forget that their objective was to gain Irish reform. Although Biggar could not compete with Butt's speaking skills, his strength of character won through.

Another of Biggar's tactics was to block bills under the 'half-past twelve' rule, which stopped motions that had been opposed being taken after that time. All he had to do was to continue speaking until then and propose a motion of adjournment as there was now insufficient time for proper discussion. This delayed bills until the next session. Not only did their public speaking become more practiced, but, by breaking the rules of the House, they became intimately acquainted with what they could get away with. The skill was to ensure that speeches remained logical to the debate to avoid accusations of irrelevance and frivolity. On 25 July 1877, Parnell and another fellow obstructionist, Mr. Jenkins, disrupted and delayed the passage of the South Africa bill. With Jenkins's intervention being dubbed obnoxious, he was accused of abusing the forms of the House, which he strenuously denied. When he moved that criticisms against him should 'be taken down' [for later review], Parnell immediately seconded his motion, claiming that the language of opposing members had reached the limits of forbearance. Sir Stafford Northcote, Chancellor of the Exchequer, immediately called for Parnell's words 'to be taken down'. The Chairman of the Committee quite irregularly declared that the words said to Jenkins were not a breach of order and asked Parnell to withdraw his statement, accusing him of intimidation. When Parnell stood, he denounced the bill, despite constant interruption, arguing that it was 'mischievous both to the colonists and to the native races', and likening their treatment to English interference in Ireland. He then claimed 'a special satisfaction in preventing and thwarting the intentions of the Government in respect to this bill'.[10] Northcote leapt on this and again called for his words 'to be taken down'. When the Speaker was called, he moved that Parnell should face parliamentary censure and be suspended for obstruction until the following Friday. When called upon to defend his action, Parnell remained defiant, making the House 'beside itself with rage'. Northcote interrupted to accuse him of contempt of the House for wilfully obstructing its business. Parnell was required to withdraw to the Speaker's gallery, where he argued that his objective was to obstruct the *will* of the Government (which as an opposition member he was perfectly entitled to do), not of the House (which would have been obstruction). Northcote was forced to defer the censure debate until the following Friday. Parnell thus resumed his speech where he had been interrupted.

On the following Friday, the Government proposed two motions: that any member called to order twice by the Speaker or the Chairman of Committees could be suspended for the remainder of the sitting, and that no member could propose more than once in the same sitting a motion for reporting progress or the adjournment of a debate. Although these two motions were adopted, Parnell avoided censure. With the Government's legislative programme considerably behind, it attempted to push through the South Africa bill over the night of 31 July. The obstructionists, including Parnell, delayed it until 2pm on the following afternoon by speaking in relays for twenty-six hours. This again caused outrage. Butt, who voted in favour of the bill, threatened to resign unless they came to heel.

Meanwhile, Parnell continued to foster his Fenian following in Britain and Ireland. He gained some notoriety by claiming that Fenians had not been involved in the Manchester murders. In August 1877, he visited Paris to meet their leaders, but realised that his parliamentary influence would be compromised if he strongly supported their armed strategies. Although he explained that he could not be seen to join a secret society, he backed their calls for Irish self-government, for vigorous promotion of peasant proprietorship and for resistance to coercive legislation.

Although Biggar and Parnell received little initial support from other Nationalist members in Parliament, they were praised by its rank and file, particularly the Irish now living in England. At a meeting of the Home Rule Confederation (which included English members) in Dublin at the end of 1877, Parnell replaced Butt as President. Although Butt offered to resign as the Nationalist leader in Parliament, this was not immediately accepted, but he was old, ill and in desperate financial straits. A subscription to assist him raised little money, and he died on 5 May 1879. It was Parnell who now had the public's attention.

When it came to the election of a new Nationalist parliamentary leader, Parnell's parliamentary approach told against him, and the Whig-orientated William Shaw was chosen. Yet obstructionist tactics continued. In 1879, during the passage of the Army bill, Parnell spoke frequently and at length to abolish flogging. When he was supported by Joseph Chamberlain and other radical Liberals, the obstructionists found their work being done for them. It was Chamberlain who now faced the odium of both the House and orthodox Liberals, but his persistence gained Liberal support.

Chamberlain had been Mayor of Birmingham before becoming a Member of Parliament. As a self-made industrialist, he had little time for the aristocracy, but he became influential, serving as a notable President of the Board of Trade from 1880 to 1885, and making staunch attacks on the Tory leader, Robert Gascoyne-Cecil, 3rd Marquess of Salisbury. In 1886, his growing opposition to Irish home rule brought about his resignation from Gladstone's third Government, helping to engineer a split within the Liberal Party and making him a key member of the Liberal-Unionists.

Although obstructionist tactics were achieving practical results, Biggar and Parnell remained unpopular. *The World* reported:

> Mr. Biggar, though occasionally endurable, is invariably grotesque ... But Mr. Parnell has no redeeming qualities, unless we regard it as an advantage to have in the House a man who unites in his own person all the childish unreasonableness, all the ill-regulated suspicion, and all the childish credulity, of the Irish peasant, without any of the humour, the courtliness, or dash of the Irish gentleman.

Meanwhile rack-renting continued, and the level of tenant evictions doubled. Both the Courts and the law had always stood on the landlords' side. Although Gladstone had wanted evicted tenants to be compensated, once evicted they had no means of generating income. Compensation did not resolve their difficulties. Although farmers from the Irish west coast made seasonal trips for the English harvest each year, their earnings merely settled what they owed to their landlord. Emigrants had to repatriate parts of their wages to support those left behind. It is estimated that they returned £800,000 to Ireland each year.

The famine's impact was worsened by the incompetence of the Chief Secretary for Ireland, Mr. James Lowther. He refused to accept that there was a problem. His attitude drove Parnell into the ranks of the Irish National Land League, a group aiming to protect tenant rights. He rapidly became their idol. He was determined that the fate of those who had suffered in 1846 and 1847 should not be repeated in 1879 and 1880. From now on, he wanted not just tenant rights, but the removal of the landlord, so that the tenant retained his own produce on his own land. On 8 June 1879, he addressed a meeting of tenants at Westport, saying: 'You must show the landlords that you intend to hold a firm grip of your homesteads and land.'[11] At a meeting at the Imperial Hotel in Dublin on 21 October, the following resolutions were approved:

I.   That the objects of the League are, first, to bring about a
     reduction of rack-rents; second, to facilitate the obtaining of
     the ownership of the soil by the occupiers

II. That the objects of the League can best be attained (1) by
     promoting organisation among the tenant farmers; (2) by
     defending those who may be threatened with eviction for
     refusing to pay unjust rents; (3) by facilitating the working of
     the Bright Clauses of the Land Act during the winter; and (4)
     by obtaining such reform in the laws relating to land as will
     enable every tenant to become the owner of his holding by
     paying a fair rent for a limited number of years.

When Parnell was elected President, the league rapidly increased its
membership by holding meetings all over Ireland. T. P. O'Connor has
graphically explained the choice available to the rural Irish:

> It was clear that the time had come when Ireland must make
> a tremendous step either of advance or retrogression. Either
> distress was to develop into famine, and famine to lead to
> wholesale eviction, and another lease of landlord power and
> oppression, or the Irish people were to throw off the chains
> of centuries, to revolt against the perpetuation of their
> miseries and of their servitude, and to dash forward in an
> effort for a new and better era.[12]

Although Parnell discouraged violence, he encouraged tenants to follow
the Land League's resolutions. This linked it to the mass agitation being
organised in Parliament. From 1873 to 1896 there was a renewed period
of agricultural hardship. Grain arrived from America in ever-increasing
amounts, both cheaper and of better quality than that produced locally.
Meat transported in refrigerated ships from Argentina and New Zealand
competed with Irish production. In 1873 there was a recurrence of potato
blight. In 1879, the crop was 35 per cent of normal. Tenants unable to pay
their rents had no protection from eviction. The Land League extended
its agitation, with outrages becoming known as the 'Land War'.

When Parnell travelled to America to raise money, he received an enthusiastic reception from thousands of Americans in sixty-two cities. He was influenced by two Irish Americans, John Devoy, a leading member of *Clan na Gael*, closely affiliated to the Fenians, and Patrick Ford, who preached militant republicanism and hatred of England through his newspaper, *The Irish World*.[13] He now explained:

> When we have undermined English mis-government we have paved the way for Ireland to take her place amongst the nations of the earth. And let us not forget that that is the ultimate goal at which we Irishmen aim. None of us, whether we be in America or in Ireland … will be satisfied until we have destroyed the last link which keeps Ireland bound to England.[14]

He was granted an audience with the President, Rutherford B. Hayes, and, quite exceptionally, was permitted to address the House of Representatives. This laid the foundation for an Irish Land League in America. He raised about £144,000, half to be allocated for promotion and half to relieve distress.

Although Lowther was still denying the existence of distress, a relief committee was formed by the Duchess of Marlborough, wife of the Lord Lieutenant. Both she and the Lord Mayor of Dublin, Edmund Dwyer Gray, began fund-raising. With the famine becoming an admitted fact, both Lowther and Parliament were at last compelled to listen. The Tory Government passed The Relief of Distress Act to require landlords to distribute relief to their tenants. £1,092,985 was made available to offer employment to those affected by famine. While this reduced eviction levels, 500,000 tenants remained unable to pay their rents, despite the receipt of charity.

When Disraeli called a General Election in March 1880, it was won by Gladstone and the Liberals, but Gladstone remained oblivious to the scale of Ireland's growing distress. Much later, in 1884, he admitted:

> I had had much upon my hands connected with the doings of the Government in almost every quarter of the world,

and I did not know – no one knew – the severity of the crisis
that was already swelling upon the horizon, and that shortly
after rushed upon us like a flood.[15]

Parnell had hurried back from America for the election campaign,
but the Nationalists had little money and often adopted mediocre
candidates. Although Home Rulers won sixty-three seats, many of
those elected were of doubtful use to the Nationalist cause, leaving
Parnell with twenty-seven supporters in a minority. On 17 May 1880
the elected members met at the City Hall in Dublin to choose a leader.
With Shaw still opposing 'peasant proprietary', they were determined
to replace him. With most of Parnell's parliamentary supporters being
little known and new to politics, he did not seem an obvious choice,
but, at a private discussion held at the Imperial Hotel beforehand, he
received strong backing. When offered the leadership, he seemed to
favour Justin McCarthy, a well-known journalist, but, when a vote was
taken at the City Hall, Parnell received 23 votes and Shaw 18.

Gladstone adopted a confrontational approach against the
Nationalists. In November 1880, the Attorney-General filed a suit
against Parnell and other Nationalist leaders for having formed
combinations of tenants to incite unrest and encourage non-payment
of rents. Parnell was also accused of conspiring against landlords and
deterring the takeover of lands from evicted tenants. Parnell's objective
was to end tenant hardship by providing 'a new birth of political hope
and power', and the charges against him were not progressed.[16]

At the opening of Parliament on 6 January 1881, the proposals in
the Queen's Speech for legislation on coercion and an Irish land bill
were eagerly awaited. When the Nationalists took their seats, Shaw
and his clique sided with the Liberals, who seemed to sympathise
with Irish issues. With the Land League becoming progressively
more powerful, Parnell kept his supporters independent of both
major parties and sat with the opposition. It was already recognised
that the Land League's ploy to prevent tenants from outbidding
each other for land prevented rack-renting. In 1880, it had proposed
a Department or Commission of Land Administration to supervise

land transfers from landlord to tenant. The Commission could either advance the purchase money to the tenant repayable by an annuity based on twenty years' purchase of the annual rental or purchase the land from the landlord for reletting at a rate equal to $3\frac{1}{2}$ per cent of its cost. Although both proposals were fiercely attacked in the British Press, they were later supported by the Tories.

With American funding, the Land League was now backed by four-fifths of the Irish population. It was no longer a few agitators, but the whole Irish nation. Despite this, the Liberals had not addressed the land problem, and the Queen's speech failed to clarify the Government's intentions. Gladstone argued that the 1870 Act had been 'fairly successful' and that new legislation would be a development of its principles. He was generally polite about landlords, denying that any general increase in rents had taken place. He proposed a tribunal to settle fair rents and land sale prices but avoided any mention of fixity of tenure.

In the debate on the Queen's speech, the Nationalists argued that the 1870 Act had been unworkable, and the proposals would achieve nothing. When Parnell called for an amendment, he was cheered by Liberal radicals. Although Shaw's group argued that the Government needed time to develop a policy, Parnell wanted the issue brought forward immediately, fearing that delay would cause the tenantry's wholesale destruction and the issue would be forgotten. His speech set out the situation in Ireland, but 'was listened to with more curiosity than sympathy'. He was still branded 'a very violent and irrational man, who represented nothing but a small and irresponsible knot of senseless irreconcilables'.[17] Shaw undercut his stance by speaking from the Government benches immediately after him 'in welcome contrast to the heat and exaggeration of Mr. Parnell'.[18] Nevertheless, it was Parnell and his colleagues with whom the Government had to contend. With annual evictions increasing from 1,238 in 1879 to 2,110 in 1890, agrarian outrages grew correspondingly from 863 to 2,590 cases.

Parnell's calls for a commission of enquiry into the working of the 1870 Act were at last heeded, but his proposal to include a tenant farmer on it was opposed. Hartington demanded 'a set of honest and impartial men to make enquiry on the spot'. Parnell had no confidence in it achieving reform of land ownership, fearing that this would take a state bordering on revolution. Yet, in 1881, the Commission, headed by Frederick Ponsonby, 6th Earl of Bessborough, confirmed that the Act provided no real protection for tenants. Compensation for tenant improvements could only be claimed on a lease's termination. Tenants were forced to accept rent increases on renewal to avoid losing the land on which their improvements had been made. The Commission even confirmed its support for 'the three Fs' as demanded by the Land League.[19]

To prevent evictions by landlords during a period of crop failure, the Parnellites promoted a Suspension of Evictions bill. To ensure that it received attention, Parnell tabled it at 2am, forcing Gladstone to concede that he would make it one of the 'chief and primary questions of the session'.[20] When the Government revealed that evictions were increasing, the full horror started to dawn. Gladstone admitted that 'a sentence of eviction might be regarded as equivalent to a sentence of death'.[21] Despite fierce Tory opposition, the House of Commons overwhelmingly carried the bill, only to have it thrown out with contempt in the House of Lords. Although the Liberals wanted to avoid being seen to condone injustice, they did not want another General Election so soon after their recent victory. A modified Relief of Distress bill was tabled and approved, again providing landlords with money to relieve hardship.

Gladstone became alarmed at the Land League's growing power. Although the Queen's speech proposed coercion to end unrest, Parnell tabled a series of amendments, arguing that 'the peace and tranquillity of Ireland cannot be promoted by suspending any of the constitutional rights of the Irish people'.[22] McCarthy proposed that Her Majesty should:

> refrain from using the naval, military and constabulary forces of the Crown in enforcing ejectments for the non-payment of rent in Ireland, until the measures proposed to be submitted to her Majesty with regard to the ownership of land in Ireland have been decided upon by Parliament.[23]

The unprecedented delays in gaining approval of the Queen's Speech exasperated members on all sides. Yet, the 'little Irish phalanx' fought on, backed by the Land League and 'the rising temper of their own country'.[24] Crowds of peasants, with pitchforks, scythes and pike heads began frustrating landlord evictions. With the Government defending its law enforcement procedures, Shaw and his allies resigned from the Nationalist party to join its benches.

Despite the efforts of Parnell and his colleagues, on 24 January 1881 a new Coercion bill was introduced by Forster, now Ireland's Chief Secretary. Its objective was to prevent public meetings and to curb violence. He justified his action by outlining a massive increase in Irish crime, although his evidence was shown to be fabricated. After a protracted debate lasting forty-one hours, the Speaker ended the proceedings with the Nationalists complaining that he was out of order. When Gladstone tried to speak, he could not be heard above continuing interruptions. With the Nationalists being suspended and forcibly ejected from the House, the Coercion bill was enacted without further dissent. In March 1881, a Peace Preservation bill was also approved despite Nationalist opposition. This led to another wave of emigration to the United States, Australia and New Zealand and the ever-expanding cities of Victorian Britain.

Extra police were drafted into Mayo and Galway 'to carry out the unjust [Coercion] law to its bitterest end' with taxes being raised to pay for them.[25] The Protestant press in Ulster depicted the unrest as a vast Catholic conspiracy. Ulster Protestants formed an Orange Emergency Committee to uphold landlord property rights. The Land League countered this by forming a Property Defence Association. The English press blamed sectarian unrest on calls for tenant rights, which only inflamed growing resentment between England and Ireland. Yet several Cabinet members opposed coercion. Bright again called on the Government to provide relief, complaining that the use of force offered no remedy. Nevertheless, the next session of Parliament again advocated coercive legislation.

Parnell was already pushing for a new Land Act. The Land League held mass meetings to promote 'peasant proprietorship', where Parnell claimed that the only way to govern Ireland was for it to govern itself. Without landlordism, the Irish Parliament could be restored, making Home Rule inevitable. There was unparalleled attendance at meetings. Parnell encouraged farmers to stand together to achieve reform by their own actions and organisations. He discouraged the payment of unjust rents but called on tenants to remain firmly in control of their own homesteads, boycotting those bidding to take over farms of evicted neighbours. His 'No Rent Manifesto' was widely supported. The British Government was forced to listen, when he accepted the principle of tenants paying landlords fair compensation in instalments over thirty-five years at a rate which did not exceed a fair rent.

In April 1881 the Government tabled a new bill to offer peasant proprietorship. Gladstone hoped that its terms would end the Land League's agitation. It was enacted as the Land Law (Ireland) Act 1881. It established a Land Commission to reduce unreasonable rents and to allow tenants, up-to-date with their rents, to acquire their freeholds. For the first time, the principle was conceded that fair rents could be determined judicially. In effect, this guaranteed the value of tenant rights, making the tenant a co-proprietor. 'Landlords had a right to draw an income from the land, but tenants had limited property rights in the same land.'[26] Unquestionably, it was the Land League's greatest achievement.[27] Initially, it was welcomed by Nationalists with 'pleased surprise', and it received general support.[28] The principle of dual ownership by landlord and tenant gave legal status to the Ulster practice of compensating tenants for improvements when a lease ended. This was now extended over the whole of Ireland. Gladstone argued that this would end 'landlordism'.[29] The Act also provided a formula for tenants to purchase land based on twenty times the annual rental. The Land Commission would advance three-quarters of the purchase price repayable over 35 years at 5 per cent interest. It seemed to offer the three Fs, which Parnell had been fighting for. Furthermore, landlords were now assured of being paid for what they were selling.

The sting came in the detail. When tenants' rents were assessed under its Fair Rent clause, the Land Commission generally reduced them by 15 or 20 per cent. With this reduction, a tenant's incentive either to buy or to improve productivity was diminished. Yet, without the tenant becoming the proprietor, absentee landlordism would remain. Tenants also considered that their purchase price should be based on the reduced rental, but landlords found this unacceptable. When they recognised the problem, the Nationalists baulked. Opponents of 'peasant proprietorship' argued that the cost of purchasing a freehold left the tenant depleted of capital for land improvement. This was flawed economics, as tenants had always been able to borrow on the security of their tenant rights. Parnell took a middle line. He discouraged tenants from seeking rent reductions through the Land Commission, but some agitators were still advocating adherence to the Land League's 'No Rent Manifesto' by deferring rental payments to the bitter end.[30] After concluding that the bill failed to meet tenant objectives, the Nationalists agreed to boycott its debate (although some took part anyway), as they did not want it recognised as the final solution on the land ownership. The principle objections to the Act were that:

1. it attempted to create a partnership between landlord and tenant, which was impracticable,
2. the Land Commission would not make a reduction in rents sufficient to resolve the hardship that poor tenants were facing,
3. as many tenants were completely unable to pay off their rental arrears arising from the Great Famine and recent poor weather, the legislation left them at the landlords' mercy,
4. there was no benefit for those continuing as leaseholders,
5. in setting revised rents, due provision was not made for tenant improvements,
6. it encouraged emigration, and
7. it made no provision for the plight of agricultural labourers.

With the Land bill having received Parliamentary support, Forster introduced his Coercion bill. This made non-payment of rent a criminal offence and permitted the forcible eviction of tenants, even though they might be starving. While some tenants had heeded Land

League advice to defer rental payments, the effect of poor harvests and lower prices for produce meant that most tenants were unable to pay. When the Coercion bill was enacted, administrators 'raged through the population arresting extremists with a perfect frenzy of insult, lawlessness and cruelty'.[31] Police and troops broke into houses, disrupting meetings and arresting the occupants. Buckshot fired indiscriminately into crowds by police caused several deaths. When the Ladies' Land League erected huts to shelter those evicted, its members were jailed, some for six months, for attempting to intimidate the authorities. The measures only aggravated matters and juries refused to convict purported offenders. The Irish believed that:

> the Coercion Act, coming as it did on the threshold of the Land Bill would inspire the landlords with the idea that the tenants, once more terrorised and broken, could be treated with the cruelty of old times.[32]

With so many tenants refusing to pay rents, there were complaints in Parliament at the Land League's approach, and eviction numbers again started to rise. Gladstone believed that the line taken by Parnell and his supporters lacked the backing of the Irish at large, who were supportive of the Act. With Parnell having support from only 35 of the 103 Irish Members, this concern was understandable. Yet his middle line had gained a rapturous following throughout Ireland. On 22 August, when the 1881 Land Act received Royal assent, the Land League continued to agitate for rent-paying tenants to be financed to become peasant proprietors.[33]

In October 1881, Parnell returned to Ireland to promote Home Rule, leaving O'Brien's *United Ireland* to continue its attack on the Land Act. Forster persuaded the British Cabinet to order Parnell's arrest under the Coercion Act 'for sabotaging the Land Act'. Forster arrived in Dublin with an armed escort and sent 100 police to surround Parnell's house in Foster Place. When Parnell was woken, he dressed and was escorted to Kilmainham jail by two police in a cab surrounded by police vehicles. The Irish saw this as a national calamity.

> The country was swept by a passion of anger and grief, the more bitter because it had to be suppressed. Troops were poured into the country, and, by way of striking wholesome terror, Dublin was given over for two days to the police; and then occurred scenes of brutality the records of which it is not possible to read even at this distance without bitter anger.[34]

Police with batons charged into a crowd in Sackville (later O'Connell) Street, kicking anyone who fell. 'No quarter was given. The roadway was strewn with the bodies of the people.'[35] Some threw stones, but otherwise there was little resistance. The Dublin Corporation sent a deputation to complain at the use of force, but there was no apology. 'Ireland and England now confronted one another in universal and undisguised hatred.'[36]

Three more Nationalist members of parliament, John Dillon, O'Kelly, and Sexton, were apprehended. Although there were warrants to arrest Timothy Healy, Arthur O'Connor and Biggar, Parnell warned them to stay out of sight. This was a victory for the extremists, who Parnell was opposing. O'Brien was accused of 'seditious libel', and the *United Ireland* was suppressed. During his trial, a parliamentary vacancy arose in Mallow, his home town. He was determined to wrest it from the Whigs and won comfortably. Other popular journalists and public speakers were targeted. The Land League was suppressed, and its members arrested. During 1881, without its protection, 17,341 tenants were evicted. It was not until Forster's resignation that the *United Ireland* was revived, allowing O'Brien to begin 'a long and lonely duel' with Government, which lasted three years.[37]

As has been seen, tenants' rental arrears were not just politically motivated. The exceptionally poor harvests of 1878 and 1879 confirmed that few tenants could pay off their rental backlogs. With Nationalists determined to protect tenants, unrest was aggravated when extremists were imprisoned under the Coercion Act. It was hardship, which was the principal cause of rising agrarian crime. Gladstone continued to promote relief efforts. His Land Law (Ireland) Act (44 and 45 Victoria.

Cap. 49) proposed a system of fair rents with tenants free to sell their occupancy and tenancy rights. 'Rules were made to stop intimidation of squatters occupying land from which tenants had been evicted.'[38] In Ulster, a land committee was set up to represent tenants' rights. Local authorities were empowered to borrow to build dwellings for agricultural labourers.

While in Kilmainham, Parnell and his colleagues signed the 'No Rent Manifesto' and called for a tenant farmer rent strike. With rents remaining in arrears, his political stock was growing. Nationalist resistance was forcing landlords to heed the tenants' plight. Rack-renting was ended, with rents being reduced and evictions delayed. Forster had failed to admit the extent of the unrest to his parliamentary colleagues. This allowed the Tories to make political capital out of it. When, at last, the Liberals realised that his coercion policies were counter-productive, they reached an agreement, known as the Kilmainham treaty, with the Nationalists, brokered on their behalf by Captain William O'Shea, while Parnell and other Nationalist leaders remained imprisoned. (For the previous two years, Parnell had been conducting an affair with O'Shea's estranged wife Katherine (Kitty).) The agreement confirmed:

1. that the policy of coercion had failed,
2. Forster, the Irish Chief Secretary, would resign,
3. the Land Act would be amended so that tenants could purchase their properties in accordance with Parnell's requests,
4. the 'No Rent Manifesto' would be withdrawn, and
5. Parnell and the other Nationalists would be released from imprisonment without trial.

Quite suddenly, Parnell's diplomacy had won, and he was 'the master of the situation'.[39] With £40,000 raised to support the Nationalists' dwindling resources, they won by-elections whenever they arose. Parnell's leadership was unquestioned, except in eastern Ulster. The Land Act now allowed tenants, even those in arrears, to finance the purchase of their freeholds with Government loans, repayable on terms less than their existing rents. Gladstone supported the changes and promised to deal with matters immediately, but, even he recognised that landlords lacked the 'moral force' to support his objectives. At last, in 1882, the Government tabled an Arrears bill, an earlier version of which had been drafted by Parnell at Kilmainham. Parnell's victory was a 'veritable triumph'; he was now 'the most potent political force in the British Empire'.[40] Even Forster admitted that 'he is the greatest power in Ireland today'.[41] Yet his use of diplomacy had lost him the support of Fenians and other radicals.

On 6 May 1881, Forster's successor as Chief Secretary for Ireland, Lord Frederick Cavendish, and the Permanent Under-Secretary, Thomas Henry Burke, were assassinated in Phoenix Park in Dublin, horrifying Parnell and his Nationalist colleagues in Parliament. When Parnell went to Gladstone offering to resign his seat, they developed a private working relationship for the future. Yet the Tories believed (or professed to believe) that Forster had been vindicated, although he had caused much of the unrest, and there were renewed calls for coercion. When a Crimes bill was brought before the House, Nationalists resorted to filibustering in all night sittings to delay its passage. Irish members were declared guilty of obstruction, even those who had not been involved, and one who had not even been at the House.

Parnell faced another difficulty. James Carey, chief of the 'Invincibles', a gang claiming responsibility for the Phoenix Park murders, declared that they had been funded by the Land League. With gang members having disappeared to America, Forster renewed his attacks on Parnell in the House of Commons. Parnell now severed his links with radicals including the Irish Republican Brotherhood.

In Ulster, which remained strongly loyalist, the Nationalists held meetings to rally inarticulate Roman Catholics and registered them to vote. Orangemen promptly argued that they were disseminating 'pernicious doctrines' and disturbing the peace of Ulster.[42] They gained landlord support to disrupt meetings, carrying revolvers and inciting murder. The Government used police to clamp down on these attacks and to disperse the Orangemen. This left the Nationalists seemingly unstoppable. When Forster proposed a reduction in the number of seats allotted to Irish members of Parliament by the Act of Union from 103 to 8, Gladstone gained almost universal assent to retain the *status quo*.

Although coercion had always been a Tory policy, the Tories, particularly Lord Randolph Churchill, stood 'solidly together' with the Nationalists to end it, taking political advantage of Liberal disagreements.[43] During 1880, Churchill declared that 'demand for peculiar penal laws ... would be an act in the highest degree impolitic unless supported by overwhelming and overpowering evidence which no one could resist'.[44] Yet it took another four years for the Coercion bill to be defeated. When Gladstone resigned in January 1885 (over his failure to relieve General Gordon at Khartoum), a General Election was delayed by planned boundary changes until November.

Peasant proprietorship now depended on how the Land Commission interpreted the Land Act legislation. Judge O'Hagan, the chief of the Court, and his colleagues, Mr. Litton and Mr. Vernon, were criticised in Parliament when their decisions 'lacked any boldness or initiative'.[45] With the Land Commission under landlord pressure, both Houses of Parliament ensured that neither landlord rights nor property values were diminished by negotiated rent reductions.

Chapter 30

The thwarting of calls for Home Rule
1882 – 1889

Parnell now focused on Irish home rule. In October 1882, the Land League was resurrected as the Irish National League (INL) to combine moderate policies for agrarian reform with a programme for home rule. With the Reform Act of 1884 extending the voting franchise to householders in country districts, the electorate had nearly doubled, and Parnell could expect even greater voting support. He was also backed by Roman Catholic bishops, as home rule 'alone can satisfy the wants, the wishes, as well as the legitimate aspirations, of the Irish people'.[1] He worked with them to achieve endorsement from the Catholic electorate. The day-to-day running of the INL, which operated through 1,200 branches, was left to Timothy Harrington, its Secretary, O'Brien and Healy. Parnell reorganised the Nationalist party (or Irish Parliamentary Party as it became known) with a system of 'whips' to create a cohesive and focused group with professionally selected candidates. (This was the first party in British politics to adopt a whip system to ensure that members followed the party line.) It now became far more Catholic and middle class, with many journalists and lawyers among its members.

With Parnell having every expectation of leading between eighty and ninety members after any future election, he was a force to be reckoned with. In retrospect, it can be seen that the Tories realised that their only hope of winning the June 1885 election was to form an alliance with him. When Henry Herbert, 4th Earl of Carnarvon came to meet him, it was Parnell's understanding that, if their coalition was successful, Ireland would be offered a statutory legislature with legislation supporting Government finance for land purchase on a large scale. Nationalists thus encouraged Irish electors in England to vote Tory. With the Tories failing to gain an overall majority, Salisbury formed a minority Government with Nationalist support. Yet Tory 'Unionists' pressurised the Government not to accede to Irish home rule. With falling agricultural prices causing renewed distress and unrest in Ireland, the Tories reverted to coercion, and promises of home rule were forgotten.

After their earlier election promises, Gladstone had expected Irish home rule to have Tory support. In December 1885, his son, Herbert, wrote a letter in *The Times*, later known as the Hawarden Kite (named after Gladstone's home at Hawarden Castle), in which he expressed his father's view that Ireland should be offered parliamentary independence. Gladstone seemed to be testing which way the wind was blowing. Parnell switched the allegiance of his eighty-two Nationalist members to the Liberals and brought down the Tory Government.

In February 1886, the Nationalists won eighty-six Irish seats in the general election, and Gladstone needed to support home rule to retain their backing and form a government. Although Gladstone personally supported it, Liberal 'Unionists' did not support him. Hartington, their leader, refused to serve in the Government. Gladstone managed to ameliorate the Nationalists by stifling calls for coercion and bringing forward a bill, which became the Purchase of Land (Ireland) Act (48 and 49 Victoria. Cap. 73). This adopted the Land League's proposals for tenant land ownership. Government loans now enabled tenants to purchase their holdings, with annual repayments less than their former rents. This irretrievably weakened the Irish landlords' position and ended the London Livery Companies' involvement in Ulster. Hostility in Ireland was rapidly brought under control, and Carnarvon, who had been appointed Lord Lieutenant by the Tories, could travel through the country unattended, dispensing with large numbers of dragoons and police.

When Gladstone tabled his Home Rule bill, the proposals fell far short of Fenian aspirations, but Parnell accepted them as a basis for achieving a settlement, and its introduction has to be seen as his personal triumph. Yet the gulf between Liberal Unionists and Home-

Rulers widened, irretrievably damaging their party. The Tories, who had shown every sign of supporting the bill, turned firmly against it, hoping to bring down Gladstone's Government with support from the ninety-three Liberal Unionist members.

The House was packed for the Home Rule debate. Gladstone set out the proposals in a brilliant speech lasting three hours. It went into great detail, outlining a 'constitution of an Irish Parliament sitting in Dublin, with the Queen at its head'.[2] This was to be divided into two 'orders' with an elected assembly initially made up of Ireland's 103 former Westminster members, together with a further 103 to be elected from each constituency. There was to be an upper order, initially to include Ireland's 28 representative peers but with a further 75 elected members. The Crown would continue to appoint a Lord Lieutenant. He would be non-political and could be either Catholic or Protestant. The majority parliamentary group would form an executive. The Westminster parliament retained rights to maintain the dignity and succession to the Crown, to supervise foreign and colonial relations, matters relating to trade and navigation, the defence of the realm, and the creation of titles and honours. The new Parliament would control law and order including the appointment of judges and other officials and the raising of police forces under local control. It would raise and collect all taxes (other than excise duty, from which an estimated £6,180,000 was to be made available to fund Ireland's contribution to the armed forces and to the national debt) and raise loans for public works. It was to regulate education, and to legislate on all local Irish matters other than changes to religious freedoms or rights of property. Despite the Irish assembly's subordinated status, the bill received strong Nationalist support.

On 16 April 1886, Gladstone also brought forward a bill to allow tenants to buy their holdings from landlords at prices to be approved by Land Commissioners. This was generally to be at twenty years' purchase of the net rental, although the Commissioners had some discretion. Net rental was to be established after deducting rates, tithes and other charges paid by the Landlord, and an allowance for bad debts (which made it extremely difficult to calculate). Rental arrears were to be added to the agreed value. The State was to be authorised to acquire small holdings, receiving rents from tenants or, if unviable, holding them for resale. Critics have suggested that 'land reform in Ireland was much more a wealth-redistribution program financed by Britain that a serious effort to improve the efficiency of agriculture'.[3]

From the outset, it was clear that the complications in the Land bill greatly increased Gladstone's difficulty in gaining approval for Home Rule. His opponents expressed concerns at the cost of financing land purchase on the British Exchequer (although this proved hugely exaggerated). He was inundated with appeals to drop the Land bill but believed that he had 'the obligations of honour and the necessities of public interest', to carry through with it.[4] His opponents now played politics to bring him down. Although he allowed plenty of time for amendment, so long as the principle was approved, it was defeated by thirty votes at the second reading, when Liberal Unionists led by Hartington and Chamberlain voted against it. Its defeat was to be the principal cause of the Irish troubles that followed.

The split within the Liberal Party bewildered the country. Confident that Unionists would soon return to the fold, Gladstone called a general election. During the campaign, both Liberal Unionists and Tories pledged opposition to renewed coercion in Ireland as an alternative to home rule. Although some professed support for a measure of home rule, their aim was to bring Gladstone down. This led to home rule objectives being misrepresented. Parnell pulled back from active participation in the debate. He did not want to be seen as Gladstone's 'poodle' in demonstrating support for what he considered less than ideal proposals, and he was unwell. After waiting to see which way the wind blew, Churchill advised an Irish member privately: 'I have done my best for you, and failed; and now, of course I'll do my best against you.'[5] He visited Belfast to incite Orangemen into a sectarian war against home rule. This led to brutal rioting.

At the election in July 1886, many Liberal Unionists voted for Salisbury's Tories. They later admitted having reached a bargain, so that Liberal candidates voting against home rule would not be opposed by a Tory candidate. The combined Liberal Unionist and

Tory coalition won a majority of 118 over the rump of the Liberals and Nationalists, and they formed a Government. To maintain Liberal Unionist loyalty, Salisbury proposed Hartington as Premier, but he declined, preferring to promote traditional Liberal policies from outside Government. His followers even sat beside Gladstone on the opposition benches. Yet, Chamberlain now served under his former opponent, Salisbury, as Secretary of State for the Colonies. It was Churchill, still under forty, who showed 'conspicuous ability' as Chancellor of the Exchequer and Leader of the House.[6]

This was a Parliament of 'broken pledges'.[7] The Government adopted a scheme for Irish land purchase financed by British credit, which they had rigorously opposed under Gladstone. Yet they called for sale prices to be based on actual rents receivable, even if inflated by rack-renting. Although the Land Commissioners had some discretion to reduce values to equitable levels, they did not always do so. This inflated prices payable by the tenant and increased the finance needed from the British Government. It was this that Gladstone and the Land League had wanted to avoid and had caused Parnell and his colleagues to be jailed. The new terms also debarred tenants in arrears from receiving Government finance. Although some arrears were part of a Land League protest, most tenants had no means of paying. Poor weather had again reduced yields, and falling agricultural prices were causing genuine economic hardship. (It is estimated that Irish agricultural produce fell in value by 18½ per cent in 1885 and 1886, compared to an average of the four preceding years.)[8]

Parnell brought forward a bill proposing concessions for defaulting tenants who were suffering genuine economic difficulties. This would have allowed them to purchase their holdings on a basis set by the Land Commissioners, if they contributed at least half of their arrears in advance. The balance was to be funded as part of the purchase price. This was misunderstood in Parliament, where Parnell was thought to be seeking to halve the rental arrears properly due, which was not the case. Although Gladstone, who had been recuperating in Germany, returned to support the bill, it again failed.

Faced with 'brute force' from the British Government, the Nationalists incited civil disobedience to achieve fair rent reductions, complaining that Ireland's needs were not being addressed. Their 'Plan of Campaign' called for tenants on each estate to form a Management Committee made up of seven tenants chaired by the local priest. This was to collect each half-year's rent from tenants as it fell due. Tenants were instructed not to negotiate with their landlord except through the Committee. They were to act with the majority and accept nothing unless it was offered to all. If the Landlord's agent refused their proposals, the Committee was to retain what had been collected. Although these proposals were extreme, the Nationalists considered them morally justified for tenants with a real grievance or facing abnormal agricultural difficulties.

Many landlords offered a rent abatement of between 15 and 25 per cent without recourse by the tenants to a Plan of Campaign, but others would not concede. Although there were relatively few estates left in conflict, these filled the courts with prosecutions for rental arrears to support eviction processes. In the words of Mr Frederic Harrison in an appeal to Liberal Unionists, it was a 'gigantic, permanent systematic wickedness which you cover with the name of morality, justice and honour'. When the absentee Hubert de Burgh-Canning, 2nd Marquess of Clanrickarde, refused concessions, his agent, John Blake, was shot dead. He now obtained an injunction to prevent publication of the agent's correspondence with tenants, which would have revealed his greed. He commenced an eviction process, but when the new agent considered abatement to be fair, Clanrickarde was denounced in *The Times*.[9]

When Sir Michael Hicks-Beach was appointed Chief Secretary in Ireland he immediately recognised the need for rent abatement. Despite having opposed Parnell's bill in Parliament, he encouraged landlords to admit the economic reality of the crisis. He saw Plans of Campaign as 'an extra-legal method of settling difficulties' and refused to provide military and police support for landlords seeking tenant eviction.[10] In Kerry, Sir Redvers Buller was another official who refuse to provide rack-renting landlords with protection.

Salisbury saw Hicks-Beach's approach as conflicting with Government policy. He was replaced as Chief Secretary by Salisbury's nephew, the inexperienced Arthur Balfour, an ally of Churchill.[11] In 1887, Balfour introduced a Perpetual Crimes Act, under which hundreds were arrested and imprisoned without trial. He also introduced a new and savage Coercion bill to be enacted in perpetuity. Conflict between tenant and landlord was made illegal. The holding of meetings and writing articles needed advance approval from the Irish Executive. To overcome Irish juries' failure to convict, he proposed that prosecutions should be transferred to the Old Bailey (although this was subsequently abandoned). Tribunals were now to take place without a jury under two resident magistrates, whom Balfour appointed.

When the Coercion Act passed into law on 23 August 1887, tenants attempting to form combinations faced imprisonment. This was enforced almost universally. If an association was involved in or incited 'crime', defined as 'serious offences against the person', the Lord Lieutenant could declare it a 'dangerous association', membership of which was a criminal offence. He immediately indicted the National League, despite lacking evidence of any criminal involvement. To justify this, he claimed that the League 'promoted and incited acts of violence and interfered with the administration of the law'.[12] Yet, this was not 'crime' as defined. In September, two hundred League branches were suppressed in cos. Cork, Kerry, Limerick, Clare, Wexford and Galway. Anyone involved in incitement faced six months' imprisonment.

For some time, police reporters had been attending public meetings to report on their proceedings. This had never previously caused a problem. On 9 September 1887, O'Brien, who had been Balfour's formidable opponent in editorials in the *New Ireland*, and John Mandeville, a 'cheerful' local gentleman farmer, arranged a meeting at Mitchelstown, also attended by Dillon, the Nationalist Member of Parliament. Their objective was to support a group of tenants in their plan for a combination to reduce rents charged by their landlord, the Dowager Countess of Kingston. Although the meeting was called before the Coercion Act came into in force, it took place afterwards and was by then illegal. Tenants had already turned down the landlord's offers of a reduction of 15 per cent and later of 17½ per cent, and the meeting was to discuss what further action could be taken.

When the meeting started, police arrived unannounced, pushing their way through the throng with batons to put their reporter in place. With some of the audience on horses, the police were driven back. When they returned in greater numbers, there was a 'scuffle'. Having retired to their barrack, they opened fire, killing three men. Although they later claimed that the crowd threw stones, the barrack door was undamaged, and only six out of 160 panes of the barrack's glass were broken, probably by the police to enable them to use their rifles. When Dillon arrived to calm the crowd, he found 'not 10 men within 60 yards of the barrack.' The 'Mitchelstown massacre' caused an outrage, and Balfour was reduced to lying to justify what had happened. When a coroners' jury returned a verdict of wilful murder against the police, Balfour had it quashed. Although the police authorities called an investigation, no one was prosecuted. Yet a policeman injured in the scuffle received £1,000 raised as a tax on the locality.

After the Mitchelstown meeting, O'Brien and Mandeville were arrested and jailed at Cork for three and two months respectively. On their second morning in jail, they were woken at about 4am and moved without notice to the more remote Tullamore, out of range of the Mayor and magistrates in Cork, who sympathised with their political views. At Tullamore, the magistracy was made up mainly of Tory 'political stooges', who were unlikely to interfere. Yet there were two Nationalists among them, and Dr Moorehead protected O'Brien, who still suffered poor health. Mandeville was less lucky. He was treated as a common criminal, but he retained his own clothing and refused to don prison garb or to clean his cell. He was placed on bread and water, and later faced solitary confinement. Despite his strong constitution, he was soon suffering 'symptoms of physical decay' and complained of a sore throat.[13] His diet caused him diarrhoea, but his punishment continued so long as he shunned prison garb. At last, his sore throat was seen by the prison doctor, Dr Ridley, who claimed that he was not ill (although Dr Moorehead disagreed). After seventy-two hours of further punishment, his violent diarrhoea required treatment. Although the doctor substituted white bread for brown, Mandeville remained very ill. Eventually, the Governor came to his cell, where warders forcibly tore off his clothes, leaving him with the choice of prison garb or 'the temporary cover of his bed clothes'.[14] After twenty-four hours wrapped in his quilt and sheet in winter weather, he submitted to prison clothing.

On his release on Christmas Eve, Mandeville's wife found him thin and weak, hardly being able to write or to walk to his house a mile away in Mitchelstown. His sore throat continued, and he never recovered his strength. Although he exhorted the locality not to pay compensation for the injured policeman, he died six months later.

The reporting of the Mitchelstown massacre and of Mandeville's death spread consternation through Tory ranks. Many called for Irish prisons to provide more humane treatment. On 1 March 1889, Gladstone made a brilliant speech in the House of Commons warning the Government that the writing was on the wall. He gained support for an amendment to the Queen's speech and pointed out that in the sixty by-elections since the 1886 General Election, the Tory candidate had either been defeated by the Liberal or his majority had been significantly reduced. Yet the Tories continued to support coercion.

Despite a promise to maintain Press freedom, Balfour prosecuted any journal reporting on meetings of suppressed branches of the National League, arguing that freedom of the press was limited to editorial comment. They could comment on, but could not record, events! When Timothy Daniel Sullivan, the Lord Mayor of Dublin, was prosecuted, Mr. C J O'Donel, the Chief Magistrate, refused to convict him. Although he was found guilty when Balfour prosecuted him in a higher court, he faced only a nominal sentence. Similar treatment was meted out to O'Brien, to other newspaper proprietors and Nationalist supporters making political speeches. Some were jailed for booing Balfour. This was political tyranny at its worst.

Although Tories had rejected the tenant relief proposals of Parnell's bill, they came forward with their own bill in 1888, to provide £5 million to fund tenants' land purchases. Yet relief was to be limited to an 'irreducible minimum' and was not available to those in arrears. Although it would have 'afforded some relief, [it would have] aggravated some of the very worst difficulties of the Irish situation'.[15] It would have prevented Land Commissioners from amending rents set judicially, even though they might have been set five years earlier when economic circumstances had been very much better. This left the terms for selling land from landlord to tenant not particularly attractive to either party. Eventually the Government relented, and Land Commissioners were authorised to adjust rents, but only to the extent of the fall in produce prices. They had no powers to take falling yields into consideration. This was at odds with Scottish legislation, where rents were generally lower. 'The [Scottish] Land Commission had the power not merely to reduce the rent, but to reduce or extinguish the arrears'.[16] The bill proposed that tenants in arrears should be allowed to go bankrupt. This not only left the landlord out of pocket, but the tenant's other creditors, particularly shopkeepers, who had often provided support during a difficult period.

Eventually, increasing Liberal and Nationalist pressure caused the bill to be dropped. Despite this, no alternative measures to relieve the tenants' financial plight were brought forward, and the arrears problem was left unresolved. Nevertheless, many landlords voluntarily reduced rents by up to 50 per cent (25 per cent on rents set judicially). With Land Courts now reducing valuations set by Land Commissioners, rental abatement became almost universal, heralding an 'extraordinary reduction' in agricultural crime. Yet plot sizes often remained below subsistence levels. At last, in 1891, the Government organised Congested District Boards with the goal of amalgamating and restructuring holdings in the poorest parts of the north and west of Ireland to create areas sufficient to support a family.

Chapter 31

Attempts to blacken Parnell's name
1886 – 1891

As if by chance, on the day of the Coercion bill's debate, *The Times* published a letter purportedly written and signed by Parnell four years earlier, which related to the Phoenix Park killings. This included the words: 'Though I regret the accident of Lord F. Cavendish's death, I cannot refuse to admit that Burke got no more than his deserts.' Although the letter was printed by *The Times* in facsimile with assurances of authenticity, Parnell protested that it was a malicious forgery. Nevertheless, the Tory Government turned down his request for a full investigation by a House of Commons committee. When it proposed that the Attorney-General should prosecute *The Times*, Parnell would not agree, as the Attorney-General was a member of the Government (and subsequently led *The Times's* prosecution against the Irish members). With the Government continuing to make political capital, Parnell contemplated prosecuting *The Times* himself, but did not want the decision resting with a London jury with possible Tory sympathies. The matter seemed to rest there until Frank Hugh O'Donnell, a former Irish Member with a grudge against Parnell, sued *The Times* for libel without consulting him, even though he was not particularly implicated. With Parnell taking no part, the libel case ended in fiasco, and he had to defend himself. As it was a political issue, he again asked for investigation by a Parliamentary committee, but the Government proposed a tribunal of judges, which Parnell reluctantly accepted.

By this time, *The Times* had published further letters, apparently signed by Parnell, implying his incitement of the Phoenix Park murders. When the Government refused to limit the investigation's scope, it became a trial of the Nationalist movement. Although the Attorney-General was acting as Counsel for *The Times,* quite improperly he nominated the tribunal's judges. When it began, the letters were put on one side, and the investigation's focus was on evidence that the Nationalists had used the Land League to incite tenant unrest. A Government spy, Major Le Caron, claimed that Parnell had told him that it would take an armed insurrection to free Ireland. This must have seemed an unlikely comment for him to make to a perfect stranger. When at last the letters were discussed, *The Times* editor admitted having no evidence to authenticate those purportedly written by Parnell. They had been provided by a Mr Houston, who obtained them from Richard Pigott, a rogue journalist. From the witness stand, Pigott claimed to have received them in Paris. Under cross-examination he was asked to spell 'likelihood' and 'hesitancy' and he misspelt them as they were misspelt in the letters. He was then shown to have a previous record of attempted blackmail, and eventually confessed to writing them himself. He immediately fled, but was traced to Madrid, where he shot himself through the mouth during attempts to arrest him. In an out-of-court settlement, Parnell received £5,000 from *The Times,* but the Nationalists were not cleared of criminal involvement in the murders.

With Parnell otherwise occupied in the libel action, the passage of the Coercion bill was greatly eased, although need for it was hard to fathom. Crime was at about one quarter of the level of five years earlier. In Limerick, Mr Justice O'Brien told the grand Jury at the assize: 'There is no criminal business to be done'.[1] Although Balfour manipulated statistics to make crime look worse, the objective was to end 'Plans of Campaign' (as both Salisbury and Hartington subsequently admitted), thereby preventing combinations of tenants challenging their landlords.

The effect of the letters published in *The Times* being shown to be fraudulent only added to Tory consternation. When Parnell returned to the House of Commons, Liberals and Nationalists gave him a standing ovation lasting several minutes. Money to fight the Irish cause was being raised in America and it was seen that his 'demands were entirely within the accepted parameters of Liberal thinking'.[2] It was the high point of his career, and it seemed that Irish home rule would be achieved as soon as the Liberals were back in office. Once more, Irish hopes were to be dashed.

In 1886, Parnell had agreed to promoted O'Shea as member for Galway, apparently after pressure from the liberal Joseph Chamberlain (who may have been trying to undermine Parnell's authority), but it was against the advice of Healy, Dillon and O'Brien. O'Shea had brokered the Kilmainham treaty with the Liberals, which had resulted in Parnell and others being freed. His election as a Member of Parliament required him to move to London, where his wife Kitty, from whom he had been estranged for some time, had arrived in the previous year. She had acted as a liaison between the Nationalists and Gladstone during his first Home Rule bill. She had also been Parnell's mistress since 1880, although he had only recently taken up residence with her. Although her separation from O'Shea had arisen long before this, she was in expectation of a substantial inheritance from an aunt and he would not divorce her. It was common knowledge in Westminster circles that Parnell had fathered three of her children, but if generally known, it would cause him political embarrassment. In December 1889, O'Shea at last cited Parnell in divorce proceedings. The case was not heard until November 1890. Although Parnell was confident of riding out the storm, his extra-marital relationship was bound to cause a scandal. He did not contest the proceedings and the divorce was granted, leaving him free to marry Kitty, but the Court placed his two surviving children in O'Shea's custody. Although he received initial backing from both Nationalists and the Catholic Church (which professed that it was a political issue), Gladstone was shocked. He had not believed rumours of the affair but feared that Parnell's retention as Nationalist leader would undermine the Liberals' non-conformist vote, which was at the core of its support. If the next election were lost, their alliance with the Nationalists to achieve home rule would end. Although Parnell was re-elected leader by his Nationalist colleagues, they were not aware of Gladstone's views, which were published on the following day.

With Parnell determined to hold the Nationalists together, he refused to stand down as leader, even temporarily. Eventually McCarthy, with Liberal party encouragement, walked out of a National party meeting with forty-four other members to form the Irish National Federation. He was a distinguished journalist, having become editor of the *Morning Star* in 1860, but in 1868 he retired to lecture in the United States. In 1870, he returned as leader writer of the *Daily News*. With his journalistic pedigree, he made an obvious caretaker leader, but was not an active politician. John Dillon soon took over, having gained crucial Catholic Church support. Yet he was a republican at heart and resisted all attempts to reach accord with the Unionists. Parnell was left with twenty-eight supporters in the Irish National League, headed by John Redmond. Despite having been Parnell's stalwart supporter, Healy, an ardent Catholic, viciously attacked his leadership, forcing his resignation. The split tore Ireland apart, particularly when Parnell turned once more to the Fenians for support, causing the Irish National League to lose several crucial by-elections.

Parnell married Kitty on 25 June 1891 and they moved to Brighton, but he was suffering from kidney disease and deteriorating health. Although he continued to campaign in Ireland to restore his fortunes, he was completely exhausted when he returned to Kitty in England and died of pneumonia at Hove on 6 October. He was aged forty-five. His funeral in Dublin was attended by 200,000 people.

Chapter 32

The legacy left by Gladstone and Parnell 1891 and thereafter

In the 1892 General Election, Gladstone again promised home rule, and the Liberals gained sufficient seats to form a minority Government. In February 1893, he introduced his second Home Rule bill, but the former understanding developed with Parnell was never recovered. Dillon, lacking the same *rapport*, and the divided Nationalists did not become involved in promoting it. The drafting was similar to enactments for confederation in Canada. It would have allowed eighty Irish members to continue to sit and vote at Westminster. Although it was passed by narrow majorities at the second and third readings in the House of Commons, it remained seriously flawed and needed further debate. With Gladstone becoming 'increasingly disengaged', it lost credibility, and, in September, the Tory-dominated House of Lords voted it down by 419 votes to 41. It has been suggested that Gladstone was the author of his own defeat, and he resigned soon after.

With the return of a Tory Government in 1895, home rule was again moved to the back burner. Gladstone was a broken man and died in 1898. The successors of Gladstone and Parnell lacked their statesmanship. Dillon's policy was to pressurise landlords and Government with continued agrarian agitation. He fell out with many of his Nationalist colleagues. When Healy advocated conciliation, Dillon expelled him from the party. He also fell out with O'Brien, who, in 1898, launched the National Ireland League seeking reconciliation through agrarian reform. Eventually Dillon was forced into taking a more moderate line and his 'doctrine of conciliation' gained considerable support. In 1900, the Nationalists reunited under John Redmond, with Dillon retained as Deputy. While Dillon loyally supported Redmond, he attacked O'Brien during the 1902 Land Conference. For Dillon, conflict had always been more important than victory, and he focused the home rule movement on a class war against landlords. When, in November 1903, O' Brien resigned, Dillon regained control of the National Ireland League, and continued his attack on the 'traditional enemy'.

The Act of Union had become the most divisive issue in British politics. The Tories rebranded themselves as the Conservative and Unionist Party, introducing a range of constructive reforms, hoping to 'kill home rule by kindness'. The man who rose to the Unionist cause was Sir Edward Carson, the charismatic leader of the Ulster Unionist Party. He was from a wealthy Dublin-based Protestant family and had become an eminent barrister. Most notably, he had acted for the Marquess of Queensbury when accused of libel by Oscar Wilde. In 1892, he became Ireland's Solicitor-General, despite not having a seat in the House of Commons but was elected for Dublin as a Liberal Unionist soon after.

Although Dillon poured scorn on Carson and took an uncompromising stance against him, Carson mounted an effective campaign to maintain the union, backed by the Conservative leader Bonar Law. He also strongly opposed Orangeism, describing it as 'the unrolling of a mummy. All old bones and rotten rags'.[1] With the Liberal Party disillusioned by the defeats of the Home Rule bills in 1886 and 1893, it failed to support renewed Nationalist demands for home rule, and the House of Lords remained fervently opposed to it. Yet steps were being taken to limit the powers of the upper house (culminating in the Parliamentary Act of 1911). When Herbert Asquith was forced to call a General Election in 1910, he needed Nationalist support to retain a Commons majority. This led to a third Home Rule bill in 1912. With the House of Lords being curbed, there was every expectation of it coming into force. Yet, it was opposed by Carson, who was in fear of a Catholic dominated Dublin government, and by thousands of Ulstermen, who signed a Solemn League and Covenant to resist it. Carson formed the Ulster Volunteers as a loyalist paramilitary group to co-ordinate armed resistance. This undertook military training and, controversially, Carson approved the purchase of arms from Imperial Germany, which was eager to promote political tension in the United Kingdom. To meet the challenge from Ulster, the Irish Republican Brotherhood raised the Irish Volunteers to advance separatist ends. With their arms again being provided from Germany, Ireland was on the brink of civil war. In September, Carson announced that, if home rule came into effect in the rest of Ireland, Ulster would establish its own provisional Government.[2] When both Asquith and the Nationalists tried to resist him, this only strengthened Unionist resolve. Voting in Down, Antrim, Armagh and Londonderry showed large Unionist majorities. Although Fermanagh and Tyrone had small home rule majorities, they too linked with Ulster's provisional Government.

Nationalist hopes of establishing Ireland as a single republican state were now doomed. To allow the bill to progress, Redmond and O'Brien would have to concede a large measure of local autonomy to Ulster, but Dillon was reluctant to allow the six counties to opt out. When the Government of Ireland Act was passed in 1914, Redmond was greatly praised for at last achieving home rule for southern Ireland. He even agreed that Royal Assent for its implementation should be suspended for the war's duration and raised 150,000 National Volunteers to support the British war effort. Although he persuaded Dillon to support the allies, Dillon abstained from backing the use of Irish military divisions.

Had land ownership reform been successful? The Wyndham Land Purchase Act of 1903 offered generous terms for tenants seeking to buy their properties. This had made the initiative extremely popular, but expensive for the British taxpayer. By the First World War, finance for Irish land purchase had been ended, but, by then, about half of Ireland's agricultural land was held by its occupiers. At partition, landlords were finally compelled to sell.

One of the undoubted disappointments of the Land Acts is that it did not act as a massive boost to Irish farming productivity. Despite tenants being able to obtain finance under the Land Acts to acquire their freeholds, agriculture achieved only a 7 per cent increase in production between 1870 and 1910. The rate of increase in farming investment was less than between 1850 and 1870 before the Acts were in place. Although the legislation ended landlord absenteeism, it failed to incentivise Irish farmers either to increase productivity or to invest further in their infrastructure. With annual costs being reduced, small farmers no longer needed to seek additional agricultural work by travelling to Britain during the harvest, and the declining availability of farm labour pushed up agricultural wages. There was another reason. Guinnane and Miller in the *Chicago Journals* of 2010, have argued that the great majority of agricultural land had remained for generations in the occupation of the same more substantial tenant families and smaller freeholders.[3] They felt no sense of insecurity and could borrow when needed against their tenant rights', which the Irish Land Acts extended from Ulster all over Ireland. From 1850 to 1870 bigger farmers enjoyed great economic prosperity, with the value of output increasing far faster than the cost of rent. Most Irish farmers generated surpluses, which they retained for themselves. This, of course, meant that, while farmers with larger land areas happily acquired their freeholds, this had no impact on the way that they farmed. In retrospect, calls for land ownership reform proved more successful in achieving Irish nationalism than in improving its productivity.

Guinnane and Miller go on to say that the precariousness of land tenure immediately prior to the Land Reform Acts was grossly exaggerated and reports were politically motivated. While this may be partially correct, there is no doubt of the genuine deprivation suffered by small holders on areas of land that were not sustainable, nor of the obnoxious treatment meted out on behalf of absentee landlords. Without freehold ownership, rent paid by a tenant to an absentee landlord in Britain was lost to the Irish economy.

The British Government has to shoulder the lion's share of the blame for its mismanagement of Ireland. Its primary objective in introducing the Irish Land Acts was not land ownership reform but the pacification of rural unrest. Certainly, this was Gladstone's motive. The Acts were successful in redistributing wealth from landlords to sustainable tenants, but this came at substantial cost to the British taxpayer. Smallholders remained out in the cold. Their choice was to remain on the same plots as before, with the same inefficiencies as in the past, or to emigrate. The legislation failed to establish land banks (as on the Continent) to provide them with farming finance. When they found borrowing costs to be prohibitive, they had no way to better themselves.

Postscript

History has shown that Ireland's problems have not ended here, particularly in the North. This narrative has outlined many of the causes of Irish unrest; it would be invidious to offer solutions. Given the extent of past outrages, it is understandable that old sores have taken time to heal, but heal they need to do, as history cannot be rewritten. In all 'colonial' regimes set up within the British Empire, the achievement of independence has always proved the most sensitive aspect. It is the settlers who have had most difficulty in reconciling themselves to the democratic process of self-government, particularly those who have been there for many generations. It was never so much of a problem in Canada or Australia, or even the United States (although by then the British colonisers had lost control), where the indigenous populations were small, often having been decimated by European diseases. Natives were simply overwhelmed by arriving settlers. Yet in Africa and Asia, independence has tended to cause settlers to come off worst, even if not forced out completely. In larger Commonwealth countries, there has always been the potential for unrest between groups of settlers from differing locations or with differing sectarian backgrounds. Good examples have been French settlers in Quebec and Boers in South Africa. Although perceived differences between rival groupings have sometimes led to calls for partition, economic common sense generally prevails.

The British have always been sensitive to Irish aggression, because Ireland's proximity threatens British security, particularly if supported by hostile aggressors from elsewhere. The Gaelic-speaking Irish have always been seen as alien; they had no historic links with the English, differing not just in speech, but in clothing, in custom and later in religious belief. In a land where deprivation has led to a burgeoning of petty atrocities, there is an unfortunate perception that rivalries are divided down sectarian fault lines, which, as has been seen, has not always been the case.

Much of Ireland's tragedy can be laid at the feet of absentee British landlords, who milked their Irish estates for all they were worth, without any attempt to improve the land's infrastructure or to provide support for their impoverished and often starving tenants. With British landowners dominating the Westminster Parliament, particularly the House of Lords, it is hard to find any mitigation for the greed which promoted their protectionist policies. Fear that cheap Irish labour would undercut English prices led to controls on Irish agricultural exports and an embargo on the development of an Irish manufacturing industry able to employ the surplus rural population.

Religious difference has become blurred by time. It was the Dissenters who promoted the republican rebellions of 1798 and 1803, while preaching religious tolerance for all. Yet the British preferred to depict it as Catholic unrest. It is an irony that it was the Dissenters' descendants who became the 'Loyalists' wedded to the union with Britain. No religious denomination has done much to mitigate continuing conflict. The Established Church of Ireland, which professed Anglican dogma, saw its role as supporting the Protestant 'Ascendancy'. It was never able to count a high proportion of the population as part of its flock, but it usurped Catholic churches and Church lands. Its bishops lived with the wealth of princes and its clergy enjoyed life at the social pinnacle of each locality, funded out of Church lands and from tithes and hearth taxes. These were paid by all denominations regardless of creed, particularly by impoverished Catholics and Presbyterians, who did not attend their services. The Irish Catholic church has remained extraordinarily resilient after the drubbing it faced from penal legislation. When, at last, it could flex its wings, it actively enforced segregation, preventing Catholic children from contamination by attending schools with their Protestant counterparts. It also failed (and still fails) to encourage modern forms of birth control, leaving a growing Catholic population with less land to be shared between each generation of farmer.

There was a time when population growth was controlled in many other ways. War and internecine conflict played their part, and very often crops were ravaged or failed, resulting in deaths from starvation. Deaths also arose from disease, often imported by soldiers and other arrivals from overseas, but just as often caused by poor sanitation. Outbreaks of cholera, typhoid and plague brought a devastating loss of life, but the rural Irish were slow to become familiar with the reasonable standards of hygiene essential among larger population groups. The uncertain climate caused crop failures, often the result of extended periods of cold weather or drought. The failure of the potato crop from *Phytophthora Infestans* famously caused the Great Famine starting in 1845, but the potato crop failed on numerous occasions, often from poor weather. The disaster caused by the Great Famine has been shown to be the result of British Government ineptitude. Whether delays in providing welfare were used as a means of achieving a reduction in the rural peasant population is difficult to judge. With the nineteenth century bringing with it better hygiene and medical care, the peasant population was able to grow freely, but the shortage of land led to inevitable deprivation. In Ireland, this could only be solved by emigration. In Ulster, the growing numbers of Catholics when compared to Protestants is disturbing the uneasy balance in its more western counties by providing them with a majority Catholic population.

Ireland has many geographic shortcomings. It is at the outer perimeter of the European continent resulting in longer transportation distances to the disadvantage of its trading relationships. It lacks significant mineral resources, with little oil or gas and a dearth of iron and coal, but perhaps a potential abundance of wind power. It faces inclement weather, but, nevertheless, attracts visitors to its soft and emerald countryside as a sought-after tourist destination. It is blessed with beautiful buildings in unparalleled settings, both rugged castles and Georgian mansions, generally the remaining vestiges of British settlement. The partition of Northern Ireland has brought its own problems, leaving Londonderry as an *entrepôt* with only half of its original hinterland. Economically, Ulster depends heavily on the rest of Ireland as a trading partner. It does not need these links to be damaged by BREXIT. Assuring its continuing trading links may reopen old sensitivities, but common sense needs to prevail; Ulster needs to overlook the sectarian difficulties of the past and recognise the economic realities and opportunities of its future.

Bibliography

Adelman, Paul, and Pearce, Robert, *Great Britain and the Irish Question, 1798 – 1922,* London, Hodder Murray, 2005 – 'Adelman and Pearce'

Agnew, Jean, ed., *The Drennan McTier Letters 1776 – 1819* (3 Vols.), Dublin, Irish Manuscript Commssion, 1998, 1999 – 'Agnew'

Apprentice Boys of Derry web site – *'Apprentice Boys of Derry'*

Armstrong, Rev. James, M.A., *Presbyterian Congregations in Dublin, in the Ordination Service of James Martineau,* Dublin, 1829 – 'Armstrong'

Bardon, Jonathan, *The Plantation of Ulster, The British Colonisation of the North of Ireland in the Seventeenth Century,* Gill and MacMillan, Dublin 2011 – 'Bardon'

Barnard, Toby, *The Kingdom of Ireland 1641 – 1760,* New York, Palgrave, 2004 – 'Barnard'

Barrington, Sir Jonah, *Historic Memoirs of Ireland; comprising Secret Records of the National Convention, the Rebellion, and the Union,* London, Henry Colburn, 1835 – 'Barrington'

Bartlett, Thomas, *Theobald Wolfe Tone,* Dublin, Lilliput, 1998 – 'Bartlett'

Bartlett, Thomas, *Revolutionary Dublin 1795 – 1801: The Letters of Francis Higgins to Dublin Castle,* Dublin, Four Courts, 2004 – *'Higgins'*

Beresford, William, Ed., *The Correspondence of The Right Honourable John Beresford,* London, Woodfall and Kinder, 1854 – 'Beresford'

Betts, John, *The Story of the Irish Society,* 1913, The Honourable The Irish Society – 'Betts'

Blake, Robert, *Disraeli,* University Paperbacks, St Martin's Press, 1967 – 'Blake'

Boyd, Andrew, *Holy War in Belfast,* Tralee, Anvil, 1969 – 'Boyd'

Brown, Michael, *Francis Hutcheson in Dublin,* Dublin, Four Courts, 2002 – 'Brown'

Campbell, Flann, *The Dissenting Voice, Protestant Democracy in Ulster from Plantation to Partition,* Belfast, Blackstaff, 1991 – 'Campbell'

Carroll, Francis M., *The American Presence in Ulster: A Diplomatic History, 1796 – 1996,*Washington, The Catholic University of America Press, 2005 – 'Carroll'

Childe-Pemberton, William S., *The Earl Bishop. The Life of Frederick Hervey, Bishop of Derry, Earl of Bristol,* London, Hurst & Blackett, 1924 – 'Childe-Pemberton'

Clifford, Brendan, *Belfast and the French Revolution,* Belfast, Historical and Educational Society, 1989 – 'Clifford 1989'

Clifford, Brendan, *Scripture Politics, The Works of William Steel Dickson,* Belfast, Atholl, 1991 – 'Clifford 1991'

Cobban, Alfred, and Smith, Robert A., Eds. *The Correspondence of Edmund Burke,* Vol. 7, Chicago, University of Chicago Press, 1967 – 'Cobban and Smith'

Cochrane, Feargal, *The Unionists of Ulster: An Idealogical Analysis,* Cork, Cork University Press, 1997 – 'Cochrane'

Communist Party of Ireland, *Remember '98: The Man from God Knows Where: Thomas Russell (1767 – 1803)* – 'Thomas Russell'

Communist Party of Ireland, *The Man of No Property: Jemmy Hope (1764 – 1847)* – 'Jemmy Hope'

Connell, K. H., *Peasant Marriage in Ireland: Its Structure and Development since the Famine, Economic History Review,* 2nd Series – 'Connell'

Connolly, S. J., *Divided Kingdom: Ireland 1630 – 1800,* Oxford, Oxford University Press, 2008 – 'Connolly'

Crymble, Adam, *The United Irishmen's Allies,* United Irishmen Online – 'Crymble'

Curl, James Stevens, *The Londonderry Plantation, 1609 – 1914*, Chichester, Phillimore & Co. Limited, 1986 – 'Curl 1986'

Curl, James Stevens, *The Honourable The Irish Society and the Plantation of Ulster, 1608 – 2000*, Chichester, Phillimore & Co. Limited, 2000 – 'Curl 2000'

Curl, James Stevens, *The City of London and the Plantation of Ulster*, BBCi History on Line, 2001 – 'Curl BBCi 2001'

Curtin, Nancy, *The United Irishmen: Popular Politics in Ulster and Dublin, 1791 – 1798*, Oxford, Clarendon Press, 1998 – 'Curtin'

Curtis, Edmund, *A á*, Dublin, Methuen & Co., 1945 – 'Curtis'

Devine, T. M., Scotland's Empire 1600 – 1815, London – 'Devine'

Dictionary of National Biography, 1917 – 'DNB'

Drennan Letters, Public Record Office, Northern Ireland – 'Drennan Letters'

Drummond, William, ed., *Autobiography of Archibald Hamilton Rowan*, Dublin, Thomas Tegg, 1840 – 'Drummond'

Encyclopaedia Britannica

Fitzpatrick, W. J., *The Sham Squire and the Informers of 1798*, Dublin, M. H. Gill and Son, 1865 – 'Fitzpatrick'

Fitzwilliam, Earl, *Letters of a Venerated Nobleman, recently retired from this country to the Earl of Carlisle, explaining the cause of that event*, Dublin, 1795 – 'Fitzwilliam'

Garret, Clarke, *Joseph Priestley, the Millennium and the French Revolution*, Journal of the History of Ideas 34.1, 1973 – 'Garret'

Gilbert, J.T., ed., *History of the Irish Confederation and the War in Ireland, 7 Vols.*, Dublin, 1882 – 9 – 'Gilbert'

Gordon, The Rev. James Bentley, *A History of the Rebellion in Ireland in 1798*, Dublin, 1801 – 'Gordon'

Grattan, Henry (son), *Memoirs of the Life and Times of the Rt. Hon. Henry Grattan, Esq. M.P.*, London, Henry Colburn, 1839 – 'Grattan Memoirs'

Grayling, A.C., *The Quarrel of the Age: The Life and Times of William Hazlitt*, London, Phoenix, 2001 – 'Grayling'

Gregg, Pauline, *Freeborn John: The Biography of John Lilburne*, Phoenix, 2000 – 'Gregg'

Gribben, Crawford, *God's Irishmen: Theological Debates in Cromwellian Ireland*, New York: Oxford University Press, 2007 – 'Gribben'

Guinnane, Timothy W., and Miller, Ronald I., *The Limits to Land Reform, 1870 – 1909*, Chicago, University of Chicago Press, vol. 45(3) – 'Guinnane and Miller'

Gwynn, Denis, *Daniel O'Connell, The Irish Liberator*, Ireland, Hutchinson & Co., 1929 – 'Gwynn'

Hallinan, Conn, *Coin of Empire. Too Costly for Israelis, Palistinians and US Taxpayers*, Foreign Policy In Focus, 2003 – 'Hallinan'

Hames, Jane Hayter, *Arthur O'Connor: United Irishman*, Cork, Collins Press, 2001 – 'Hames'

Harris, James, 3rd Earl of Malmesbury, ed., *Diaries and Correspondence of James Harris, 1st Earl of Malmesbury* – 'Malmesbury'

Hay, Edward, *History of the Insurrection of the County of Wexford, A.D. 1798*, Dublin, John Stockdale, 1803 – 'Hay'

Hays-McCoy, G. A., *Irish Battles: A Military History of Ireland*, London, 1969 – 'Hays-McCoy'

Healy, Timothy, *Why there is an Irish land question and an Irish Land League*, Dublin, M.H. Gill, 1881 – 'Healy'

Hickey, D. J., and Doherty, J. E., *A New Dictionary of Irish History from 1800*, Land Acts, Gill and MacMillan, 2003 – 'Hickey and Doherty'

Hill, Jacqueline, *Dublin Corporation, Dissent and Politics, 1660 – 1800*, in Herlihy, Kevin, ed., *The Politics of Irish Dissent 1650 – 1800*, Dublin, Four Courts Press, 1999 – 'Hill'

Historical Collections relating to the Town of Belfast, 1817 – 'Historical Collections'

Hope, Jemmy, *The Memoirs of Jemmy Hope: An Autobigraphy of a Working Class United Irishman*, British & Irish Communist Organisation, 1972 – 'Hope'

Houston, Alan Craig, *Algernon Sidney and the Republican Heritage in England and America*, Princeton, Princeton University Press, 1991 – 'Houston'

Irish Democrat, Napper Tandy: forgotten patriot – 'Tandy'

Irish Society, The, *A Concise History of The Irish Society*, G. Bleaden 1842 – 'Irish Society'

Joy, Henry, *Belfast Politics*, Belfast, 1794 – 'Joy'

Kennedy, Brian, *The Scots-Irish in the Mountains of Tennessee*, Londonderry, Causeway, 1995 – 'Kennedy'

Kilroy, Phil., *Protestant Dissent and Controversy in Ireland, 1660 – 1714*, Cork, Cork University Press, 1994 – 'Kilroy'

King, William, *The State of the Protestants*, London, 1691 – 'King'

Larkin, John, *The Trial of William Drennan*, Dublin, Irish Academic Press, 1991 – 'Larkin'

Lecky, W. E. H., *History of Ireland in the Eighteenth Century*, London, 1892, Vol. I – 'Lecky'

Leland, Thomas, *History of Ireland*, London and Dublin, 1773 – 'Leland'

Litton, Helen, *The Irish Famine: An Illustrated History*, University of California, Wolfhound Press, 1994 – 'Litton'

Lyons, Francis Stewart Leland, *Charles Stewart Parnell*, New York, Oxford University Press, 1973 – 'Lyons'

McCracken, Henry Joy, *The McCracken Letters* – 'McCracken Letters'

MacDonnell, Michael F. J., *Ireland and the Home Rule Movement*, Fáilte Romhat, 1908 – 'MacDonnell'

McDowell, R. B., *Grattan a life*, Dublin, Lilliput, 2001 – 'McDowell'

McDowell, R. B., ed. *The Correspondence of Edmund Burke*, Vol. 8, Chicago, University of Chicago Press, 1970 – 'McDowell, Ed., Vol. 8'

McNeill, *The Life and Times of Mary Ann McCracken,* 1960, Allen Figgis and Company Limited – 'McNeill'

Madden, Richard Robert, *Antrim and Down in '98,* Cameron & Ferguson Edition, London, Burns Oates & Washbourne Ltd. – 'Antrim and Down in '98'

Madden, Richard Robert, *The United Irishmen, their lives and times,* 3 series, 1842, J. Madden & Co., London, – 'Madden'

Maher, Maura, *Oliver Bond, Dublin Historical Record, September – November 1950* – 'Maher'

Mahon, Lord (later Earl Stanhope) and Cardwell, Rt. Hon. Edward, Trustees, *Memoirs by the Right Honourable Sir Robert Peel,* London, John Murray, 1857 – 'Peel Memoirs'

Marshall, P. J. and Woods, John A., Eds. *The Correspondence of Edward Burke,* Chicago, University of Chicago Press, Vol. 7, 1968 – 'Marshall and Woods'

Marshall, W.F., *Ulster Sails West,* 5th Ed. 1976 – 'Marshall'

Miller, Kerby A., et al., *Irish Immigrants in the Land of Canaan: Letters and Memoirs from Colonial and Revolutionary America, 1675 – 1800,* Oxford, Oxford University Press, 2003 – 'Miller'

Millin, Samuel Shannon, *Sidelights on Belfast History,* W. & G. Baird, 1932 – 'Millin'

Millingen, John Gideon, *The History of Duelling,* London, Richard Bentley, 1841 – 'Millingen'

Morgan, W., *Memoirs of the Life of Rev. Richard Price,* London, 1823, in *Enlightenment and Dissent,* vol. 22, 2003 – 'Morgan'

Morley, John, *The Life of William Ewart Gladstone,* London, MacMillan & Co. 1903 – 'Morley'

Nelson, Craig, *Thomas Paine: Enlightenment, Revolution, and the Birth of Modern Nations,* New York, Viking, 2006 – 'Nelson'

O'Connell, M., ed., *The Correspondence of Daniel O'Connell,* 8 Vols., Dublin, Blackwater, 1972 – 80 – 'O'Connell correspondence'

O'Connor, T. P., and Page, T. N., *Parnell Movement*, New York, Cassell Publishing Company, 1891 – 'T. P. O'Connor'

O'Ferrall, Fergus, *Daniel O'Connell*, Dublin, Gill and MacMillan, 1981 – 'O'Ferrall'

O'Riorden, Rev. M., *Catholicity and Progress in Ireland*, London, Kegan Paul, Trench, Trübner & Co., Ltd., 1906 – 'O'Riorden'

Perceval-Maxwell, M., *The Outbreak of the Irish Rebellion of 1641*, Dublin, 1994 – 'Perceval-Maxwell'

Phillips, Charles, *Recollections of Curren and some of his contemporaries*, London, Milliken, Dublin 1818 – 'Phillips'

Pincus, Steve, *1688: The First Modern Revolution*, Newhaven and London, Yale University Press, 2009 – 'Pincus'

Price, Rev. Dr Richard, *Discourse on the Love of our Country*, 1789 – 'Price'

Reid, J. Seaton, *History of the Presbyterian Church in Ireland*, Belfast, 1867 – 'Reid'

Robbins, Caroline, *The Eighteenth-Century Commonwealthman*, Indianapolis, Liberty Fund, 1987 – 'Robbins'

Ryan, Desmond, *The Fenian Chief: A Biography of James Stephens*, Dublin, Hey Thom Ltd., 1967 – 'Ryan'

Smith, E. A., *Whig Principles and Party Politics. Earl FitzWilliam and the Whig Party. 1748 – 1833*, Manchester, Manchester University Press, 1986 – 'Smith'

Stanhope, Earl, *The Life of The Right Honourable William Pitt*, Vol. II, London, John Murray, 1879 – 'Stanhope'

Stedall, Robert *Men of Substance: The London Livery Companies' Reluctant Part in the Plantation of Ulster*, Austin Macauley Publishers Limited, 2016 – '*Men of Substance*'

Stewart, A. T. Q., *A Deeper Silence: The Hidden Origins of the United Irishmen*, Belfast, Blackstaff, 1993 – 'Stewart'

Sullivan, A.M., *New Ireland*, New York, Peter F. Collier, 1878 – 'Sullivan'

Teeling, Charles Hamilton, *Personal Narrative of the "Irish Rebellion" of 1798*, London, Henry Colburn, 1828 – 'Teeling'

Tillyard, Stella, *Citizen Lord: Edward FitzGerald 1763 – 1798*, London, Chatto & Windus, 1997 – 'Tillyard'

Todd, Janet, *Daughters of Ireland; The Rebellious Kingsborough Sisters and the Making of a Modern Nation*, New York, Ballentine Books, 2005 – 'Todd'

Tone, Washington, ed., *Life of T. W. Tone*, 1826 – 'Tone'

Treadwell, Victor, ed., *The Irish Commission of 1622*, Dublin, 2006 – 'Treadwell'

Trinity College Dublin, MMS – 'Trinity College'

Quinn, John, *Soul on Fire, a Life of Thomas Russell*, Dublin, Irish Academic Press, 2002 – 'Quinn'

Whelan, Fergus, *Dissent into Treason*, Brandon Books, London, 2010 – 'Whelan'

Whelan, Kevin and Bartlett, Thomas, eds. *The Memoirs of Miles Byrne*, Wexford, Duffy Press, 1998 – 'Whelan and Bartlett'

Woodham-Smith, Cecil, *The Great Hunger, Ireland 1845 – 1849*, New York, Signet, 1991 – 'Woodham-Smith'

Woodward, Richard, Bishop of Cloyne, *The Present State of the Church in Ireland*, Dublin, 1787 – 'Woodward'

Young, R. M., *Historical Notices of Old Belfast and its Vicinity*, 1896, Belfast, Marcus Ward & Co. Limited – 'Young'

References

Part 1 The Reformation and its impact on British efforts to dominate Ireland

Chapter 1: The arrival of British settlers in Ireland c. 1540 – c. 1635

1. Treadwell, pp. 607–8; cited in Bardon, p. 250
2. Devine
3. Bardon, p. 253

Chapter 3: The effect of Presbyterianism on British political thinking c. 1567 – c. 1649

1. Whelan, p. 17
2. Whelan, p. 23
3. Whelan, p. 52
4. Whelan, p. 53
5. Whelan, p. 23
6. Whelan, p. 22

Part 2 Events leading up to the English Civil War

Chapter 4: Growing conflict between Charles I and the English Parliament 1625 – 1641

1. Perceval-Maxwell, p. 43; cited in Bardon, p. 270
2. Bardon, p. 260

Chapter 5: The Great Rebellion in Ireland 1641 – 1649

1. Bardon, p. 271
2. Perceval-Maxwell, p. 218; cited in Bardon, p. 275

3. Bardon, p. 273
4. Bardon, pp. 270–1
5. Lecky, pp. 46–89; cited in Curl 1986, p. 91
6. Curl 1986, p. 90
7. Gilbert 1879 – 80, Vol 2, pp. 465–6 from a speech by Colonel Audley Mervyn; cited in Bardon, p. 275
8. Bardon, p. 280
9. Bardon, p. 275
10. Bardon, p. 276
11. Bardon, p. 276
12. Bardon, p. 281
13. Bardon, p. 275
14. Trinity College MMS 866; cited in Curl 1986, p. 91
15. Bardon, p. 282
16. Bardon, p. 283
17. Bardon, p. 281
18. Bardon, p. 283
19. Bardon, p. 284
20. Hays-McCoy, p. 193; cited in Bardon, p. 284
21. Bardon, p. 282
22. Bardon, p. 283
23. Bardon, p. 283

Chapter 6: The War of the Three Kingdoms 1642 – 1649

1. Gregg, p. 160; cited in Whelan, p. 22
2. Whelan, p. 28
3. Bardon, p. 284
4. Bardon, p. 284
5. Whelan, p. 28
6. Whelan, p. 22
7. Gregg, p. 220; cited in Whelan p. 24
8. Whelan, p. 29

Chapter 7: Ireland under Parliamentary control 1649 – 1660

1. Whelan, p. 22
2. Bardon, p. 285
3. Curl 1986, p. 93
4. Bardon, p. 285
5. Bardon, p. 285
6. Gribben, p. 15; cited in Whelan, p. 36
7. Bardon, p. 287
8. Bardon, p. 286
9. Bardon, p. 289
10. Bardon, p. 286
11. Bardon, p. 286
12. Bardon, p. 291
13. Madden, p. 15
14. Bardon, p. 291
15. *Men of Substance*, p. 275
16. Whelan, p. 51
17. Madden, p. 15
18. Bardon, p. 288
19. Bardon, p. 288
20. *Men of Substance*, p. 276
21. Bardon, p. 292
22. Curl 1986, p. 94
23. *Men of Substance*, p. 276

Part 3 The Restoration and the Williamite Wars

Chapter 8: Backlash against Dissenters following the Restoration 1660 – 1685

1. Connolly, p. 124; cited in Whelan, p. 43
2. Madden, p. 16
3. 12 Charles II, Cap.11; cited in Curl, p. 96
4. Connolly, p. 128; cited in Whelan, p. 45

5. Cited in Betts, p. 84
6. *Men of Substance,* p. 283
7. Bardon, p. 293
8. Madden, p. 17
9. Madden, p. 17
10. Bardon, p. 295
11. Kilroy, p. 231; cited in Whelan, p. 48
12. McNeill, p. 65
13. Bardon, p. 295
14. Whelan, p. 49
15. Whelan, p. 49
16. Whelan, p. 49
17. *Men of Substance,* p. 287
18. *Men of Substance,* p. 287
19. Whelan, p. 54
20. Whelan, p. 53
21. *Men of Substance,* p. 288
22. Curl 1986, p. 97
23. *Men of Substance,* p. 288
24. *Men of Substance,* p. 288
25. *Men of Substance,* p. 289
26. Bardon, p. 295
27. *Men of Substance,* p. 290
28. *Men of Substance,* p. 290
29. King, p. 42; cited in Curl 1986, p. 98
30. Curl 1986, p. 98
31. William Brooke; cited in Bardon, p.298
32. Richard Dobbs; cited in Bardon, p. 298
33. *Men of Substance,* p. 291
34. Curl 1986, p. 98
35. *Men of Substance,* p. 292
36. *Men of Substance,* p. 293

Chapter 9: James II and the Williamite Wars 1685 – 1691

1. *Men of Substance,* p. 294
2. *Men of Substance,* p. 294
3. *Men of Substance,* p. 294
4. Whelan, p. 60
5. Houston, p. 8; cited in Whelan, p. 61
6. Whelan, p. 62
7. Whelan, p. 62
8. Curl 1986, p. 98
9. *Men of Substance,* p. 295
10. Curl 1986, p. 98
11. Bardon, p. 299
12. Curl 1986, p. 99
13. Curl 1986, p. 99
14. *Men of Substance,* p. 296
15. Whelan, p. 63
16. Pincus, p. 141; cited in Whelan, p. 63
17. *Men of Substance,* p. 297
18. *Men of Substance,* p. 297
19. *Men of Substance,* p. 297
20. Bardon, p. 299
21. *Men of Substance,* p. 298
22. *Men of Substance,* p. 298
23. *Men of Substance,* p. 298
24. *Men of Substance,* p. 299
25. *Men of Substance,* p. 300
26. *Men of Substance,* p. 300
27. Bardon, p. 299
28. Bardon, p. 300
29. *Men of Substance,* p. 300
30. *Men of Substance,* p. 300
31. *Men of Substance,* p. 301
32. Madden, p. 18
33. Leland; cited in Irish Society, p. 12

34. Curl 1986, p. 101
35. *Men of Substance*, p. 302
36. *Men of Substance*, p. 302
37. *Men of Substance*, p. 303
38. *Men of Substance*, p. 303
39. Curl 1986, p.102
40. *Men of Substance*, p. 303
41. *Men of Substance*, p. 303
42. Curl 1986, p. 102
43. *Men of Substance*, p. 304
44. From *Apprentice Boys of Derry*
45. *Men of Substance*, p. 305
46. From *Apprentice Boys of Derry*
47. *Men of Substance*, p.305
48. *Men of Substance*, pp. 305-6
49. *Men of Substance*, p. 306
50. Curl 1986, p. 102
51. *Men of Substance*, p. 306
52. *Men of Substance*, p. 306
53. *Men of Substance*, p. 306
54. Curl 1986, p. 101
55. *Men of Substance*, p. 307
56. Curl 1986, p. 101
57. Bardon, p. 300
58. *Men of Substance*, p. 307
59. Curl 1986, p. 103
60. *Men of Substance*, p. 308
61. *Men of Substance*, p. 308
62. *Men of Substance*, pp. 308-9
63. *Men of Substance*, p. 309
64. *Men of Substance*, p. 309
65. Madden, p. 18
66. *Men of Substance*, p. 310
67. Bardon, p. 300
68. Curl 1986, p. 103

69. *Men of Substance,* p. 310
70. *Men of Substance,* p. 310
71. Whelan, p. 68
72. *Men of Substance,* p. 310
73. *Men of Substance,* p. 310
74. Curl 1986, p 104
75. Bardon, p. 301
76. *Men of Substance,* p. 310
77. Curl 1986, p. 104
78. Bardon, p. 300
79. *Men of Substance,* pp. 211-2
80. Curl 1986, p. 104
81. Bardon, p. 310
82. *Men of Substance,* p. 312
83. *Men of Substance,* p. 313
84. Curl 1986, p. 104

Chapter 10: The Protestant Ascendancy's assertion of its authority 1691 – 1714

1. *Men of Substance,* p. 317
2. *Men of Substance,* p. 335
3. Whelan, p. 70
4. Whelan, p. 71
5. *Men of Substance,* p. 317
6. Whelan, p. 74
7. Whelan, p. 75
8. *Men of Substance,* p. 313
9. Curl 1986, p. 107
10. *Men of Substance,* pp. 317-8
11. Madden, p. 21
12. Madden, p. 21
13. *Men of Substance,* p. 318
14. Whelan, p. 74
15. Whelan, p. 71

16. Curl 1986, p. 107
17. Curl 1986, p. 105
18. *Men of Substance,* p. 313
19. Bardon, p. 329
20. Bardon, p. 330
21. *Men of Substance,* p. 313
22. Curl 1986, p. 108
23. Curl 1986, p. 107
24. Curl 1986, p. 107
25. Bardon, p. 303
26. Bardon, p. 305
27. *Men of Substance,* p. 318–9
28. McNeill, p. 62
29. Madden, p. 22
30. *Men of Substance,* p. 319–20
31. McNeill, p. 62
32. Bardon, p. 308
33. *Men of Substance,* p. 319
34. *Men of Substance,* p. 320
35. Reid, Vol. 3, pp. 68–70; cited in Bardon, p. 307
36. Bardon pp. 307 and 325
37. *Men of Substance,* p. 321
38. Curl BBCi 2001, p. 8
39. *Men of Substance,* pp. 320–1

Part 4 The development of Dissenter theology in the cause of republicanism

Chapter 11: The development of Dissenter thinking in Ireland c. 1690 – c. 1760

1. Whelan, p. 75
2. Whelan, p. 76
3. Whelan, p. 76
4. Whelan, p. 76

5. Barnard, p. 166; cited in Whelan, p. 79
6. Whelan, p. 82
7. Whelan, p. 81
8. Whelan, p. 78
9. Whelan, p. 79
10. Brown, p. 84; cited in Whelan, p. 90
11. Whelan, p. 91
12. Robbins, p. 163; cited in Whelan, p. 98
13. Armstrong, p. 60; cited in Whelan, p. 98
14. Miller, p. 488; cited in Whelan, p. 100
15. Whelan, p. 100
16. Hill, p. 22; cited in Whelan, p. 107
17. Hill, p. 91; cited in Whelan, p. 108
18. Connolly, p. 240; cited in Whelan, p. 108
19. Whelan, p. 109
20. Whelan, p. 110
21. Drummond, p. 75; cited in Whelan, p. 111

Chapter 12: Growing seeds of Dissenter unrest c. 1714 – c. 1782

1. Whelan, p. 114
2. Whelan, p. 114
3. Whelan, p. 115
4. Whelan, p. 115
5. Whelan, p. 117
6. Whelan, p. 116
7. Whelan, p. 116
8. Madden, p. 29
9. Whelan, p. 118
10. Whelan, p. 116
11. Kennedy, p. 29; cited in Whelan, p. 118, and Marshall, pp. 29–38
12. Madden, p. 130
13. Clifford 1991, p. 15; cited in Whelan, p. 118
14. Whelan, p. 118

15. Whelan, p. 131
16. Whelan, p. 121
17. Whelan, p. 122
18. McNeill, p. 63
19. McNeill, p. 63
20. Whelan, p. 124
21. Whelan, p. 124
22. DNB (1917), ix, p. 732; cited in Curl 2000, pp. 212–3
23. Childe-Pemberton, vol. I, pp. 238, 219; cited in Curl 2000, p. 216
24. Whelan, p. 125
25. Madden, p. 45

Chapter 13: The development of the Unitarians' political objectives c. 1755 – c. 1791

1. Whelan, p. 94
2. Woodward; cited in Whelan, p. 96
3. Whelan, p. 123
4. Whelan, p. 123
5. Morgan, p. 83; cited in Whelan, p. 143
6. Whelan, p. 138
7. Price; cited in Whelan, p. 134
8. Whelan, p. 135
9. Whelan, p. 135
10. Whelan, p.137
11. Whelan, p. 185
12. Grayling, p. 28; cited in Whelan, p. 185
13. Quinn, p. 99; cited in Whelan, p. 186
14. Garret, p. 51; cited in Whelan, p. 223
15. Whelan, p. 189
16. Whelan, p. 189
17. Whelan, p. 189

18. Clifford 1989, p. 53; cited in Whelan, p. 188
19. Madden, pp. 27–8

Part 5 Britain's determination to retain control over Irish Government

Chapter 14: The rise to influence of Henry Grattan and the Irish Whigs c. 1770 – 1791

1. Madden, p. 27
2. Madden, p. 30
3. Madden, p. 27
4. *Morning Herald,* 6 March 1782; cited in McDowell, p. 28
5. Curl 1986, p. 98
6. McDowell, p. 50
7. *Hibernian Journal* 5 May 1780; cited in McDowell, p. 51
8. *Dublin Evening Post* 25 April 1780; cited in McDowell, p. 50
9. McDowell, p. 54
10. McDowell, pp. 54–5
11. McDowell, p. 52
12. McDowell, p. 52
13. McDowell, p. 55
14. McDowell, pp. 56–7
15. McDowell, p. 59
16. McDowell, p. 79
17. McDowell, p. 90
18. McDowell, p. 91
19. *McCracken Letters;* cited in McNeill p. 98
20. McDowell, p. 117
21. McDowell, p. 117
22. McDowell, p. 119
23. Whelan, p. 126
24. Tone, p. 41; cited in McNeill, p. 63
25. Madden, p. 31
26. Madden, p. 31

Chapter 15: British Government efforts to end the Dissenter threat c. 1780 – 1797

1. Whelan, p. 148
2. Clifford 1989, p. 63; cited in Whelan, p. 144
3. Clifford 1989, p. 41; cited in Whelan, p. 189
4. Whelan, p. 147
5. Whelan, p. 190
6. Thomas W. Copeland; cited Whelan, p. 148
7. Whelan, p. 148
8. McNeill, p. 65
9. Whelan, p. 151
10. Bartlett, p. 119; cited in Whelan, p. 150
11. Curtin, p. 22; cited in Whelan, p. 150
12. Nelson, p. 221; cited in Whelan, p. 151

Chapter 16: Divergent political views in England on how to manage Catholic emancipation c. 1792 – c. 1795

1. Smith pp. 137–8
2. Cobban and Smith, p. 402
3. Marshall and Woods, p. 107
4. Smith pp. 134–5
5. Malmesbury, Vol. II, pp. 453–4
6. Smith, p. 159
7. Smith, p. 163
8. Smith, p. 164
9. Smith, pp. 165–6
10. Smith, pp. 166–7
11. Smith, pp. 168–9
12. Smith, pp. 169
13. Smith, pp. 169–70
14. Madden, p. 82
15. *Grattan Memoirs,* Vol. IV, p. 173
16. McDowell, p. 125

17. McDowell, p. 126
18. Madden, pp. 82–3
19. Smith, p. 179
20. Smith, p. 182
21. McDowell, p. 127
22. McDowell, p. 127
23. Smith, pp. 185–6
24. McDowell, p. 128
25. McDowell, Ed., Vol. 8, p. 78

Chapter 17: Fitzwilliam's Lord Lieutenancy in Ireland and its aftermath 1795

1. McDowell, p. 124
2. *Encyclopaedia Britannica*
3. Smith, p. 192
4. Smith, pp. 190–1
5. Stanhope, p. XXIII
6. Smith, p. 197
7. Smith, p. 193
8. Smith, p. 195
9. Madden, p. 89
10. Madden, p. 90
11. Smith, pp. 193–4
12. Fitzwilliam; cited in Madden, p. 85
13. Fitzwilliam; cited in Madden, pp. 85–6
14. Madden, p. 88
15. Madden, p. 89
16. McDowell, p. 136
17. Madden, p. 85
18. Portland to Fitzwilliam, 21 February 1795
19. Smith, p. 199
20. Smith, p. 199
21. Smith, p. 200
22. Smith, pp. 205–6

23. Smith, p. 207
24. *Historical Collections*, p. 442, cited in McNeill, p. 103
25. McMillan in *Swords*, 1997, p. 88; cited in Whelan, p. 202
26. McDowell, p. 142
27. McDowell, p. 143
28. *Historical Collections*, p. 433; cited in McNeill, p. 103
29. Beresford, Vol. II, p. 111
30. Beresford, Vol. II, p. 114
31. Beresford, Vol. II, pp. 117–9
32. McDowell, Ed. Vol. 8, p. 281

Part 6 The seeds of revolution to establish republicanism in Ireland

Chapter 18: The formation of the Society of United Irishmen 1783 – 1794

1. Madden, p. 25
2. Carroll, p. 25
3. Madden, p. 31
4. Madden, p. 36
5. Madden, p. 36
6. Whelan, p. 126
7. Whelan, p. 126
8. Stewart, p 22; cited in Whelan, p. 127
9. Madden, p. 68
10. *Historical Collections*, p. 293; cited in McNeill, p. 63
11. Whelan, p. 159
12. Larkin, p. 8; cited in Whelan, p. 159
13. Millin, p. 82; cited in McNeill, p. 34
14. Drennan Letters No. 434
15. Whelan, p. 161
16. Whelan, p. 162
17. Madden, p. 116
18. McNeill, p. 68

19. McNeill, p. 68
20. *Ulster Magazine,* January 1830, Sketch of Thomas Russell; cited in McNeill, p. 72
21. *Historical Collections,* p. V; cited in McNeill, p. 65
22. *Historical Collections,* p. 347; cited in McNeill, p. 67
23. Cited in Jemmy Hope
24. Agnew; cited in Whelan, p. 161
25. Curtin, p. 43; cited in Whelan, p. 161
26. McNeill, p. 74
27. Tone, p. 51; cited in McNeill, p. 71
28. Whelan, p. 164
29. Tone, p. 149, cited in McNeill, p. 75
30. Whelan, p. 165
31. Whelan, p. 164
32. Joy, p. 141; cited in McNeill, pp. 86–7
33. McNeill, p. 87
34. Madden, p. 137
35. Tone, p. 222; cited in McNeill, p. 86
36. Young, p. 188; cited in McNeill, p. 56
37. Cited in Thomas Russell
38. Whelan, p. 128
39. Madden, p. 137
40. Madden, p. 137
41. Cited in Tandy

Chapter 19: United Irish efforts to influence reform in the Irish Parliament 1792 – 1797

1. Drennan Letters, No. 396
2. Drennan Letters, No. 351; cited in Mc Neill, p. 92
3. Madden, p. 138
4. Curtin, p. 31; cited in Whelan, p. 168
5. Whelan, p. 168
6. Whelan, p. 169
7. McNeill, p. 87

8. Madden, 1st Series, 2nd Ed., p. 234; cited in McNeill, pp. 87–8
9. Agnew, Vol. I, p. 35; cited in Whelan, p. 220
10. Drennan Letters, No. 391a; cited in McNeill, p. 99
11. Madden, p. 153
12. Madden, p. 148 and p. 36
13. Madden, p. 36
14. Wikipedia, Thomas Russell
15. Whelan, p. 168
16. Drennan Letters, No. 698
17. Bartlett, p. 78; cited in Whelan, p. 224
18. Whelan, p. 225
19. Maher, p. 33n; cited in Whelan, p. 224
20. Maher, p. 98; cited in Whelan, p. 224
21. Bardon, p. 332
22. Drennan Letters, No. 463
23. Curtis, p. 376; cited in McNeill, p. 93
24. McNeill, p. 99
25. Madden, p. 118
26. McNeill, p. 99
27. Drennan Letters, No. 391a; cited in McNeill, p. 99
28. Drennan Letters, No. 397
29. Drennan Letters, Nos. 410 and 411; cited in McNeill, pp. 99–100
30. Drennan Letters, No. 411; cited in McNeill, p. 100
31. Drennan Letters, No. 513; cited in McNeill, p. 101

Chapter 20: United Irish efforts to obtain French backing for a republican rebellion 1795 – 1798

1. Drennan Letters, No. 618; cited in McNeill, p. 107
2. McDowell, p. 141
3. McDowell, p. 141
4. McNeill, p. 104
5. Young, p. 191; cited in McNeill, p. 103
6. McNeill, p. 97

7. Whelan, p. 173
8. Whelan, p. 263
9. Hames, p. 89; cited in Whelan, p. 204
10. Tillyard, p. 139; cited in Whelan, p. 205
11. Hames, p. 84; cited in Whelan, p. 204
12. Hames, p. 120; cited in Whelan, p. 207
13. Cited in Jemmy Hope
14. McNeill, p. 95
15. McNeill, p. 95
16. Madden, p. 149; cited in McNeill, p. 96
17. Antrim and Down in '98, p. 108; cited in McNeill, p. 94
18. Antrim and Down in '98, p. 104
19. Antrim and Down in '98, p. 98; cited in McNeill, p. 96
20. Cited in Jemmy Hope
21. McNeill, p. 96
22. McNeill, p. 98
23. Cited in Jemmy Hope
24. McNeill, p. 107
25. McNeill, p. 108
26. McNeill, p. 85
27. Madden, p. 35
28. O'Connell correspondence, Vol. I. Letter No. 24a
29. O'Ferrall, p. 12
30. Gwynn, p. 71
31. Gwynn, p. 71
32. O'Ferrall, p. 12
33. Madden, p. 35
34. Whelan, p. 209

Chapter 21: The rebellion of 1798

1. Madden, p. 168
2. Madden, p. 169
3. Sir Jonah Barrington; cited in Madden, p. 373
4. Madden, p. 373

5. Fitzpatrick, p. 11; cited in Whelan, p. 221
6. Bartlett, p. 182; cited in Whelan, p. 223
7. Maher, p. 106; cited in Whelan, p. 219
8. Bartlett, p. 78; cited in Whelan, p. 227
9. Hames, p. 123; cited in Whelan, p. 208
10. Whelan, p. 208
11. Agnew, Vol. II, p. 6; cited in Whelan, p. 229
12. Whelan, p. 216
13. Maher, p. 101; cited in Whelan, p. 216
14. *Higgins*, p. 48; cited in Whelan, p. 228
15. Whelan, p. 233
16. McNeill, p. 171
17. McNeill, p. 173
18. Madden, 2nd Series, Vol. II, p. 487; cited in McNeill, p. 181
19. McNeill, p. 187
20. State Paper Office, Dublin; cited in McNeill, p. 190
21. Madden, 2nd Series, Vol. II, p. 497
22. Whelan, p. 234
23. Hames, p. 183; cited in Whelan, p. 234
24. Todd, p. 254; cited in Whelan, p. 234
25. Gordon, p. 142; cited in Madden, p. 414
26. Hay; cited in Madden, p. 413
27. Madden, p. 413
28. Hay, p. 153; cited in Madden, pp. 414–5
29. Madden, p. 165
30. Campbell, p. 74; cited in Whelan, p. 236
31. Boyd, p. 2; cited in Whelan, p. 236
32. Tone, p. 384
33. Crymble
34. Whelan and Bartlett; cited in Whelan, p. 240
35. McNeill, p. 195
36. Madden
37. Hope
38. Madden, p. 213
39. Teeling, p. 138; cited in Madden, p. 358

40. Madden, p. 344
41. Barrington, p. 248; cited in Madden, p. 346
42. Hay, p. 181; cited in Madden, p. 349
43. Cited in Madden, pp. 356–7
44. Gordon, p. 76; cited in Madden, p. 347
45. Madden, p. 363
46. Teeling, p. 15; cited in Madden, p. 356
47. Rufus King to the Duke of Portland, 13 September 1798; cited in Carroll, p. 17

Part 7 Events leading to Union and emancipation
Chapter 22: The Act of Union 1789 –1801

1. Madden, p. 96
2. Madden, p. 118
3. Madden, p. 119
4. Madden, p. 40
5. Madden, p. 41
6. McNeill, p. 198
7. Bardon, p. 334

Chapter 23: The rebellion of 1803

1. Madden, 3rd series, Vol. II, p. 202; cited in McNeill, p. 210
2. McNeill, p. 214
3. Whelan, p. 252
4. *Memoirs of the examination of the State Prisoners*; cited in Madden, p. 148
5. *Memoirs of the examination of the State Prisoners*; cited in Madden, p. 149
6. Phillips
7. Cited in Jemmy Hope
8. McNeill, p. 225
9. Carroll, p. 26

10. O'Connell Correspondence, Vol. 1, Letter No. 97
11. Whelan, p. 253

Chapter 24: The Liberator 1806 – 1841

1. Whelan, p. 261
2. Whelan, p. 272
3. Gwynn, pp. 138–145
4. Millingen, p. 215
5. T. P. O'Connor, p. 11
6. Adelman and Pearce, p. 33
7. *Men of Substance*, p. 348
8. *Men of Substance*, p. 348
9. T. P. O'Connor, p. 7
10. T. P. O'Connor, pp. 7–8
11. T. P. O'Connor, p. 7
12. O'Riorden, p. 26
13. Hallinan
14. Curl 1986, p. 114
15. *Men of Substance*, p. 349
16. T. P. O'Connor, p. 9
17. Curl 1986, p. 115
18. *Men of Substance*, p. 348
19. T. P. O'Connor, p. 9
20. T. P. O'Connor, p. 8
21. T. P. O'Connor, p. 9
22. T. P. O'Connor, p. 11
23. T. P. O'Connor, p. 12
24. T. P. O'Connor, p. 12
25. T. P. O'Connor, p. 12
26. T. P. O'Connor, p. 47
27. T. P. O'Connor, p. 74
28. T. P. O'Connor, p. 15
29. T. P. O'Connor, p. 73
30. T. P. O'Connor, p. 13

31. T. P. O'Connor, p. 46
32. T. P. O'Connor, p. 51

Part 8 Famine, destitution and agitation for independence

Chapter 25: Famine c. 1800 – c. 1870

1. *Men of Substance*, p.349
2. T. P. O'Connor, p. 16
3. T. P. O'Connor, p. 22
4. T. P. O'Connor, p. 23
5. *Men of Substance*, p. 351
6. *Men of Substance*, p. 351
7. Woodham-Smith, p. 24; cited in *Men of Substance*, p. 351
8. T. P. O'Connor, p. 24
9. Healy, p. 55; cited in T. P. O'Connor, p. 24
10. Rev. Philip Skelton; cited in Bardon p. 324
11. *Men of Substance*, p. 350
12. Cited in T. P. O'Connor, p. 23
13. *Men of Substance*, p. 351
14. *Men of Substance*, p. 350
15. *Men of Substance*, p. 351
16. *Men of Substance*, p. 342
17. *Men of Substance*, p. 343
18. *Men of Substance*, p. 343
19. Curl BBCi 2001, pp. 8–9; cited in *Men of Substance*, p. 344
20. Curl BBCi 2001, p. 9; cited in *Men of Substance*, pp. 344–5
21. Curl BBCi 2001, p. 9; cited in *Men of Substance*, p. 345
22. *Men of Substance*, p. 346
23. Woodham-Smith, p. 22; cited in *Men of Substance*, p. 331
24. *Men of Substance*, p. 349
25. Woodham-Smith, p. 31; cited in *Men of Substance*, p. 353
26. T. P. O'Connor, p. 17; cited in *Men of Substance*, p. 351
27. *Men of Substance*, p. 351

28. T. P. O'Connor, pp. 23–4; cited in *Men of Substance*, p. 350
29. T. P. O'Connor, p. 18; cited in *Men of Substance*, p. 352
30. T. P. O'Connor, p. 20; cited in *Men of Substance*, p. 352
31. *Men of Substance*, pp. 352–3
32. T. P. O'Connor, p. 18
33. *Men of Substance*, p. 353
34. *Men of Substance*, p. 352
35. T. P. O'Connor, p. 16; cited in *Men of Substance*, p. 351
36. Litton, p. 95: cited in *Men of Substance*, p. 352
37. *Men of Substance*, p. 353
38. *Men of Substance*, p. 353
39. Blake, p. 179; cited in *Men of Substance* p. 353
40. *Men of Substance*, p. 353
41. Cited in T. P. O'Connor, p. 23; cited in *Men of Substance*, p. 353
42. Woodham-Smith, p. 24; cited in *Men of Substance*, p. 353
43. The Commission Report, p. 226; cited in T. P. O'Connor, p. 23
44. T. P. O'Connor, p. 53
45. Census Commissioners, p. 317; cited in T. P. O'Connor, p. 53
46. *Men of Substance*, p. 353
47. *Men of Substance*, p. 354
48. Curl BBCi 2001, p. 10
49. Census Commissioners, p. 245; cited in T. P. O'Connor, p. 39
50. Cited in T. P. O'Connor, p. 40
51. Cited in T. P. O'Connor, p. 40
52. Cited in T. P. O'Connor, p. 40
53. Report of the Inspectors-General of Prisons: Census Commissioners' 'Tables of Deaths', p. 30; cited in T. P. O'Connor, p. 41
54. T. P. O'Connor, p. 43
55. *Men of Substance*, p. 354
56. Connell, 14, No. 3, 1962, p. 521
57. T. P. O'Connor, p. 26; cited in *Men of Substance*, p. 354
58. *Men of Substance*, p. 354
59. *Men of Substance*, p. 355

60. T. P. O'Connor, p. 27; cited in *Men of Substance,* p. 354
61. Cited in T. P. O'Connor, p. 27
62. Cited in T. P. O'Connor, p. 28
63. *Men of Substance,* pp. 354–5
64. *Men of Substance,* p. 354
65. *Men of Substance,* p. 354
66. *Men of Substance,* p. 355
67. *Men of Substance,* p. 355
68. *Men of Substance,* p. 354
69. *Men of Substance,* p. 354
70. *Men of Substance,* p. 354
71. T. P. O'Connor, p. 28
72. *Men of Substance,* pp. 355–6
73. *Men of Substance,* p. 356
74. T. P. O'Connor, p. 71
75. Cited in T. P. O'Connor, p. 72
76. *Hansard,* lxxxvii, p. 516; cited in T. P. O'Connor, p. 71
77. *Hansard,* lxxxiv, p. 694; cited in *Men of Substance,* p. 358
78. *Hansard,* C., p. 943; cited in T. P. O'Connor, p. 73
79. Captain Wynne; cited in T. P. O'Connor, p. 31
80. *Men of Substance,* p. 356
81. *Men of Substance,* p. 356
82. T. P. O'Connor, p. 82
83. T. P. O'Connor, p. 82
84. *Men of Substance,* p. 356
85. Cited in T. P. O'Connor, p. 34
86. Cited in T. P. O'Connor, p. 35; cited in *Men of Substance,* p. 356
87. Cited in T. P. O'Connor, p. 35
88. T. P. O'Connor, p. 34; cited in *Men of Substance* pp. 356–7
89. Leland, ii, p. 215; cited in T. P. O'Connor, p. 36
90. Sullivan, p. 64; cited in T. P. O'Connor p. 36
91. *Men of Substance,* p. 357
92. T. P. O'Connor, p. 36
93. T. P. O'Connor, p. 37

94. Census Commissioners, p. 273; cited in T. P. O'Connor, p. 31
95. Census Commissioners, p, 243; cited in T. P. O'Connor, p. 31
96. Census Commissioners, p. 310
97. Census Commissioners, p. 277
98. T. P. O'Connor, p. 32
99. Curl 1986, p. 115
100. *Men of Substance,* p. 357
101. T. P. O'Connor, p. 75
102. T. P. O'Connor, p. 76
103. *Men of Substance*, p. 357
104. *Men of Substance,* p. 357
105. *Men of Substance, p. 357*
106. Leland, ii, p. 215; cited in T. P. O'Connor, p. 37; cited in *Men of Substance,* p. 357
107. Men of Substance, p. 357
108. T. P. O'Connor, p. 43
109. T. P. O'Connor, p. 44
110. Census Commissioners, p. 310; cited in T. P. O'Connor, p. 52
111. T. P. O'Connor, p. 52
112. Census Commissioners, p. 315; cited in T. P. O'Connor, p. 52
113. T. P. O'Connor, p. 42
114. T. P. O'Connor, p. 78
115. Peel Memoirs, Part III, p. 143; cited in T. P. O'Connor, p. 78
116. *Men of Substance*, p. 359
117. *Men of Substance*, p. 359
118. T. P. O'Connor, p. 61
119. Curl 1986, p. 116; cited in *Men of Substance,* pp. 358–9
120. T. P. O'Connor, p. 57
121. Curl 1986, p. 115
122. T. P. O'Connor, p. 67
123. Cited in T. P. O'Connor, p. 69
124. *Men of Substance,* p. 358
125. *Men of Substance,* p. 359
126. Cited in T. P. O'Connor, p. 27; cited in *Men of Substance,* p. 358

127. Litton, pp. 98–9; cited in *Men of Substance,* p. 358
128. *Hansard,* p. 8 June 1849; cited in T. P. O'Connor, p. 68
129. *Men of Substance,* p. 358
130. T. P. O'Connor, p. 69
131. *Men of Substance,* p. 358
132. *Men of Substance,* p. 359
133. T. P. O'Connor, p. 45
134. *Men of Substance,* p. 359
135. *Men of Substance,* p. 359
136. T. P. O'Connor, p. 44
137. *Men of Substance,* p. 359
138. *Men of Substance,* p. 359
139. Sullivan, pp. 67–8; cited in T. P. O'Connor, p. 83
140. T. P. O'Connor, p. 83
141. Gavan Duffy; cited in T. P. O'Connor, p. 83
142. Curl 1986, p. 116
143. *Men of Substance,* p. 359

Chapter 26: Continuing evictions despite calls for tenant rights 1850 – 1870

1. T. P. O'Connor
2. T. P. O'Connor, p. 87
3. T. P. O'Connor, pp. 121–2
4. T. P. O'Connor, p. 124
5. *The Nation,* 23 April 1853; cited in T. P. O'Connor, p. 103
6. T. P. O'Connor, p. 126
7. T. P. O'Connor, p. 126
8. T. P. O'Connor, p. 128
9. T. P. O'Connor, p. 127
10. T. P. O'Connor
11. T. P. O'Connor, p. 111
12. T. P. O'Connor, p. 117
13. T. P. O'Connor, p. 120
14. *Journals,* Vol. ii, pp. 85–6; cited in T. P. O'Connor, p. 129

15. T. P. O'Connor, p. 129
16. T. P. O'Connor, p. 130
17. T. P. O'Connor, p. 132
18. T. P. O'Connor, p. 132
19. T. P. O'Connor, p. 133
20. T. P. O'Connor, p. 133

Chapter 27: The Fenian movement 1848 – 1879

1. T. P. O'Connor, p. 46
2. T. P. O'Connor, p. 49
3. T. P. O'Connor, p. 134
4. Ryan, p. 107
5. T. P. O'Connor, p. 137
6. Curl 1968, p. 117
7. T. P. O'Connor, p. 137
8. T. P. O'Connor, p. 254
9. T. P. O'Connor, p. 254

Part 9 Parliamentary agitation for Irish Home Rule

Chapter 28: Gladstone's initial approach to reform in Ireland 1867 – 1874

1. *Encyclopaedia Britannica*
2. Morley, Vol. II, p. 293
3. *Encyclopaedia Britannica*
4. *Encyclopaedia Britannica*
5. Curl 1986, p. 117
6. *Encyclopaedia Britannica*
7. Curl 1986, p. 116
8. T. P. O'Connor, p. 138
9. T. P. O'Connor, p. 140
10. T. P. O'Connor, p. 140
11. T. P. O'Connor, p. 141

12. T. P. O'Connor, p. 142
13. T. P. O'Connor, p. 145
14. T. P. O'Connor, p. 146

Chapter 29: The rise of Charles Stewart Parnell 1874 – 1882

1. T. P. O'Connor, p. 149
2. Gladstone, *Hansard,* Vol. cclxxvii, p. 482; cited in T. P. O'Connor, p. 150
3. T. P. O'Connor, p. 152
4. T. P. O'Connor, p. 154
5. T. P. O'Connor, p. 154
6. T. P. O'Connor, p. 154
7. T. P. O'Connor, p. 155
8. T. P. O'Connor, p. 155
9. T. P. O'Connor, p. 158
10. T. P. O'Connor, p. 159
11. *Freeman's Journal,* 8 June 1879; cited in T. P. O'Connor, p. 172
12. T. P. O'Connor, p. 197
13. *Encyclopaedia Britannica*
14. Lyons, p. 186
15. *Hansard,* Vol. cclv, pp. 1415–16; cited in T. P. O'Connor, p. 198
16. T. P. O'Connor, p. 207
17. T. P. O'Connor, p. 199
18. T. P. O'Connor, p. 199
19. MacDonnell, pp. 61–2
20. T. P. O'Connor, p. 200
21. *Hansard,* Vol. ccliii, p. 1663; cited in T. P. O'Connor, p. 201
22. T. P. O'Connor, p. 213
23. T. P. O'Connor, p. 213
24. T. P. O'Connor, p. 214
25. T. P. O'Connor, p. 206
26. Guinnane and Miller
27. *Encyclopaedia Britannica*
28. T. P. O'Connor, p. 228

29. Hickey and Doherty, Land Acts, p. 287
30. T. P. O'Connor, p. 228
31. T. P. O'Connor, p. 229
32. T. P. O'Connor, p. 230
33. T. P. O'Connor, p. 232
34. T. P. O'Connor, p. 238
35. T. P. O'Connor, p. 239
36. T. P. O'Connor, p. 239
37. T. P. O'Connor, p. 255
38. *Men of Substance,* p. 361
39. T. P. O'Connor, p. 148
40. T. P. O'Connor, p. 148
41. T. P. O'Connor, p. 248
42. T. P. O'Connor, p. 262
43. T. P. O'Connor, p. 264
44. T. P. O'Connor, p. 266
45. T. P. O'Connor, p. 133

Chapter 30: The thwarting of calls for Home Rule 1882 – 1889

1. *Freeman's Journal,* 22 February 1886; cited in Curl 1986, p. 118
2. Mr. Gladstone's Irish Bills, pp. 13,18; cited in T. P. O'Connor, p. 276
3. Guinnane and Miller
4. T. P. O'Connor, p. 282
5. T. P. O'Connor, p. 274
6. T. P. O'Connor, p. 292
7. T. P. O'Connor, p. 292
8. T. P. O'Connor, p. 304
9. T. P. O'Connor, p. 299
10. T. P. O'Connor, p. 301
11. T. P. O'Connor, p. 306
12. T. P. O'Connor, p. 324
13. T. P. O'Connor, p. 328
14. T. P. O'Connor, p. 329

15. T. P. O'Connor, p. 313
16. T. P. O'Connor, p. 317

Chapter 31: Attempts to blacken Parnell's name 1886 – 1891

1. T. P. O'Connor, p. 311
2. Wikipedia

Chapter 32: The legacy left by Gladstone and Parnell 1891 and thereafter

1. Cochrane
2. *Encyclopaedia Britannica*
3. Guinnane and Miller, p. 599

Index